ROUTLEDGE LIBRARY EDITIONS: LIBRARY AND INFORMATION SCIENCE

Volume 89

SERIALS CATALOGING

SERIALS CATALOGING
The State of the Art

Edited by
JIM E. COLE AND JACKIE ZAJANC

LONDON AND NEW YORK

First published in 1987 by The Haworth Press, Inc.

This edition first published in 2020
by Routledge
2 Park Square, Milton Park, Abingdon, Oxon OX14 4RN

and by Routledge
52 Vanderbilt Avenue, New York, NY 10017

Routledge is an imprint of the Taylor & Francis Group, an informa business

© 1987 The Haworth Press, Inc.

All rights reserved. No part of this book may be reprinted or reproduced or utilised in any form or by any electronic, mechanical, or other means, now known or hereafter invented, including photocopying and recording, or in any information storage or retrieval system, without permission in writing from the publishers.

Trademark notice: Product or corporate names may be trademarks or registered trademarks, and are used only for identification and explanation without intent to infringe.

British Library Cataloguing in Publication Data
A catalogue record for this book is available from the British Library

ISBN: 978-0-367-34616-4 (Set)
ISBN: 978-0-429-34352-0 (Set) (ebk)
ISBN: 978-0-367-36212-6 (Volume 89) (hbk)
ISBN: 978-0-367-36214-0 (Volume 89) (pbk)
ISBN: 978-0-429-34462-6 (Volume 89) (ebk)

Publisher's Note
The publisher has gone to great lengths to ensure the quality of this reprint but points out that some imperfections in the original copies may be apparent.

Disclaimer
The publisher has made every effort to trace copyright holders and would welcome correspondence from those they have been unable to trace.

Serials Cataloging: The State of the Art

Jim E. Cole
Jackie Zajanc
Editors

The Haworth Press
New York • London

Serials Cataloging: The State of the Art has also been published as *The Serials Librarian*, Volume 12, Numbers 1/2, 1987.

© 1987 by The Haworth Press, Inc. All rights reserved. No part of this book may be reproduced or utilized in any form or by any means, electronic or mechanical, including photocopying, microfilm and recording, or by any information storage and retrieval system, without permission in writing from the publisher. Printed in the United States of America.

The Haworth Press, Inc., 12 West 32 Street, New York, NY 10001
EUROSPAN/Haworth, 3 Henrietta Street, London WC2E 8LU England

Library of Congress Cataloging-in-Publication Data

Serials cataloging.

"Has also been published as The Serials librarian, volume 12, numbers 1/2, 1987."
Includes bibliographies and index.
1. Cataloging of serial publications. I. Cole, Jim E. II. Zajanc, Jackie.
Z695.7.S47   1987   025.3'432   87-2877
ISBN 0-86656-619-8

Serials Cataloging: The State of the Art

The Serials Librarian
Volume 12, Numbers 1/2

CONTENTS

Introduction
    Jim E. Cole
    Jackie Zajanc
	ix

THE INTERNATIONAL ARENA

National and International Serial Standards *Mary S. Price*	1
Serials Cataloguing in Sweden *Sten Hedberg*	11

AACR2: BASIC CONCERNS

AACR2's Effect on Public Services
    Cindy Hepfer, BA, MLS
    Will Hepfer, BA, MLS
	19

Serials Cataloging with AACR2: The Primary Problems and Concerns *James W. Williams, BS, MSLS*	27
The Descriptive Cataloging of Serials: Library of Congress' Application of AACR2 *Dorothy J. Glasby*	43

Bilingual Serial Cataloguing at the National Library of Canada
    Wayne Jones, BA (Hons), MA, MLS
    John Clark, BA, MLS
	53

POTENTIAL FOR CHANGE

Multiplication of Serial Titles Forever?   63
    Günter Franzmeier

Corporate Names as Qualifiers in Uniform Titles   73
    Jim E. Cole

The First Shall Be Last: Earliest Entry Cataloging   83
    Jim E. Cole

Title Changes in an Automated Environment:
  The Last Shall Be First   93
    Jackie Zajanc

SPECIAL APPLICATIONS OF SERIALS CATALOGING

Serials Cataloging from the Union List Standpoint   101
    Lori L. Osmus, BA, MSLS

The Iowa Newspaper Project: A Field Report   117
    Nancy Kraft

AUTOMATION OF SERIALS CATALOGING

The CONSER Editing Guide   131
    Linda K. Bartley
    Jean L. Hirons

Life After Input: Original Serials Cataloging Using OCLC   147
    Beth R. Barrett, MLS
    Olivia M. A. Madison, MA

The Use of RLIN for Serials Cataloging   157
    Mary Monson, MA

EDUCATION OF SERIALS CATALOGERS

The Education of Serials Catalogers   169
    Mary Ellen Soper

Index   181
    Compiled by Nancy S. Hanks

Introduction

The last quarter of a century has witnessed a revolution in the cataloging of all library materials, including serials. The International Conference on Cataloguing Principles and its resultant "Statement of Principles," the automation of the cataloging process, the ever-increasing importance of universal bibliographic control—these and other factors have shaped and molded the cataloging record. Libraries' dependence upon bibliographic utilities for cataloging data has led to an acceptance of cataloging standards that conform closely to internationally accepted principles.

The purpose of the present collection of papers is to assess the state of the art of serials cataloging, especially in two areas: the rules by which the cataloging record is created and the automation of that record. The second edition of the *Anglo-American Cataloguing Rules* has now been applied for over half a decade. This has allowed libraries time to gain a thorough understanding of the rules and their implications for the processing of serials, to develop a pragmatic approach to the application of the code, as witnessed by the various Library of Congress rule interpretations, and to reflect upon the benefits and difficulties caused by the code as experienced both by technical services personnel and by other users of the cataloging record. Several bibliographic utilities, as well as the CONSER Project, are involved in the automation of serials cataloging, oftentimes providing enhanced online access to their machine-readable records by means of Boolean, keyword, and other search strategies. Off-line products, such as printed union lists, receive wide circulation; nonparticipants using these products may need to understand the practices followed in creating and editing the records on-line.

This collection is arranged by theme in several different sections. Since any classification scheme is to some extent arbitrary, other groupings of the papers would have been possible. The editors therefore beg the indulgence of the reader in this matter.

The first section, "The International Arena," consists of two papers. Mary S. Price first discusses the International Standard Serial Number, the relationship between the International Serials Data System and ISBD(S), and the standards for serial holdings statements. Next, Sten Hedberg describes serials cataloging in Sweden, where a cataloging code based on AACR2 was published in 1983. This code, although similar in many respects to AACR2, rejects the concept of corporate main entry for serials, favoring instead key title as main entry.

In the second section, "AACR2: Basic Concerns," Cindy and Will Hepfer examine the advantages, disadvantages, and implementation of AACR2 from the public services viewpoint. James W. Williams then discusses the various problems and concerns of serials cataloging under AACR2 as reflected in the literature, the Library of Congress rule interpretations, and the work of the American Library Association's Committee to Study Serials Cataloging. Dorothy J. Glasby looks at the application of AACR2 to the descriptive cataloging of serials at the Library of Congress, providing an in-depth discussion of various rule interpretations and their background. Finally, Wayne Jones and John Clark describe the policies regarding bilingual serials cataloging at the National Library of Canada.

"Potential for Change" begins with a paper by Günter Franzmeier, in which is presented a convincing argument in favor of corporate main entry for serials with generic titles. Jim E. Cole discusses problems caused by the current guidelines for uniform titles for serials, proposing alternate rules for recording corporate names used as qualifiers. Cole and Jackie Zajanc next focus on earliest and latest entry cataloging of serials.

Under the rubric "Special Applications of Serials Cataloging," Lori L. Osmus presents a detailed description of serials cataloging issues as they affect union lists. Nancy Kraft then discusses the planning and implementation process of the Iowa Newspaper Project.

In the section "Automation of Serials Cataloging," Linda K. Bartley and Jean L. Hirons discuss in detail the creation, development, and content of the *CONSER Editing Guide*, and point out significant changes from the earlier second CONSER edition of the *MARC Serials Editing Guide*. Beth R. Barrett and Olivia M. A. Madison examine CONSER's use and modification of serial records input by non-CONSER libraries. They also discuss the impact the Oxford Project will have on the input of serial records into the OCLC database. Last, Mary H. Monson describes the use of the RLIN in serials cataloging, giving specific information about searching and cataloging in the RLIN environment.

The last section, "Education of Serials Catalogers," consists of an article of the same title by Mary Ellen Soper, in which are set forth the results of a 1986 survey of serials cataloging courses and units offered by library schools.

The editors wish to express their gratitude to the authors who through their time and talent have made this collection possible, and also to Peter Gellatly and Jean G. Cook, whose assistance, advice, and encouragement made their task enjoyable.

Jim E. Cole
Jackie Zajanc

THE INTERNATIONAL ARENA

National and International Serial Standards

Mary S. Price

SUMMARY. This paper addresses the development and promulgation of the International Standard Serial Number, the relationship between the International Serials Data System and the *International Standard Bibliographic Description for Serials*, and emerging standards for serial holdings statements. The author discusses how these developments emerged at the national level here in the U.S. as well as internationally, and demonstrates how the national and international efforts converged to the mutual benefit of both arenas.

I. INTRODUCTION

The variety of standards activities that have emerged during the past ten to fifteen years in support of serials control has been noteworthy. This article will address three particular areas of standards activities that relate specifically to serials; discuss how these developments emerged at the national level here in the U.S. as well as internationally; and then demonstrate how the national and international efforts converged to the mutual benefit of both arenas.

By way of introduction, it might be helpful to discuss very briefly the standards organizations that will be referenced in this report.[1] Starting at the national level, the American National Standards Institute (ANSI) is the primary nationwide standards-setting organization in the United States. ANSI is a "voluntary" standards organization in that the members participate by choice and the standards are used by choice. The actual

---

Mary S. Price is Director for Bibliographic Products and Services at the Library of Congress, Washington, D.C. 20540.

© 1987 by The Haworth Press, Inc. All rights reserved.

work in developing an ANSI standard takes place through American National Standard Committees and their supporting subcommittees. The committee perhaps most important and well-known to the library community is the American National Standards Committee on Library and Information Sciences and Related Publishing Practices, Z39—also known as NISO (National Information Standards Organization). NISO has a large voting membership, including the American Library Association and other library-related professional associations.

At the international level, ANSI's counterpart, so to speak, is the International Organization for Standardization (ISO). Like ANSI, ISO is a voluntary standards-developing organization. Its members are the national standards institutes from countries all over the world (including ANSI from the U.S.). Similar to the approach taken by ANSI, the actual development of standards by ISO is performed by technical committees and their supporting subcommittees and working groups. The technical committee that most closely parallels the functions and responsibilities of NISO is ISO TC46 (Documentation). This committee concerns itself with the standardization of practices relating to libraries, documentation and information centers, indexing and abstracting services, archives, information science, and publishing.

Both ANSI and ISO achieve standardization through consensus, which involves considerable effort on the part of their committees in the preparation of draft standards for comment or vote and an extensive review process. However, one of the major organizational differences between ANSI and ISO lies in the makeup of their respective voting memberships. In ANSI, a member may be a private firm, government agency, trade association or even another standards-making organization. In ISO, a member must be the leading national standards body from each member country. The practical effect of this difference is that the American Library Association (which is a leading library association in the U.S.) can be a member of ANSI and help formulate library comments on standards developed within that framework, whereas IFLA (the International Federation of Library Associations and Institutions) cannot be a voting member of ISO. Therefore, the natural overlap of international standards activities and interests between ISO and IFLA must necessarily be coordinated through liaison relationships, informal reports, and the review of ISO draft standards by IFLA.

With this background in place, the three specific developments or topics to be covered in this article are: (1) the development and promulgation of the International Standard Serial Number (ISSN); (2) the relationship between the International Serials Data System (ISDS) and the *International Standard Bibliographic Description for Serials, ISBD(S)*; and (3) emerging standards for serial holdings statements. This order of presentation is not accidental or capricious, but instead represents the chronological development of these serial activities.

II. INTERNATIONAL STANDARD SERIAL NUMBER (ISSN)

Interest in formulating a standard numeric identifier for serials evolved at about the same time in both the national and international arenas. In the United States, an ANSI Z39 subcommittee was organized in 1968 to develop a standard numbering code, and the work of that subcommittee subsequently resulted in a U.S. national standard in 1971 for a Standard Serial Number (SSN). At its June 1970 meeting, ISO TC46 recommended an international review of the then proposed ANSI standard. In 1974 an ISO draft standard for the ISSN was ratified as ISO 3297 and accorded full status as an internationally accepted standard.[2]

There were some differences at that time between the ISO and ANSI standards, but these were not differences stemming from conflict. Rather, they resulted from stipulations included in the ISO standard that were not present in the ANSI standard. As an example, the ISO standard identified the International Serials Data System (ISDS) as the maintenance agency for the ISSN, while the ANSI standard recognized the need for a maintenance agency but did not name one. Furthermore, the ISO standard referenced bibliographic conventions and data elements (including the concept of a "key title") to be used in support of the ISSN registration process, while the ANSI standard alluded to the need for such conventions but was not specific regarding their structure or function.

Therefore, during the mandatory five year review of the ANSI standard, it was determined that the ANSI standard should be revised to allow for full compatibility with the respective ISO standard. This revision was completed in 1978,[3] and there are now ANSI and ISO standards for serial identification systems that are fully compatible with each other. Moreover, the ISSN has now become a commonly accepted element for the identification of serial publications in national bibliographies, catalog entries (especially those provided by national cataloging agencies), and various serial control operations. In a way this represents almost the ideal scenario for standards development—an orderly, timely progression from a national development to an international effort, reconciling the two as necessary, and then acceptance and compliance with the standard by the appropriate communities.

III. ISDS AND ISBD(S)

As indicated in the previous section, both the ISO and ANSI standards for the ISSN identify the International Serials Data System (ISDS) as the authorized agency responsible for administering this program. Established in 1972 as an intergovernmental organization, ISDS is an international network of national or regional centers with an International Centre in Paris, which serves as the central coordinating agency of this worldwide system. Blocks of ISSNs are allocated to each national or regional center by the International Centre for subsequent assignment to serial publications as they are published in the respective countries. In support of this activity, the ISDS network required the kind of international bibliographic conventions for identifying serial publications that were referenced in the ISO standard for the ISSN. Detailed specifications that provided ISDS centers with guidance on how ISSNs should be assigned were developed during 1972-1973 and published in 1974 as the *Guidelines for ISDS*. In order to regulate the allocation of ISSNs within the ISDS network, it was internationally agreed that a citation acceptable to all participants in the system would be used for serials to which ISSNs are assigned. The concept of the "key title" as a control element was incorporated in the ISO standard as the citation to which an ISSN is assigned in any given ISDS bibliographic record. Detailed specifications for the transcription and construction of the key title were also included in *Guidelines for ISDS*, including the requirement that a new ISSN must be assigned when the key title of a serial changes. To document properly the ISSN and key title as identifiers in a bibliographic record, the *Guidelines* also specified additional data elements required to describe the serial publication adequately, including place of publication and publisher, beginning and ending dates of publication, abbreviated and variant forms of title, as well as any related titles (such as former titles, supplements, etc.).

At about the same time, in 1971, a Joint Working Group on the International Standard Bibliographic Description for Serials was set up by the IFLA Sections on Cataloging and on Serial Publications. After a number of meetings, a final draft was published in 1974 as the recommendations of the Joint Working Group. This not only incorporated the basic structure and concepts as the ISBD for Monographs but also reflected some of the principles of ISDS in the title and statement of responsibility areas. This included the concept of a "distinctive title" rather than the title proper of *ISBD(M)* as a more comprehensive citation, one that reflected more completely the key title concept of ISDS.

As IFLA's ISBD program expanded, and as the Joint Steering Committee for Revision of *AACR* progressed with its efforts, some discrepancies or incompatibilities were noted in the ISBD texts. This led to the formulation of the *International Standard Bibliographic Description (General)*, *ISBD(G)*, which provided a general framework for the description of all library materials and served as a model for all other ISBDs. A revision of the 1974 draft *ISBD(S)* was undertaken in light of this development. After considerable discussion and debate on the relative merits of closer alignment with the ISBD principles on the one hand and the *Guidelines for ISDS* on the other, it was finally decided that *ISBD(S)* should conform to the *ISBD(G)* framework. This meant in particular that Area 1 of *ISBD(S)* would be restricted to elements of description, with the title proper replacing the concept of "distinctive title," and with the key title of ISDS included as an identifying element in Area 8 (ISSN and Terms of Availability Area). Reflecting these conventions, the first standard edition of *ISBD(S)* was published in 1977.[4] Many of these same principles were also subsequently incorporated into *AACR2*.

As most serial librarians know, there were substantive differences between these two international standards — the IFLA sponsored *ISBD(S)* and the *ISDS Guidelines* developed in support of maintaining the ISO standard for the ISSN. As national cataloging agencies endeavored to accommodate both systems, these differences became more and more troublesome. A growing impetus to rectify this situation came not only from the Anglo-American communities but from other countries as well (most notably the Scandinavian countries which were striving to follow *AACR2* and *ISBD(S)* and at the same time beginning to embark on a major union-list project utilizing the conventions of ISDS). Reflecting the concerns of many national bibliographic agencies that were also host institutions for national ISDS centers, the ISDS Directors and Governing Board passed a resolution in 1981 urging improved compatability between ISBD(S) and the ISDS bibliographic conventions.

The expanding ISDS network recognized the need to revise the *Guidelines for ISDS* in order to represent current procedures as well as appropriate practices and policies found in related international documentation, including *ISBD(S)*. A draft revision of the *Guidelines* was circulated to all ISDS Centers in 1981. Incorporating comments received as a result of this review, the *ISDS Manual* was published in 1983 (replacing the 1973 edition of the *Guidelines*).[5] At about the same time, in accordance with agreed upon procedures, IFLA initiated a five year review of *ISBD(S)* in 1981 (as part of the overall review of all ISBD texts). A primary focus of this review involved the "harmonization" of *ISBD(S)* with the conventions of ISDS wherever possible. A draft revision of *ISBD(S)* was distributed for worldwide comment in 1984, with a subsequent review of the final text conducted by the review committee during the 1985 IFLA Conference in Chicago. Upon completion of final editing of the document, publication is now anticipated for late 1986 or early 1987.

Many of the original conflicts and discrepancies between ISDS and ISBD(S) have been satisfactorily resolved — and certainly most of the major problems have been addressed. Among the more noteworthy compromises or resolutions represented in these two international standards which contribute to improved compatibility between the two systems are the following:

- Early efforts to make the key title of ISDS completely identical to the title information in an *ISBD(S)* description were dropped when it was agreed that they served two different functions: the key title of

ISDS being a major identifying access point, and the title proper of *ISBD(S)* being an important and universally applicable element of the description of an item. However, as originally formulated, the ISDS guidelines did not allow for the inclusion of the *ISBD(S)* title proper in an ISDS record. Recognizing that this severely handicapped the ability to build an *ISBD(S)* description from ISDS data and vice versa, the title proper was added as a valid data element to the ISDS record (and generally is incorporated in these records when the ISDS key title is different from the *ISBD(S)* title proper).

- When present on a serial, *ISBD(S)* requires the edition statement to be carried in the Edition Area, while ISDS includes such information as part of the key title. Originally the edition statement was not separately delimited when part of the key title; but this has now been changed, and such edition statements are now separately delimited as qualifying information, which improves the "mapping" of data elements between ISDS and *ISBD(S)*.
- Consistent practices for determining title changes were considered critical in order to ensure a one-to-one ratio between the bibliographic entity described by *ISBD(S)* and that defined by ISDS. *ISBD(S)* originally contained no guidelines in this area (referring instead to national cataloging practices), while the original *ISDS Guidelines* reflected title change conventions that were troublesome for some national cataloging agencies. The specifications for major and minor title changes within ISDS were subsequently modified considerably, and the same basic specifications have also been incorporated into *ISBD(S)*, thereby allowing for greatly improved compatibility in this area.
- Linking entry information was originally handled quite differently in the two systems, with ISDS requiring the key title and ISSN of the related record, while the original *ISBD(S)* required either the title proper or the appropriate "catalog main entry" of the related record. The specifications within *ISBD(S)* were subsequently modified to allow for carrying the key title and ISSN in linking entry notes, which again permitted considerably more consistency between the two systems (especially for national cataloging agencies attempting to accommodate both).
- Consistent or compatible punctuation between the two systems was also a concern. While the "space-hyphen-space" continues to be a trademark so to speak of the ISDS key title (when it is necessary to add the issuing body to the key title), and the space-slash-space continues to separate the statement of responsibility from the title proper in an *ISBD(S)* description, these differences can be tolerated somewhat more easily now that the functions of the ISDS key title and *ISBD(S)* title proper have been better defined. The use of brack-

ets to indicate supplied information is also an area where ISDS and *ISBD(S)* had considerable differences—with *ISBD(S)* requiring a stricter approach because of its concern with accurate description while ISDS could operate under a more liberal approach because of its emphasis on identification rather than description. Some discrepancies still exist between the two standards, but there is far more compatibility now than in earlier versions of the two.

- Recording of the imprint was one of the more troublesome areas in that major discrepancies existed between ISDS and *ISBD(S)*. To some degree this is still a problem in that the conventions for recording place of publication and publisher continue to be somewhat different for the two systems. However, ISDS is able to allow for some flexibility in order to accommodate national practices based on *ISBD(S)*.

In view of these compromises or resolutions, it is obvious that there is not yet a perfect or absolute compatibility between the guidelines presented in the *ISDS Manual* and the conventions prescribed by *ISBD(S)*. And indeed this may never be achieved. Nevertheless, it is important to note that this ten year effort on the part of IFLA, ISDS, and many national agencies has resulted in a workable harmonization of the two systems.

IV. EMERGING STANDARDS FOR SERIAL HOLDINGS STATEMENTS

Although not a topic immediately pertinent to the subject of serials cataloging, the need for a national standard for serial holding statements has nevertheless been a growing concern for serial librarians and technical service administrators for quite some time. Indeed, the history of this development is almost as long and complicated as that of ISDS and *ISBD(S)*.

An ANSI standard for serial holdings statements at the summary level was published in 1980, following six years of work by Subcommittee 40 of Z39. While this standard proved useful for union list projects and other related activities, it was also evident that a standard was needed for serial holding statements at the detailed level. Recognizing this need, Z39 Subcommittee E was set up in 1979 to formulate such a standard and submitted a draft detailed serial holdings standard for vote in 1982. A number of negative votes were received, reflecting a strong concern that this draft standard for detailed holdings was not consistent with the existing standard for summary holdings. The following discrepancies between the two standards were particularly troublesome to the American library community:

- The standard for summary statements prescribed the recording and display of enumeration and chronology data separately (e.g., 1-10 1950-1959)—while the draft standard for detailed statements required that they be recorded and displayed together, (e.g., No. 1 [1950:Jan]-no. 10 [1959:Dec]).
- Captions (e.g., volume, number, etc.) were not allowed under the conventions of the summary holdings standard but were required in the draft standard for detailed holdings.
- Different physical forms of material could be accommodated in one summary holdings statement, while the draft detailed standard required separate holding statements for each physical form.
- The summary holding standard required non-Gregorian dates to be translated into Gregorian dates, while the draft detailed standard required the recording and display of non-Gregorian dates as they appeared on the publication.

If perpetuated, these differences would have prevented any automatic derivation of summary holding statements from detailed statements (which was a stated requirement for both standards).

To address this situation, a joint meeting of both Z39 subcommittees was held in 1983. (Also attending this meeting were individuals involved in designing a MARC Format for Holdings and Locations as well as a representative from the IFLA Section on Serial Publications, which at that time was beginning to investigate the need for an international standard for serial holdings.) At this joint meeting it was unanimously recommended that a single ANSI standard be developed that would not only encompass both the summary and detailed levels but also address the discrepancies cited above. Upon approval of the Z39 membership, the charge of Subcommittee E was revised accordingly, and in January 1985 a draft standard for serial holding statements was submitted for a ballot. As a result of this ballot, one negative vote could not be resolved, but it was considered a very "conciliatory" negative by both Subcommittee E and the NISO Program Committee. It should be noted that ANSI procedures allow for a negative vote as part of the concensus progress. However, in order to carry a negative vote, a reballot is required to alert the NISO membership of the negative vote and the reasons behind it. This necessary reballot was conducted in the summer of 1985, and no further negative responses were received. The proposed standard was then submitted to the entire ANSI membership for ratification as an ANSI standard; editorial work in preparation for publication was completed in the fall of 1985 and the standard was published in the spring of 1986. Detailed information regarding the resolution of the discrepancies summarized earlier can be found in Appendix D of the published standard.[6]

Although this represents a conclusion of sorts for a major national standard effort, it also must necessarily reference an emerging international development. IFLA's interest in pursuing an international standard for serial holdings was mentioned earlier, and since 1983 work in this area has been progressing under the auspices of the Association's Section on Serial Publications and its Working Group on Union Catalogues of Serials. A paper prepared by Marjorie Bloss on behalf of the section contains recommendations for an international standard for serial holdings statements at the summary level. Considerable input was received from countries all over the world, and the recommendations or guidelines contained in this paper exhibit a gratifying compatability with the ANSI standard. These guidelines have now been published by IFLA's UBC Office as *UBC Occasional Paper #11*.[7] The recommendations are being forwarded to ISO ITC46 for consideration in their forthcoming deliberations on a standard for serial holdings statements. Concurrently, the new ANSI standard for serial holdings will also be forwarded to ISO TC46 and will become part of the body of information to be considered in developing an international standard. Therefore, as indicated earlier, work at the national level may be concluded, while efforts at the international level are intensifying (which is not an uncommon pattern for the standards-development process to follow).

NOTES

1. For a more detailed discussion of standards organizations, see: "Organizations contributing to development of library standards," by Henriette D. Avram, Sally H. McCallum, and Mary S. Price, *Library Trends*, v.31, no. 2 (fall 1982), pp. 197-223.

2. International Organization for Standardization, *ISO 3297, Documentation—International Standard Serial Numbering (ISSN)*, Paris, ISO, 1975.

3. American National Standards Committee on Standardization in the Field of Library Work, Documentation, and Related Publishing Practices, Z39. Subcommittee 20: International Standard Serial Numbering. *American National Standard for International Standard Serial Numbering (ISSN)*. "ANSI Z39.9-1979." New York, American National Standards Institute, 1979.

4. International Federation of Library Associations and Institutions. Joint Working Group on the International Standard Bibliographic Description for Serials. *ISBD(S): International Standard Bibliographic Description for Serials*, prepared by the Joint Working Group on the International Standard Bibliographic Description for Serials set up by the IFLA Committee on Cataloguing and the IFLA Committee on Serial Publications. 1st standard ed. London, IFLA International Office for UBC, 1977.

5. International Serials Data System. *ISDS Manual*. Prepared by the ISDS International Centre. Edited by A. A. Mullis, Paris, ISDS International Centre, 1983.

6. American National Standards Committee on Library and Information Sciences and Related Publishing Practices, Z39. Subcommittee E: Serial Holdings Statements. *American National Standard for Information Sciences—Serial Holdings Statements*. "ANSI Z39.44-1986." New York, American National Standards Institute, 1986.

7. Bloss, Marjorie Ellin. *Serial holdings statements at the summary level: recommendations*. Prepared for the IFLA Section on Serial Publications. London, IFLA International Programme for UBC, 1985.

Serials Cataloguing in Sweden

Sten Hedberg

SUMMARY. During the past 25 years, Swedish research libraries have witnessed three changes of catalogue code and the implementation of a computer system, first intended for integrated use but recently changed into supporting local stand-alone systems. The present code, based on AACR2, rejected 21.1B2 for serials, preferring title as main entry in all cases. The reasons for this and other changes are described, and suggestions are made regarding improvement of the system of dissemination of cataloguing information.

The research libraries in Sweden have gone through three major catalogue changes since the late 1950s. The first one, performed as local efforts at each library during 1957-1965, meant the freezing of an older, typed or hand-written catalogue and of an old stack system, built on the Prussian principles and the alphabetical order. The new apparatus created was a card catalogue, produced by a whole-scale implementation of mimeograph technology, and a sequential numbering of the acquired material to rule the order in the stacks. For this change, the main reason of which was the need to reform the shelving system—most of these libraries use closed stacks with relatively small open reference collections—cataloguing rules were defined within a purely national tradition. For all material where personal authorship was not predominent, as e.g., in serials, the order of the elements on the title page decided the choice of main entry.

The next change came in 1975, when computerization of cataloguing was so advanced that the advantages of networks and of cooperative cataloguing had made themselves known. The joint venture of producing the union list of foreign acquisitions by Swedish research libraries had been computerized, although in a primitive manner, since 1968; this step soon led to the decision to introduce an integrated, nation-wide library information system, called LIBRIS, for the research library community, starting with the common bibliographic data base. Then, the comparison with the 1967 AACR and the emerging MARC formats made it evident that

---

Sten Hedberg is Deputy Librarian at Uppsala University Library and Head of the Department for Branch Library Activities. He was one of the compilers of the first modern Swedish cataloguing rules, published in 1974, and was also a member of the committee translating the AACR2 into the present Swedish code, published in 1983.

Uppsala University, Library, Box 510, S-751 20 UPPSALA, Sweden.

© 1987 by The Haworth Press, Inc. All rights reserved.

the cataloguing rules of 1957 just would not work in a computerized environment, either nationally or internationally.

New cataloguing rules, called *Svenska katalogiseringsregler* or *SKR* for short, were compiled in 1971-1974 and introduced in 1975. Their basis was the 1967 AACR and the early stages of the ISBDs, with some respect still paid to earlier national usage. Analytical description was used in full scale, since the random order of the 1957 rules outlined above had proved a failure. In form, the SKR were the first to start by the rules for description, then the choice of headings, and last the form of the headings. The SKR were intended to be introduced without breaking any of the current card catalogues, but the main intention of AACR 6B was kept, and that often meant a change in main entry for serials. This, and some changes in forms of headings, brought about an apparatus of references within the card catalogues.

The SKR code was used as the prescribed code for the cooperative input of records for new material into the LIBRIS data base for 10 years, 1975-1985. The most important of the changes made during this time was the introduction of the full ISBD(S) with the special third area in 1980.

The rules that in July 1985 succeeded the SKR are the *Katalogiseringsregler för svenska bibliotek*, or *KRS* for short, published in 1985. These are a translation of the AACR2 with changes in well defined places. Also this change was meant to be performed without retrospective activities in the existing card catalogues, but once more, publications issued in several parts have had to be handled specially.

Instead of the formal requirements of the SKR, taken over from AACR 6B, the translators had to consider the non-formal ones of AACR2, 21.1B2. A pure translation of AACR2 was seriously considered for the KRS, but it had to be abandoned. The main reason was not the rule itself, as stated, but the inherent need of a permanent system of revision to make sure that a scientific serial stays scientific, an administrative one stays administrative: for each single issue, you have to be able to discover changes in the scope and contents of each serial, regardless of the type of its title.

In that context, after fruitful discussions with active librarians, the translators had to decide either to keep the formal requirements of the SKR or to make the key title the main entry for serials in all cases, and the latter stand was ultimately chosen. Thus, we expect to achieve easy cooperation between the serials area in monographic descriptions and the serials entry. Furthermore, and more important, we felt that the key title, in full or in short, is the most commonly used identifier of a serial, and you should see to it that that form of the title is really used as an entry in all catalogues, also the single entry ones. You reach that goal only by making the title the main entry.

Since the inception of the system in the early 1970s, important changes have taken place in the LIBRIS system, and I have to describe briefly the network environment before going on to the present situation in serials cataloguing.

With the start of the SKR in 1975, the network could at last be used as a cooperative data base giving catalogue support: the first copy catalogued was the main effort, the followers coming on with a minimum of work. The primary key used, and still used, is the ISBN or ISSN if one is available; several such numbers in the same publication are equivalent, and pieces without a standardized number are input under a local number. The system was used for current acquisitions alone, so few or no current journals were recorded: for those, the 1957-1965 campaign had already given the current card catalogues what they needed.

On the other hand, current monograph serials had to be recorded retrospectively, since the rules prescribed that the series area and the series added entry be created by a link from the monograph record to the serial record. This retrospective work turned out to be rather cumbersome. It also both forced and helped in the adaptation of the current catalogues to the SKR, since the serial record according to the SKR was often different from that created under the 1957 rules, and the serial added entries followed the actual main entry of the serial. Some help in closing or bridging the gap between the different parts of the serial added entry sequence was thus obtained.

During the rest of the 1970s, the importance of the network gradually increased, and in 1980, a very considerable number of libraries and terminals were added. Also, among other facilities, British and American MARC records for the last two years are (with minor exceptions) available in the file, as is the ISDS file, and this means that the data base can be used also as a bibliography, not only a joint catalogue, and that also the cataloguing of the first copy can find reliable support from existing information.

The system as a whole is still concentrated around the bibliographic data base. The inclusion of other routines did not succeed during the 1970s, and early in the 1980s a policy was adopted to limit the LIBRIS system to union catalogue, cataloguing support and location for interlibrary loans, while the other routines are left to stand-alone systems at each university. This also means that the LIBRIS system must be used as a source for the bibliographic part of a local system: the records in question can be copied from LIBRIS into the local store equipment. For the future, a permanent system-to-system communication must be established between LIBRIS and each local system, the structure of which is not yet decided but must be so under a well-defined standard.

For the cataloguing, this recent development has at last meant that the scope of day-to-day cataloguing in LIBRIS changed from production of catalogue cards to the establishment of a computer-stored catalogue, reflecting all the active material of a collection. Also, it was at last remembered that the current journals are very badly covered by the LIBRIS system, and retrospective recording of holdings information began parallel at a number of libraries. The ISDS records present in the base proved to be an interesting support, especially when compared to older records for the serials available in the card catalogues. Some traces of earlier LIBRIS activities in the field of serials were also discovered, and I am afraid I have to admit that the quality of the data base has not always been the main concern of all parties involved. A major cleaning is in progress.

So, for example, when the main library at Uppsala University undertook this retrospective recording, some 6,000 records for current journals had to be handled. Well above 75% of the records needed were found in the data base, half of which were "raw" ISDS records, so under 25% had to be recorded from scratch. However, the work of cleaning older records proved in fact more cumbersome than that of completing ISDS records, and that is the main cause why the project has gone far more slowly than anticipated. Our main consolation is that we get a reliable data base that both we and other libraries can use permanently.

Today, accordingly, we have card catalogues where records from three different codes exist side by side and where the catalogue cards may bear signs of two changes of main entry of the serial in question. Parallel to this, we have a common data base where ISDS-based records, unchanged ISDS records and totally home-made records exist side by side and are now being reconciled, if copies of the serial exist in Sweden. This data base is now being completed retrospectively with holdings information, as a high priority. What have we learned from these two decades?

The answer is something like an area analysis divided into three parts according to the bodies and/or auxiliaries most involved. The background is our needs, in a university community where the vast majority of the serials are acquired from abroad at substantial cost and must be processed with a minimum of delay in the library.

1. *The Production, the Publisher, the Issuing Body*

It seems unlikely that very much can be done to improve the publishers or the issuing bodies in the fields of title/name changes, new layouts, mergers, splits, etc. But the sheer publicizing of the implications of the citation and use of serials should contribute to the elimination of certain simple mistakes, such as (a) continuing to print the ISSN of the former title on issues bearing a changed title, or (b) lack in consistency between various presentations of the title and authorship information between issues in different languages and/or between different parts of the same issue (cover, spine, etc.).

Furthermore, I feel sure that the same method may dissuade publishers from making minor title changes and using complicated or parallel numbering, for example. Standardization, lastly, should be invoked to help to create a better indication of the type of numbering, such as: Will Nos. 1-6, 1986, be followed by a No. 7 or a No. 1, 1987?

2. National Bibliography, UBC and All That

The concept of universal bibliographic control (UBC), to be attained by the early establishment and distribution of a universally reliable catalogue record, has for monographs taken the form of CIP records and/or early available MARC records in computerized national systems. Serials lag far behind, despite notable efforts on both the national and international level. The *British National Bibliography*, for instance, issues records for serials; the ISDS network, too, is now well established. As a rule, you do not find a CIP record with an authorized ISSN printed in the first issue of a serial. You may find the ISSN, but you will wait a long time to find a corresponding record in the distributed ISDS file, and you must go to the regional ISDS center instead. Lastly, the contents of the ISDS records are remarkably scanty, especially in the lack of the Numeric designation area and in the superficial formatting of variant titles.

The way the ISDS network is set up, there is little hope for improvement. The time necessary for reporting, validation and distribution is too long. But the success of the CIP in monographs from scholarly and/or professional publishers invites me to suggest a CIP technique also for serials, under which a reliable record be established with the help of the national ISDS agency and be printed in the first issue of the serial and then at least once a year forthwith.

3. The Library

In the library, a catalogue record must be created at the start of the acquisition process. This is to be the reliable basis for the various transactions taking place during the lifetime of the serial: issues must be recorded, as invoices; volumes must be sent to a binder; issues must be lent and circulated. When the serial dies or the subscription ends, the record is closed and continues just for circulation support until the entire set is eventually weeded out of the library. At any time, short-title or single-entry lists of serials may be produced for the benefit of the patrons.

Fast and accurate access to the record each time must be assured. It is essential that the acquisition of a serial proceed expeditiously and safely from the time the serial is requested or from its occurrence in an agent's invoice, despite the risk of other serials having the same title. The ISDS system has contributed substantially to this goal, but it is not likely that all serials acquired by libraries will ever be included in the ISDS data base, so rules compatible with the ISDS ones must be implemented by the libraries themselves. Furthermore, without the support of a prominently displayed ISSN, serials covered by the ISDS may also cause problems of identification.

On the other hand, the use of ISSN as primary key to a record in a computerized environment, the method used by LIBRIS, is not to be implemented uncritically. You must be able to use the ISSN, but the system as such should not be built around a technique that forces you to create a new record for every change of the key title, no matter how slight, and to wait for an authorization before the final record can be made.

The present stand of the Swedish research library community in serials cataloguing may be summarized as follows:

1. The libraries can gain more from networking and other cooperation in serials than in other material, provided the network information can be effectively transformed and used in the local acquisition and circulation subsystems.
2. Since serials are better covered by indexing and abstracting services than monographs are, and, if series, are also analyzed, detailed subject analysis on the serial level can be discarded. What remains of the cataloguing is description and entry, and the information for that is most easily available in the acquisitions department. Accordingly, acquisitions and cataloguing can be organized more closely together in serials than in other material.
3. The role of the ISDS as standardizers of serial titles is not yet fully realized by librarians, which leads to annoying incidents. So, e.g., if the key title for a serial is in Japanese, we must respect that also when the piece carries an English title was well. That is a matter of staff training.
4. The support in other respects from the ISDS records in cataloguing is most positively felt in the history notes (tags 760-789) while at least early records contain very little of substance in the descriptive areas. We hope for an improvement, in close collaboration with the national institutions.
5. The repeated, manifold use of the catalogue record by staff working under stress and its use in various kinds of output make it virtually imperative that the main point of access be as close as possible to the "title as it appears on the piece." Any attempt to found a choice of main entry on contents analysis or similar parameters is bound to fail, sooner or later.

REFERENCES

The 1957 rules were published in a number of local editions, e.g.: *Provisoriska katalogregler för Uppsala universitetsbibliotek*: avseende litteratur tryckt 1963 och senare. —Uppsala, 1963.

Svenska katalogiseringsregler / pa Forskningsbiblioteksradets uppdrag utarbetade av Marie-Louise Bachman och Sten Hedberg och därefter bearbetade av en särskild katalogregelkommitté. —Ny, utökad uppl. —Stockholm : Kungl. Biblioteket, 1980. —ISBN 91-7000-080-8.

Katalogiseringsregler för svenska bibliotek : svensk översätning och bearbetning av Anglo-American cataloguing rules, second edition / utgiven av SAB/DFI:s kommitté för deskriptiv katalogisering ; redaktörer: Marie-Louise Bachman och Bodil Gustavsson. —Lund : Bibliotekstjänst, 1983. — ISBN 91-7018-232-9.

AACR2: BASIC CONCERNS

ACCR2's Effect on Public Services

Cindy Hepfer, BA, MLS
Will Hepfer, BA, MLS

SUMMARY. Many objections and reservations were expressed before AACR2 was adopted by the Library of Congress, the major shared cataloging bibliographic utilities, and most American and British libraries. This article recapitulates the perceived advantages and disadvantages of the Second Edition, insofar as this affects library public services. The article then discusses alternatives to implementation and shows how sometimes the alternatives caused more problems for public service librarians than did the new code itself. The conclusion is drawn that most library users have not noticed AACR2's effects or do not care enough about them to compliment or complain.

A pleasant Sunday drive can be ruined by a torn-up stretch of roadbed preceded by a sign indicating: TEMPORARY INCONVENIENCE FOR PERMANENT IMPROVEMENT. SIX-LANE SUPERHIGHWAY UNDER CONSTRUCTION. It is a small consolation to know that conditions will be better someday, when all that's visible in the distance is a dusty expanse of bumpy gravel.

This depressing scene is not unlike the circumstances imagined by many public service librarians when their libraries announced that AACR2 would be used for cataloging library materials after a certain date. Unless their existing card catalogs were horrendously ineffective, it is difficult to envision anyone joyfully looking forward to the inevitable

---

Cindy Hepfer is Head of the Serials Department at the Health Sciences Library at the State University of New York at Buffalo.
Will Hepfer is Head of the Serials Department in Central Technical Services at the State University of New York at Buffalo.

© 1987 by The Haworth Press, Inc. All rights reserved.

bumpy period when a substantial portion of the card catalog would have to be refiled, or, if the conflicting headings were not going to be changed, library users—including the staff themselves—would be forced to do dual look-ups in many cases. Not only were they going to have to learn new principles to use the card catalog proficiently, but, alas, some would have to remember the old principles, too. Even worse, public service librarians would have a much harder time trying to explain it all.

This is not to say that everyone was antagonistic toward the new rules because they loved the pre-AACR2 rules so much.

Pinzelik says that

> finding a complex citation in a [pre-AACR2] library catalog is often accomplished by an experienced reference librarian "thinking like a cataloger," a technique which requires suppressing one's natural instincts to look in the most logical place and instead selecting the most complicated of all the possibilities. With the changing of cataloging rules from AACR1 to AACR2, however, arriving at an educated or lucky guess should no longer require suspension of normal thought processes.[1]

Indeed, AACR2 offered many more long-range benefits to libraries, and, by the time administrative decisions were handed down, the potential merits and weaknesses of the new code had been thoroughly discussed. By then, most librarians had conceded that there was more to be gained than to be lost from AACR2 in the long run. To recap:

ADVANTAGES

First, there is the altruistic advantage that AACR2 unifies the separate American and British versions of the Anglo-American Cataloguing Rules. Compromises for the sake of the international sharing of bibliographic information are easier to accept than change for the sake of change. According to Bloss,

> by adhering to the same cataloging principles, guidelines and interpretations both nationally and internationally, greater consistency will be found from one library to the next and from one union list to the next. As serials bibliographic files are shared and used for multiple purposes as is the CONSER file, libraries become inextricably linked. In a natural extension, the cataloging principles that apply to one apply to all. This can only benefit the users of those files be they librarians, researchers, or the general public.[2]

Second is the practicality involved: after the Library of Congress and the major bibliographic utilities—OCLC, RLIN, UTLAS, and WLN— declared that AACR2 would be their cataloging standard, few libraries could afford *not* to adopt the new rules. The availability of so many ready-made, machine-readable cataloging records is an alternative that few libraries can refuse.

Bibliographically, AACR2 offered numerous improvements over the original edition. It incorporated the amendments that had been made to AACR since 1967 and added or expanded rules pertaining to non-book materials. Whether libraries chose to collect outside the realm of traditional paper formats or not, the new rules effectively eliminated one of the arguments between public service librarians who wanted, say, videodiscs, and technical service librarians who objected because they weren't sure how to handle them.

Even before Lancaster did his famous study,[3] most public service librarians probably had a pretty strong hunch that library users usually approach a serial, especially a periodical, by title. Titles are the most constant access point offered by most indexes, abstracts, and online retrieval services, and AACR2 capitalized on these odds by replacing many complex corporate main entries with title main entries. Surely library users stand a much greater chance of finding *Federal Reserve Bulletin* — especially in an alphabetized collection or in a periodicals list or a union list of serials where added entries and cross-references are minimal — if it isn't hidden behind "United States. Board of Governors of the Federal Reserve System," as was the case with AACR.

AACR2 also introduced many smaller changes that were appreciated because they each simplified a point that had caused some confusion in the past. Title change terminology, for example, was much easier for library users to understand after AACR2 purged the distinction between "continues/continued by" and "supersedes/superseded by" in favor of "continues" and "continued by." Enumeration and chronology, likewise, are simplified because they're recorded as they appear on the piece, instead of being reduced to a statement of volume and date. Thus issue numbers, exact dates, and even parallel numbering schemes are noted.

Still another helpful change was the reduction of ways of recording perplexing initialisms from four to two. Although AACR2 recognizes both "ALA" and "A.L.A." as acceptable, it no longer tolerates these same forms with spaces between the letters.

AACR2 was also applauded for providing numerous alternative access points, e.g., parallel titles and running titles. Including the transcripti on of a statement of responsibility from the piece is still another way that AACR2 is more helpful than the earlier code. According to Arret, such improvements are significant because "even more than in the past, the catalog will have the capacity to serve as a *reference* tool, and not merely as a finding and bibliographic one."[4]

Perhaps the biggest advantage of AACR2 was one that was not likely to go into effect at most libraries until a while after the new rules were implemented. Many librarians perceived AACR2 to be a requisite steppingstone between an international shared-cataloging data base and their future online catalogs. Compromises were going to be necessary, of course, but the end result was (hopefully) going to be worth the (hopefully) temporary inconvenience.

DISADVANTAGES

Pre-AACR2 rules weren't terrible, and AACR2 isn't perfect, but the fact remains that the Second Edition is here to stay—at least until AACR3 or something better comes along. Although many of the objections that have been expressed about the new rules are perfectly valid, AACR2 maintains its stance on most rules in the name of consistency.

Title main entries, for example, become troublesome when someone is trying to distinguish a generic title from a large selection of "Journals," "Bulletins," or "Revistas." When confronted by a huge selection of catalog cards or a long list of "Reports," "Report ons" and "Report tos," many public service librarians have probably yearned for the good old pre-AACR2 days when most such cases could be automatically turned into nice, predictable corporate entries.

AACR2 would be easier to forgive on this count if it were totally consistent on the matter of title main entry, instead of just being *mostly* consistent. Rule 21.1B2 exempts (1) works of an administrative nature dealing with the body itself, (2) specified governmental and legal works, (3) a record of the collective thought of the body, or (4) a report on the collective activity of a conference—and it is these exceptions that complicate the efforts of librarians who would instruct library users regarding effective searching techniques.

IMPLEMENTATION

Even prior to the adoption of AACR2, Mueller acknowledged that "the problems . . . lie not so much in the changes themselves, many of which could make your professional lives easier, but in the integration of these changes into our present catalogs."[5] Indeed, all of the options for implementing the new code were fraught with the need to impose either much more work on the library staff or much more inconvenience on library users. Needless to say, neither alternative was very popular, and no implementation scheme emerged as the preference of all. Rather, libraries made highly individualized decisions based on a wide range of factors.

Some libraries chose to "freeze" their pre-AACR2 card catalogs and to begin a new file with AACR2 records. Reasons included: (1) not wanting to mix dissimilar entries in the same file and not being able to afford the staff time for an extensive changeover project, (2) wanting to discontinue the frustration of trying to maintain one or more already unwieldy card catalogs, (3) seizing a good opportunity to move from card to microform or online files.

Starting a new catalog was perceived to be a practical solution to a temporary problem that would go away when an online catalog became a reality. Nobody believed that library users would not be inconvenienced by it, but many rationalized that the money saved by not integrating AACR2 and pre-AACR2 headings would help toward getting an automated system that much sooner.

More libraries chose to integrate AACR2 into their existing catalogs. They coped by interfiling old and new headings, changing old headings to new headings, or by using extensive cross-references and/or guide cards. Some changed existing headings only under certain circumstances, such as when less than a pre-determined number of cards were affected, or the heading was a particularly important one. The latter approach appears to be practical, although the library user may not be served well by inconsistent applications of rules in the same catalog. Complete consistency may not even be possible, however. Rush contends that

> the combination of the many options provided for in the [AACR2] rules; the use of such phrases as "if appropriate," "commonly known," "predominant," "if necessary" (all giving rise to the question: In whose judgment?); and the various compromises adopted by such eminent libraries as the Library of Congress, the British Library and the National Library of Canada (which compromises differ from library to library), makes achievement of [consistency], even to a limited extent, highly improbable.[6]

Libraries that shelve periodical volumes alphabetically found themselves in a real predicament when AACR2 was implemented. It is one thing to shift a lot of catalog cards around and another to have to re-mark and relocate a large number of bound volumes. Anything less, however, was perceived to be a real disservice to library users. Alphabetical arrangements lost much of their user friendliness when old titles were left under AACR corporate headings, e.g., "Association for Computing Machinery. Special Interest Group on Language Analysis and Studies in the Humanities. *SIGLASH newsletter*," but similar new titles cataloged under

AACR2 were cataloged and shelved according to the title proper, e.g., *SIGOA newsletter*. Union lists, periodical lists, and other relevant files would have to be changed too, of course. There were no popular solutions to this dilemma.

CONCLUSION

Libraries formulated individualized approaches to AACR2 depending on a wide variety of factors. Primary considerations were the condition of the existing card file or files and how far in the future was an online catalog likely to become a reality. The 14 cases described in *Research Libraries and Their Implementation of AACR2*,[7] edited by Hopkins and Edens, are illustrative of the wide range of possibilities that were available to the decision-makers.

One would expect then that public service at these libraries would also have been affected to a widely variable extent. On the contrary, however, Hopkins and Edens, who surveyed all 104 member libraries of the Association of Research Libraries, report that "there was surprisingly little response from either the general public or public services staff, either complaining or complimenting on the results of the implementation process."[8] By extension, this suggests that the disadvantages within AACR2 did not wreak the supposed havoc—at least within the first few years after the new rules were put into effect at most libraries.

The lack of negative reactions may be for several reasons. Most pre-AACR2 catalogs had already evolved through several sets of rules and been subject to all manner of local idiosyncracies. For most library users, AACR2 is only one more twist in a mystifying tool that they really don't want to be using in the first place. They have no idea why search strategies work or don't work and probably are satisfied with the options of either asking a librarian or doing without the information. Few library users require comprehensive coverage to meet their needs.

Library users approach information from different directions and with varying degrees of library skills. The odds are that few of them will ever want or need most of the potentially confusing types of publications that are described above. A few will, however, and it is for them that catalogers continue trying to resolve the perceived shortcomings of AACR2.

Public service librarians then need to capitalize on the catalogers' efforts. Regardless of how AACR2 was implemented, studying the existing catalog for an understanding of its arrangement and interrelationships is worthwhile preparation for anyone who must use and interpret this fundamental resource. The catalog—in whatever form it may be: card, microform, electronic—cannot help but be a complex instrument, and helping library patrons to use it as effectively as possible is one of the best public services that a librarian can offer.

NOTES

1. Barbara P. Pinzelik, "The Periodical, the Patron, and AACR2," in Neal L. Edgar, ed., *AACR2 and Serials: The American View* (New York: Haworth Press, 1983), p.41.
2. Marjorie E. Bloss, "The Impact of AACR2 on Union Lists of Serials," in Neal L. Edgar, ed., *AACR2 and Serials: The American View* (New York: Haworth Press, 1983), p.108.
3. Frederick W. Lancaster, *The Measurement and Evaluation of Library Services* (Washington, D.C.: Information Resources Press, 1977), Chapter 2.
4. Linda Arret, "New Catalog/New Librarian? Reference at LC," *RQ* 19 (Fall 1979), p.46.
5. Carolyn Mueller, "Impact of AACR2 on Public Service," *Colorado Libraries* 6 (March 1980), p.31.
6. James E. Rush, "AACR2 from an Information Scientist's Point of View," in Neal L. Edgar, *AACR2 and Serials; The American View* (New York: Haworth Press, 1983), p.47.
7. Judith Hopkins and John A. Edens, *Research Libraries and Their Implementation of AACR2* (Greenwich, Conn.: JAI Press, 1986).
8. Ibid., p.14.

Serials Cataloging with AACR2: The Primary Problems and Concerns

James W. Williams, BS, MSLS

SUMMARY. To uncover the problems of serials cataloging with AACR2, an examination was made of the literature specifically focused on serials cataloging, the Library of Congress' rule interpretations and policy decisions published in *Cataloging Service Bulletin*, and the work of the ALA RTSD Serials Section Committee to Study Serials Cataloging. While entry of serials was intensely debated during code revision, it has received little attention since the publication of AACR2. The absence of a rule for uniform titles specific to serials presented a serious problem. The guidelines formulated jointly by the Library of Congress and the National Library of Canada have provided a resolution. Uniform titles continue to be a controversial issue, however, and more research is needed in this area. Various complexities of titles proper of serials and other areas of description where the code lacks explicitness have been addressed by *Cataloging Service Bulletin* and the Committee to Study Serials Cataloging. The Library of Congress has taken a very pro-AACR2 stance in its rule interpretations and policy decisions, and in recent years the Committee to Study Serials Cataloging has assumed a more aggressive role in matters pertinent to its charge.

The study from which the present article resulted was made to identify problems that have arisen in the application of the second edition of the *Anglo-American Cataloguing Rules* (hereafter referred to as AACR2) to serials publications since its general adoption in January, 1981, and to learn the concerns the code brought serials librarians, as expressed by (1) the major literature devoted specifically to serials cataloging, (2) the Library of Congress (LC) rule interpretations and policy decisions related to serials cataloging that have appeared in the quarterly issues of *Cataloging Service Bulletin*, and (3) the work of the ALA Resources and Technical Services Division Serials Section Committee to Study Serials Cataloging. The discussion is limited to printed serials and does not explore the continuing controversy surrounding microforms cataloging.

James W. Williams is Sociology/Social Work Subject Specialist, Education and Social Science Library, and Cataloging Coordinator, Social Sciences Council Libraries at the University of Illinois at Urbana-Champaign, 1408 W. Gregory Drive, Urbana, IL 61801.

LITERATURE DURING CODE REVISION

During the years of code revision, the literature pertaining to serials cataloging was primarily concerned with entry. In reviewing serials activity for 1975, James stated:

> Nearly everyone seems to agree that the rules governing the cataloging of serials need to be revised, but just what form this revision should take has been the topic of much heated debate. The present concern with rules for entry and description of serials has been stimulated by emerging international standards. . . . Of particular interest to serials catalogers is the vote of the Resources and Technical Services Division Catalog Code Revision Committee (CCRC) at the 1975 Annual Conference to request the editors of the revised *Anglo-American Cataloging Rules (AACR)* to implement a rule specifying the entry of all serials under title and the committee's subsequent adoption at the 1976 Midwinter Meeting of a recommendation for a concept of corporate authorship which would permit the limited entry of serials under corporate author.[1]

Rules for the entry of serials publications were discussed at length. The November 22, 1974, issue of the *Library of Congress Information Bulletin* included articles by Spaulding and Howard.[2,3] Spaulding defended the current rules while Howard argued for title entry for all serials, offering as an alternative title entry for all serials except those having solely generic titles. The fall 1975 issue of *Library Resources & Technical Services* included seven articles dealing with serials entry. Cole proposed the adoption of the British version of the AACR1 rule,[4] Gorman favored a separate set of rules,[5] and Carpenter advocated having no separate rules.[6] Many variations between the Gorman and Carpenter proposals were explored. Simonton provided a succinct summary of the several options suggested.[7] Carpenter's proposal was ultimately chosen by the Catalog Code Revision Committee of the Resources and Technical Services Division. A limited concept of corporate authorship was retained in AACR2, with the rule as it is written having been heavily influenced by the work of Eva Verona for the International Federation of Library Association's Committee on Cataloguing.[8]

In his review of serials work for 1976, James noted that the furor over serials entry had not abated:

> Although the time seemed long past when one could effect any substantive changes in the rules being written for the second edition of the *Anglo-American Cataloging Rules (AACR)*, any mention of entry of serials at a gathering of serials librarians was bound to draw a

crowd—and the crowd was doing more than just listening. Neal Edgar, a member of the Catalog Code Revision Committee (CCRC) Team 2 (Serials) has received six to eight inches of letters and supporting documents dealing directly with *AACR* Rule 6 (entry of serials) alone.[9]

COMMITTEE TO STUDY SERIALS CATALOGING

The ALA Resources and Technical Services Division Serials Section Committee to Study Serials Cataloging came into being as a result of the code revision, evolving from the Serials Section's Ad Hoc AACR Revision Study Committee. The ad hoc committee was created soon after code revision was begun and charged "to solicit input from serials librarians, to present this information to the RTSD Catalog Code Revision Committee (CCRC), to study the drafts of the AACR revisions and to prepare comments from the point of view of serials for the RTSD CCRC."[10] When code revision was completed, serials librarians and most particularly serials catalogers were reluctant to abandon the ad hoc committee, which had become a continuing forum for the discussion of serials cataloging and serials cataloging related questions and problems. At the 1978 Midwinter Meeting the recommendation was made that the status of the ad hoc committee be changed to a standing committee. The recommendation met with approval, and the first meetings of the Committee to Study Serials Cataloging were held at the 1978 Annual Conference.

The committee's initial work with AACR2 was the descriptive cataloging of twenty serial titles, a task undertaken to identify problems and provide guidance in the application of the new code. This work required approximately two years, with the first five titles being discussed at the 1979 Annual Conference and the final three at the 1981 Midwinter Meeting. After the thorough discussion of the selected titles (which turned out to be nineteen because one proved to be a monographic set), the committee continued to center its meetings largely on the discussion of specific serials cataloging questions sent in advance.

The original committee consisted of five members, with one member serving as chair. Two liaison members have been added. The Serials Section annual report for 1981/1982 noted:

> In order to insure that the deliberations of the Cataloging and Classification Section's Committee on Cataloging: Description and Access (CC:DA) are available to the Serials Cataloging Committee and that SS concerns are made known to CC:DA, the Serials Section representative to CC:DA has been made an ex officio member of the Serials Cataloging Committee.[11]

A liaison member to represent the Library of Congress was added in 1984 in response to the frequent need of the committee to communicate with LC concerning serials cataloging related rule interpretations and policies.

The committee's charge was also expanded somewhat in 1984 when it became recognized that license was needed to take a more active role in matters of concern to serials cataloging. The earlier charge read, in part: "To solicit contributions from librarians concerning serials cataloging problems; to discuss these problems; to forward unresolved problems to appropriate groups for action; and to report back to participants the recommended solutions."[12] The current charge is stated:

> To identify, discuss, and propose solutions to problems related to serials cataloging. To make recommendations to the Committee on Cataloging: Description and Access and other appropriate bodies regarding changes to, or the interpretations of, the catalog code and appropriate communications formats which will enhance access to serials. To distribute the minutes of the meeting through available sources. To establish liaison, as appropriate, between the committee and other bodies having similar interests.[13]

In recent years, as experience has been gained with AACR2, fewer specific questions have been addressed to the committee. And while the discussion of such questions continues to be an important function, the committee has begun to spend more time with broader issues and concerns.

GENERAL RECEPTION OF AACR2 AND MAIN PROBLEMS PERCEIVED

In the review of serials activity for 1982, the second year during which AACR2 was in general use, Weber reported:

> Serials catalogers, though still faced with unsettled or unsettling issues, adjusted to and implemented the new rules with a minimum of fanfare. Most of the literature, little though there was on the topic, and personal conversations with those most directly involved with AACR2, reflected an attitude of acceptance and an overall appreciation of the improvements of the new code as applied to serials.[14]

Indeed, the literature concerned with the application of AACR2 to serials has been quite favorable since the code became available for review in 1979. Three problems have been cited by reviewers, however, one of a general nature and two specifically related to serials cataloging. The general criticism is that the entire code is neither as sufficiently explicit nor as directive as catalogers are inclined to think it should be. The problems specific to serials are the lack of provision for uniform titles and a failure to provide adequately for the possible complexities of titles proper.

ABSENCE OF EXPLICIT DETAIL IN TEXT

In an early review of AACR2 Soper wrote:

> ... it is clearly written, though I had a feeling of things left out as I went through it. We are told that these omissions will provide more flexibility and room for adaptation to meet local needs. What is needed now is a manual containing interpretations and adding explanations that were in AACR1 but intentionally omitted from AACR2.[15]

And Weber made the following observation in the review of serials work for 1981, the first year that AACR2 was being generally used:

> Those who take comfort in the security blanket of black-and-white rules with little or no room for gray areas most likely did not cheer the events of the past year. This cataloging code will surely be dubbed as the fluid, evolving code. The interpretations and explanations of the Library of Congress practices with regard to specific rules, as published in *Cataloging Service Bulletin* during the year, can be viewed as a mandatory supplement to the rules themselves.[16]

Cummins among others has also made reference to the lack of explicitness in the text of AACR2. In a survey conducted to assess the attitudes and opinions of catalogers and educators toward the code, Musavi found strong and positive overall support for it. Nonetheless, 20 of the 39 educators (51 per cent) and 62 of the 104 catalogers (60 per cent) expressed agreement with the statement: "Many rules in AACR2 are vague and subject to local and subjective interpretations."[17]

Published quarterly by the Processing Services at the Library of Congress, *Cataloging Service Bulletin* has gradually provided much of the explanatory material excluded from AACR2, serving in essence as the manual for which Soper noted a need and becoming a *de facto* supplement to the code itself. Libraries in the United States have tended to follow the Library of Congress practices in cataloging. This was done traditionally in order that LC catalog copy could be used locally with minimal modification and, in recent years, because online bibliographic utilities such as OCLC and RLIN require certain standards and conformity from participants inputting original cataloging. The perceived vagueness of AACR2 and the consequent dependence on *Cataloging Service Bulletin* may inadvertently have served to bring a greater and desirable degree of uniformity to cataloging. With the exception of Chapter 11 (Microforms) which LC did not implement at the request of the Association for Research Libraries and other library groups,[19] the LC stance has been very pro-AACR2. The material published in *Cataloging Service Bulletin* is largely LC's interpretation of AACR2 rules that lend themselves to interpretation and LC's policy decisions on options provided by the code. The few LC directives that are contradictory to AACR2 are noted in the following discussion.

The initial work of the Committee to Study Serials Cataloging also provided helpful guidance for the application of the new code to serials. The list of titles selected for descriptive cataloging was published in the *RTSD Newsletter* and *The Serials Librarian* for anyone wishing to test their skills against those of the committee members.[20,21] Committee members worked independently, not in consultation, and kept detailed notes regarding rule interpretations and decisions. Examples of the fully cataloged titles were distributed at committee meetings and subsequently published in the *RTSD Newsletter*. The *RTSD Newsletter* also included the more complex questions that were encountered in the cataloging of specific titles along with answers that represented LC's current thinking.[22-25]

UNIFORM TITLES

Many serials publications having nondistinctive titles qualify for title main entry under the AACR2 rules. The failure of the code to provide for uniform titles by which to distinguish otherwise identical publications presented a major problem. Soper, Turner, Frost, Kovacic, McIver, and Sadowski have commented on this weakness.[26-32]

The Library of Congress and the National Library of Canada jointly formulated guidelines for the creation of uniform titles for serials. *Cataloging Service Bulletin* no. 5 (Summer 1979) stated the rationale for using uniform titles to distinguish between two or more otherwise identical serials and gave six guidelines for their construction (under rule 25.5B). Modifications or additions to the guidelines appeared in *Bulletins* no. 11 (Winter 1981), no. 12 (Spring 1981), no. 14 (Fall 1981), no. 20 (Spring 1983), no. 23 (Winter 1983), and no. 25 (Summer 1984). The most dramatic change came with no. 23, when LC announced the intention to qualify in general by place of publication instead of issuing body, which had previously been the preferred qualifier.

In addition to the information regarding the formulation of uniform titles, LC has provided other useful criteria. These include the suggestions that conflicts are not to be predicted; that uniform titles should be devised for serials being cataloged, not for those already cataloged with which they conflict; that serials catalogers may take into account any serial of the same title about which they know, whether it is in the catalog or not; and that the catalog containing an identical title is the file against which searching and cataloging are being done.

The Committee to Study Serials Cataloging has discussed some aspect of uniform titles no less than seven times, first at the Midwinter Meeting in 1980 and most recently at the 1985 Annual Conference. The earlier discussions were centered on LC policy and application of the LC guidelines. Although problems with the original guidelines were discussed and unhappiness expressed about the use of corporate body as the preferred qualifier, the committee opposed LC's change to place of publication when it was presented as a proposal to CC:DA.

Uniform titles have major implications for catalog users, serials check-in files, and union lists. Dissatisfaction continues to exist. Bloss found divergency between the LC rule interpretations governing uniform titles and the interpretations of the National Library of Canada.[33] Cole perceives a weakness in LC's method of distinguishing for main entries only and has urged the adoption of the British Library's concept of "unique titles for serials," whereby uniform titles are created for added entries as well as main entries.[34]

COMPLEXITIES OF TITLES PROPER

Sadowski has mentioned the AACR2 failure to provide for the possible complexities of serial titles as a weakness, stating his belief that this resulted in part from the lack of distinction between serial and monograph description.[35] McIver has also pointed to problems in this area, while Soper, Turner, and Frost have discussed the lack of provision for treating as minor title changes those changes that are of short duration or prove to be no more than temporary.[36-39] The necessity of creating multiple records and the confusion that such records often cause for catalog users was discussed by the Committee to Study Serials Cataloging at the 1982 Annual Conference. Turner and Frost granted the subjectivity of short duration, and Frost added the reminder that this provision of AACR1 was abandoned by the Library of Congress in 1977 because of problems it was causing with the CONSER program.

Numerous title complexities have been addressed in *Cataloging Service Bulletin*. Issues no. 10 (Fall 1980), no. 13 (Summer 1981) and no. 20 (Spring 1983) provided guidelines for determining whether a common title or a section title should be treated as the title proper (rules 12.1B3-12.1B5). No. 22 (Fall 1983) gave the instruction that parallel titles added to the chief source of information should be recorded in a note and the title proper not considered to have changed even if the choice of title proper would have been affected had the title added later appeared on the issue from which cataloging was done. No. 26 (Fall 1984) expanded the interpretation to account also for parallel titles deleted or those that vary from the issue on which the description was based (rule 12.7B5).

Change in the title proper of serials was defined in essentially the same way in both editions of AACR, but reviewers have been unanimous in their agreement that the rule (21.2A) is stated with much more clarity in the newer edition. The Library of Congress rule interpretations have described what should not be considered a change in title. *Cataloging Service Bulletin* no. 18 (Fall 1982) expanded upon the AACR2 guidelines to include changes occurring beyond the first five words that do not change the meaning of the title or indicate a change in subject coverage and changes that occur beyond the first five words that might easily be overlooked when all manifestations of the title are considered. No. 22 (Fall 1983) discussed the addition of titles and changes in the order of titles, instructing:

> Whenever the title proper of a serial (as selected from the earliest issue) continues to appear on the chief source of later issues, retain it as the title proper. Do not consider that the title proper has changed because later issues of the serial give titles in more than one language or script in a different order from the order on the earliest issue or because later issues have a parallel title that did not appear on the earliest issue.[40]

No. 25 (Summer 1984) carried guidelines concerning multiple forms of the same word and fluctuating titles. The several LC rule interpretations have included the instruction that when doubt exists as to whether the title proper has changed, a change should be considered to have taken place.

At the 1985 Annual Conference the Committee to Study Serials Cataloging discussed the aforementioned rule interpretations in conjunction with the guidelines from the draft of the second edition of the *ISBD(S): International Standard Bibliographic Description for Serials* that define minor changes in titles proper.[41] A crucial divergency between AACR2 and the *ISBD(S)* draft is the latter's treatment as a minor change in title changes that occur when the name of an issuing body is either joined to or separated from the title proper by the addition or omission of a connective phrase. At the 1986 Midwinter Meeting the committee voted to recommend a rule change that would bring the AACR2 rule into conformity with the *ISBD(S)* guidelines and incorporate the several LC rule interpretations.

ENTRY OF SERIALS

Entry of serials has received little comment in other than an appreciative context since the publication of AACR2. In an early review Turner mentioned that the problem posed by publications concerned in part with the corporate body was not addressed.[42] Both Kovacic and Turner have expressed reservation about content as a criterion for entry, with Turner reiterating her belief that title entry for all serials would have been the better rule.[43,44]

The application of the rule for corporate entry (rule 21.1B2) has caused little problem, however, since an LC rule interpretation appeared in *Cataloging Service Bulletin* no. 12 (Spring 1981). In essence the LC directive instructs that for the purpose of corporate main entry one should be guided by the primary content or main purpose of the item. The instruction included that when doubt existed, the corporate involvement should be ignored. This was subsequently reversed in *Cataloging Service Bulletin* no. 14 (Fall 1981), where the instruction was to assume corporate involvement in the event of doubt.

Both editions of AACR have provided for personal authors as the main entry for serial publications. Kovacic expressed the belief that such provision is illogical for serials, but granted that the circumstance occurs too rarely to cause serious problems.[45] The personal authorship provision nonetheless seems to be disliked by serials catalogers. Questions were raised at the 1981 Annual Conference meeting of the Committee to Study Serials Cataloging. *Cataloging Service Bulletin* has twice given pertinent directives. No. 15 (Winter 1982) stated that the entire run of the publication should be considered before a main entry for personal author was made, with personal author entry favored only when it seemed unlikely that the publication itself would continue without the involvement of the individual (rule 21.1A2). No. 23 (Winter 1983) carried the instruction for statements of responsibility for serials (rule 12.1F3): " . . . unless there is strong evidence of personal authorship, normally consider personal statements of responsibility as statements of editorship."[46]

LEVEL OF DESCRIPTION

The decision of the Library of Congress to catalog serials at an augmented first level of description is important to note because of its national influence. The LC policy decision, which appeared in *Cataloging Service Bulletin* no. 11 (Winter 1981), included the elements of description that would be added to the first level. The LC decision basically meant that other title information and secondary statements of responsibility would routinely be omitted from records, the reasoning being that these are often lengthy and subject to frequent change. Two exceptions to the general policy were stated. In the case of publications carrying both an initialism and the words represented by the initialism, whichever form was not chosen as the title proper was to be recorded as other title information. Other title information was also to be given when a statement of responsibility was "imbedded inseparably" therein.[47] *Cataloging Service Bulletin* no. 13 (Summer 1981) added another two exceptions. Other title information was also to be given for titles proper in need of having a supplied explanation added, such as conference proceedings giving only the name of the conference as the title proper, while subsequent statements of responsibility were to be recorded when they named entities for which added entries were needed.

OTHER AREAS OF CONCERN

Other areas that have been addressed by both the Committee to Study Serials Cataloging and the Library of Congress via *Cataloging Service Bulletin* include initialisms versus full form of the words represented by the initialism as choice of title proper, numeric and/or alphabetic and chronological or other designation, chief source of information, form of linking notes, and monograph versus serials treatment in cataloging. The AACR2 rules governing the cataloging of hardcover reprints and AACR2 compatibility with the draft of the second edition of the *ISBD(S)* have also been among the more important agenda items of the Committee to Study Serials Cataloging.

INITIALISMS VERSUS FULL FORM
OF WORDS REPRESENTED

The cataloging of serial publications bearing an initialism as well as words that represent the initialism in its full form was troublesome with both editions of AACR, as neither gave guidance on which representation should be chosen as the title proper. At the 1979 Midwinter Meeting of the Committee to Study Serials Cataloging Frank Sadowski reported on a survey of publishers whose journals carried both an initialism and the full form of the words thereby represented. The vast majority of publishers indicated that the full form, not the initialism, was the official title of their publication. The results of Sadowski's study were published in the Fall 1979 issue of *Library Resources & Technical Services*.[48]

Upon the basis of Sadowski's findings, the Library of Congress greatly restricted the choice of initialisms as title proper. Rule interpretations were printed in *Cataloging Service Bulletins* no. 10 (Fall 1980), no. 13 (Summer 1981), no. 14 (Fall 1981), and no. 15 (Winter 1982). A certain amount of confusion continued, however, and questions were received by the Committee to Study Serials Cataloging in 1984. At the Midwinter Meeting in 1985 the committee voted to recommend that the following rule interpretation from *Cataloging Service Bulletin* no. 15 be added as an amendment to the rule for the transcription of title proper (12.1B1): "When a title in full as well as an initialism representing the words of the title appears in the chief source, select the initialism as the title proper only when it is the sole form presented in all locations other than the chief source."[49] The amendment was approved by CC:DA at the 1985 Annual Conference and has been passed to the Joint Steering Committee for the Revision of AACR.

NUMERIC AND/OR ALPHABETIC, CHRONOLOGICAL, OR OTHER DESIGNATION

The Committee to Study Serials Cataloging has received numerous queries concerning the transcription of numeric and chronological or other designation data (rule 12.3). Questions have included the permissibility of using information taken from sources other than the serial itself (such as OCLC, NST, and ULS) and the permissibility of recording a formal closing designation in the absence of a formal beginning designation. The consensus of the committee was that both actions are permissible since neither is prohibited by AACR2. Various problems caused by publications having more than one system of designation have been discussed, with recommendations made on a case by case basis. Another problem that is brought to the committee from time to time is that posed by monographic series that undergo a title change, with a few later numbered issues subsequently appearing under the earlier title. The committee's recommendation has been that such issues should be left with the later title and appropriate notes added to both records.

The earliest LC directive appeared in *Cataloging Service Bulletin* no. 10 (Fall 1980). This directive instructed that in the case of successive designation (rule 12.3G) separate records should generally be made when numbering starts over and the old and new systems are not linked by a designation such as "New series." This is one of the rare instances where an LC policy contradicts AACR2. The policy resulted in some confusion among catalogers who sometimes interpreted it too literally. *Cataloging Service Bulletin* no. 26 (Fall 1984) stated the LC intention more clearly and specified that a new system of numbering should not be considered to have been adopted just because a change occurs in an existing system, as when either the chronological or numeric designation is dropped or added. Other directives concerning the transcription of information appeared in bulletins no. 18 (Fall 1982) and no. 23 (Winter 1983).

CHIEF SOURCE OF INFORMATION

The chief source of information for printed serials (rule 12.0B1) has been discussed by the Committee to Study Serials Cataloging several times. *Cataloging Service Bulletin* no. 15 (Winter 1982) gave directives on deciding which issue was the earliest in the absence of the earliest issue itself, with numeric designation receiving preference over a publication date. A related instruction was given for the note area for publication and distribution information (rule 12.7B9), directing that if a publication date of the first issue was later than that of a subsequent issue, the earliest publication date should be noted. No. 15 also stated that a title page published to cover multiple issues after the publication of the issues themselves, a not uncommon occurrence with periodicals, could not be used as the chief source of information. No. 16 (Spring 1982) made an exception in the order of preferred sources for the title page substitute, allowing the cataloger to select whichever substitute source was known to carry the title that did not vary from issue to issue. Sadowski has discussed the need for a standard definition for title page as applied to periodicals.[50]

FORM OF LINKING NOTES

While very comprehensive in its treatment of the potential relationships a serial may bear to other serials, AACR2 does not cover the catalog entry form in which related titles should be cited in linking notes (rule 12.7B7). Questions regarding the form of these notes was brought to the Committee to Study Serials Cataloging at the 1981 Annual Conference. In *Cataloging Service Bulletin* no. 14 (Fall 1981), LC prescribed the use of the AACR2 form of entry even if the title was in a pre-AACR2 form in the catalog. Bulletin no. 23 (Winter 1983) reversed this decision, giving preference to the catalog entry form. The AACR2 form of name is prescribed for corporate entry headings, however, and for serials not in the catalog. *Cataloging Service Bulletin* no. 18 (Fall 1982) gave information concerning the use of numeric and chronological designations in linking notes when certain data do not apply to all issues.

MONOGRAPHIC VERSUS SERIALS TREATMENT

Monograph versus serials treatment of materials in cataloging has been discussed by the Committee to Study Serials Cataloging most specifically in relation to IEEE and related publications. AACR2 perhaps appropriately provides no guidelines for decision. LC has issued very comprehensive guidelines, which first appeared in *Cataloging Service Bulletin* no. 20 (Spring 1983) and were reprinted with some revisions in no. 29 (Summer 1985). Guidelines are given for initial serial treatment, retropective serial treatment, and monograph treatment. The special problems presented by conference and exhibit publications and loose-leaf publications are explored.

HARDCOVER REPRINTS

Hardcover reprints have twice been discussed by the Committee to Study Serials Cataloging. Whether these publications should be cataloged as monographs or serials was raised at the 1982 Midwinter Meeting. The AACR2 instructions seem to present an arguable case for cataloging as multipart monographs. Rule 1.11A reads, in part: "If a facsimile, etc., is in a form of library material different from that of the original . . . use the chapter on the form of the facsimile, etc., in determining the sources of information . . . "[51] The consensus of committee members and those in attendance was that reprinted serials should be cataloged as serials, the point being made that the omission of reprinted publications from serials catalogs and serials union lists would constitute a disservice to catalog users. The LC policy has been to catalog serial reprints as serials.

Serial catalogers dislike the AACR2 provisions for the transcription of title proper and notes pertaining to the original publication. Rule 1.11B instructs, in part: "If the facsimile, etc., has a title different from the original, give the title of the facsimile, etc., as the title proper."[52] Rule 1.11F directs: "Give all of the details of the original of a facsimile, etc., in a single note. Give the details of the original in the order of the areas of the description."[53] Serial reprints not infrequently include more than one title, this circumstance most often occurring when an original publication has been successively continued by one or more subsequent titles. The title chosen by a reprint publisher may be the earliest title of the run, the latest title of the run, the title that lasted the longest, or an entirely different title. A single note can become extremely long and cumbersome, obscuring details relevant to the original publication(s), when it must account for multiple titles, changes in issuing bodies, irregularities in numbering, and other details.

At the 1985 Annual Conference meeting of the Committee to Study Serials Cataloging, Dorothy Glasby reported that the Library of Congress was formulating a policy for hardcover serial reprints. The description will be based on the original serial, with information pertinent to the reprinted publication noted.

AACR2/ISBD(S) COMPATIBILITY

In discussing the development of the *ISBD(G): General International Standard Bibliographic Description*, Gorman commented upon the unacceptably divergent features of the preliminary edition of the *ISBD(S)* that appeared in 1974.[54-56] As a general framework for all bibliographic descriptions, *ISBD(G)* was created to assure that a certain uniformity would be achieved in all of ISBD formats in the future. Both AACR2 and the first edition of *ISBD(S): International Standard Bibliographic Description for Serials* were based on *ISBD(G)*.[57] Cole nonetheless found that AACR2 and *ISBD(S)* diverged in every area of description, with major differences particularly notable in the areas for title and statement of responsibility and numeric and/or alphabetic, chronological, or other designation.[58]

At the 1984 Midwinter Meeting, the Committee to Study Serials Cataloging examined the draft of the second edition of *ISBD(S)* against AACR2 for compatibility.[59] Certain discrepancies noted by Cole were no longer present as a result of changes in the *ISBD(S)* format. Kovacic believes that the departures are still too many, however.[60] As previously mentioned, the Committee to Study Serials Cataloging has drafted a rule revision according to which the AACR2 definition of changes in titles proper would be brought into conformity with the *ISBD(S)* definition. Uniformity in this area is particularly desirable for the international exchange of cataloging records in years to come.

CONCLUSION

AACR2 represents a major advance in the formulation of an international cataloging code. The British and North American editions of AACR1 are reconciled into a single text, that conforms more closely to the Paris Principles, and has as its basis an international standard for bibliographic description. The Joint Steering Committee for the Revision of AACR exists as a mechanism by which code review and revision are a continuing process. A formal structure provides for input into the deliberations of the Joint Steering Committee by cataloging groups representing the United States, Canada, and Britain. AACR2 has widespread use throughout the English speaking world. While not an international code, it is in international use.

NOTES

1. John R. James, "Serials '75 – Review and Trends," *Library Resources & Technical Services* 20, no. 3 (Summer 1976): 259-260.
2. C. Sumner Spaulding, "ISBD(S) and Title Main Entry for Serials," *Library of Congress Information Bulletin* 33 (Nov. 22, 1974): A229-A232.

3. Joseph H. Howard, "Main Entry for Serials," *Library of Congress Information Bulletin* 33 (Nov. 22, 1974): A232-A236.

4. Jim E. Cole, "AACR6: Time for a Review," *Library Resources & Technical Services* 19, no. 4 (Fall 1975): 314-326.

5. Michael Gorman, "The Current State of Standardization in the Cataloging of Serials," *Library Resources & Technical Services* 19, no. 4 (Fall 1975): 301-313.

6. Michael Carpenter, "No Special Rules for Entry of Serials," *Library Resources & Technical Services* 19, no. 4 (Fall 1975): 327-332.

7. Wesley Simonton, "Serial Cataloging Problems: Rules of Entry and Definition of Title," *Library Resources & Technical Services* 19, no. 4 (Fall 1975): 294-299.

8. Eva Verona, *Corporate Headings: Their Use in Library Catalogues and National Bibliographies* (London: IFLA Committee on Cataloguing, 1975).

9. John R. James, "Serials in 1976," *Library Resources & Technical Services* 21, no. 3 (Summer 1977): 220-221.

10. "Resources and Technical Services Division Annual Reports, 1974/1975: Serials Section Report," *Library Resources & Technical Services* 20, no. 1 (Winter 1976): 83.

11. "RTSD Annual Reports, 1981/1982: Serials Section," *Library Resources & Technical Services* 26, no. 4 (Oct./Dec. 1982): 396.

12. *ALA Handbook of Organization, 1983/1984* (Chicago: American Library Association, 1983): 142.

13. *ALA Handbook of Organization, 1984/1985* (Chicago: American Library Association, 1984): 145.

14. Benita M. Weber, "The Year's Work in Serials: 1982," *Library Resources & Technical Services* 27, no. 3 (July/Sept. 1983): 247-248.

15. Mary Ellen Soper, "Description and Entry of Serials in AACR2," *The Serials Librarian* 4, no. 2 (Winter 1979): 174.

16. Benita M. Weber, "The Year's Work in Serials: 1981," *Library Resources & Technical Services* 26, no. 3 (July/Sept. 1982): 277-278.

17. Lynn Mealer Cummins, "Serials Cataloging in Transition," *The Serials Librarian* 10, no. 1/2 (Fall 1985/Winter 1986): 130.

18. Nurieh Musavi, "An Evaluation of AACR2," *Library Resources & Technical Services* 30, no. 2 (Apr./June 1986): 144.

19. *Cataloging Titles in Microform Sets* (Washington, D.C.: Association of Research Libraries, 1983): 60.

20. "Committee to Study Serials Cataloging Twenty Titles Selected for AACR2 Cataloging," *RTSD Newsletter* 4, no. 3 (June 1979): 8-9.

21. "Networks/Consortia and Library-Oriented Organizations," *The Serials Librarian* 4, no. 1 (Fall 1979): 106.

22. Judith Cannan and Ben R. Tucker, "Serials Cataloging under AACR2," *RTSD Newsletter* 5, no. 2 (Mar./Apr. 1980): 19-21.

23. Judith Cannan, "Serials Cataloging under AACR2, Part 2," *RTSD Newsletter* 5, no. 3 (May/June 1980): 29-32.

24. Judith Cannan, "Serials Cataloging under AACR2," *RTSD Newsletter* 5, no. 6 (Nov./Dec. 1980): 68-69.

25. Ellen Siegel Kovacic, "Serials Cataloging under AACR2," *RTSD Newsletter* 6, no. 3 (May/June 1981): 32-33.

26. Soper, "Description and Entry of Serials in AACR2," p. 171.

27. Ann Turner, "Effects of AACR2 on Serials Cataloging," *The Serials Librarian* 4, no. 2 (Winter 1979): 186.

28. Ann Turner, "AACR2 and Serials," *The Serials Librarian* 6, no. 1 (Fall 1981): 32-34.

29. Carolyn O. Frost, "A Comparison of Cataloging Codes for Serials: AACR2 and Its Predecessors," in *AACR2 and Serials: The American view*, ed. Neal L. Edgar (New York: Haworth Press, 1983): 30-31.

30. Ellen Siegel Kovacic, "Serials Cataloging: What It Is, How It's Done, Why It's Done That Way," *Serials Review* 11, no. 1 (Spring 1985): 79.

31. Carole R. McIver, "The AACRs and Serials Cataloging," *The Serials Librarian* 10, nos. 1/2 (Fall 1985/Winter 1986): 123.

32. Frank E. Sadowski, Jr., "Serials Cataloging Developments, 1975-1985: A Personal View of Some Highlights," *The Serials Librarian* 10, no. 1/2 (Fall 1985/Winter 1986): 135.

33. Alexander Bloss, "AACR2 North and South: Serials Cataloging from the Library of Congress and the National Library of Canada," *Serials Review* 9, no. 4 (Winter 1983): 87-89.
34. Jim E. Cole, "Unique Serial Title Entries," *Serials Review* 7, no. 4 (Oct./Dec. 1981): 75-76.
35. Sadowski, "Serials Cataloging Developments," p. 135-136.
36. McIver, "The AACRs and Serials Cataloging," p. 123-124.
37. Soper, "Description and Entry of Serials in AACR2," p. 171.
38. Turner, "AACR2 and Serials," p. 30.
39. Frost, "A Comparison of Cataloging Codes for Serials," p. 29.
40. *Cataloging Service Bulletin* 22 (Fall 1983): 23.
41. *ISBD(S): International Standard Bibliographic Description for Serials*. Draft 2nd ed. (London: IFLA International Office for UBC, 1983): 67.
42. Turner, "Effects of AACR2 on Serials Cataloging," p. 186.
43. Kovacic, "Serials Cataloging," p. 79.
44. Turner, "AACR2 and Serials," p. 31-32.
45. Kovacic, "Serials Cataloging," p. 79.
46. *Cataloging Service Bulletin* 23 (Winter 1983): 19.
47. *Cataloging Service Bulletin* 11 (Winter 1981): 16-17.
48. Frank E. Sadowski, Jr., "Initially, We Need Some Definitions: The Problems of Initialisms in Periodical Titles," *Library Resources & Technical Services* 23, no. 4 (Fall 1979): 365-373.
49. *Cataloging Service Bulletin* 15 (Winter 1982): 7.
50. Sadowski, "Initially, We Need Some Definitions," p. 366-367.
51. *Anglo-American Cataloguing Rules*. 2nd ed. (Chicago: American Library Association, 1978): 50.
52. Ibid.
53. Ibid., p. 51.
54. *ISBD(G): General International Standard Bibliographic Description* (London: IFLA International Office for UBC, 1977).
55. Michael Gorman, "The Anglo-American Cataloguing Rules, Second Edition," *Library Resources & Technical Services* 22, no. 3 (Summer 1978): 212-213.
56. *ISBD(S): International Standard Bibliographic Description for Serials* (London: IFLA Committee on Cataloguing, 1974).
57. *ISBD(S): International Standard Bibliographic Description for Serials*. 1st Standard ed. (London: IFLA International Office for UBC, 1977).
58. Jim E. Cole, "AACR2 and ISBD(S): Correspondence or Divergence?" *Serials Review* 8, no. 3 (Fall 1982): 67-69.
59. *ISBD(S): International Standard Bibliographic Description for Serials*. Draft 2nd ed. (London: IFLA International Office for UBC, 1983).
60. Kovacic, "Serials Cataloging," p. 82.

REFERENCES

Anglo-American Cataloguing Rules. 2nd ed. (Chicago: American Library Association, 1978).
Cataloging Service Bulletin 1 (Summer 1978)-31 (Winter 1986).

The Descriptive Cataloging of Serials: Library of Congress' Application of AACR2

Dorothy J. Glasby

SUMMARY. The application of AACR2 to the descriptive cataloging of serials in the Library of Congress and in the CONSER project is described. Some Library of Congress rule interpretations relating specifically to serials are discussed and explained.

The descriptive cataloging of serials, except newspapers, in the Library of Congress (LC) is carried out in the Serial Record Division by catalogers, over thirty of them, who work only on serials and prepare records for between ten and twelve thousand serial titles annually, together with name and series authority records as needed.

Since 1973 LC has prepared MARC records for its serials, and since 1976, with the advent of the CONSER (CONversion of SERials) project, the MARC records have been prepared by direct input to OCLC. In doing this, LC's serials catalogers have used serial records already present in OCLC's data base because of previous input by a CONSER or other OCLC participant.

In addition to being a regular CONSER participant and adding its records for new cataloging to the CONSER data base, LC is a center of responsibility in the CONSER project, and as such a group of catalogers in the Serial Record Division authenticates (reviews for conformance to agreed upon practices and policies) the records of other CONSER participants, except for Canadian imprints, which are authenticated by the National Library of Canada (NLC). Additionally, the Serial Record Division houses and administers the National Serials Data Program (NSDP), which serves as the United States center for the International Serials Data System (ISDS), and is responsible for assigning ISSN and key titles to U.S. imprints. NSDP also functions as a center of responsibility in the CONSER project, its authentication being, chiefly, of the ISDS data elements, primarily the ISSN and key title. ISDS/Canada plays a similar role in CONSER in dealing with Canadian imprints.

The MARC serial records in LC's internal online data base are CON-

---

Dorothy J. Glasby is Assistant Chief, Serial Record Division, Library of Congress, Washington, D.C. 20540.

SER authenticated records returned to LC on a weekly tape from OCLC. The records may have been authenticated by LC, NSDP, NLC, ISDS/ Canada, or, as has been the case in the last few years, by CONSER participants choosing to authenticate their own records. In addition to forming LC's internal serials data base, the authenticated records are distributed monthly by LC's MARC Serials Distribution Service, and selected records are used to prepare printed cards for serials, as entries for *New Serial Titles*, and to report to the ISDS in Paris the ISSN and key titles assigned by NSDP to U.S. imprints.

Obviously LC has a deep commitment to, and investment in, the CONSER project, and could not begin to do the descriptive cataloging of its serials according to the provisions of the *Anglo-American Cataloguing Rules*, Second Edition (AACR2), without reaching some agreement with other CONSER participants in regard to how, and for what existing records, AACR2 would be applied. Accordingly, during the period between 1978, when AACR2 was published and January 1981, when it was adopted by LC (and CONSER), CONSER participants reached agreement that all input representing new descriptive cataloging of serials would be done according to AACR2, and that in cases in which they were inputting existing cataloging into the CONSER data base, they would supply AACR2 forms of name heading. It was further agreed that no more latest entry records would be input, although those already input would be allowed to stand. Earlier CONSER policy had permitted duplication of latest entry records with successive records done under the *Anglo American Cataloging Rules* (AACR), and at the same time acceptable duplication was agreed to in regard to successive records done under AACR2. CONSER participants were given the option of using (claiming) existing records on the data base as they stood or, in cases where they had an issue of the publication in hand and had the power do to so (the records were not authenticated by a symbol that locked the record), changing a pre-AACR2 record to AACR2.

The Library of Congress affirmed its intention to do all of its descriptive cataloging of serials as of January 1981 according to AACR2, even in cases in which this required changing a record, authenticated or not, already in the CONSER data base to conform to the new set of rules. In doing this, LC would often have to reformulate the entire body of the record in order to describe the piece in hand and to drop beginning information and information about earlier places of publication or publishers into note areas, as LC might not have these earlier pieces in hand or even in its collections.

LC also proposed to CONSER participants that the normal CONSER record be somewhere between the first and the second level of description, as outlined in AACR2 rule 1.0D—an "augmented level 1." This proposal was made in order to keep from "cluttering" the body of the serial record with overly long subtitles (other title information) and statements of responsibility that would tend to obscure other data and would, in all probability, change frequently. The CONSER participants agreed to this proposal as well as to an NLC request that if items (such as subtitles) were deliberately left out of the body of the record, they would not be given as quoted notes (as had been the practice under AACR). LC documented the "augmented level 1" in a rule interpretation (RI) for 1.0D. In hindsight it is clear that the "augmented level 1" might as easily have been dubbed a "lesser level 2," as it called for a fairly complete second level of description except that statements of responsibility beyond the first would be omitted and other title information would be omitted except in special circumstances, as when it included a statement of responsibility or other data that were considered desirable for reasons of access.

During the period between publication of AACR2 and its implementation at the Library of Congress, it was realized, at LC, that since almost all series as well as the majority of other types of serials would be entered under title, according to AACR2, there would be a problem in linking notes and added entries in distinguishing between serials with the same title. If the title entry were to be used in a linking note, for example, how would anyone know to what particular *Focus* (a common serial title) a note such as "continued by Focus" referred? And how could added entries for series be filed so that all of those for a particular series were together and not intermingled with those of another series with the same title?

After many weeks of meetings and discussion, staff at LC developed the concept of entry for serials that did not have unique titles under a uniform title that would consist of the title proper of the serial plus qualifying information, such as place or corporate body, which would make the title unique. The "uniquing" concept is, of course, similar to that used in the ISDS in formulating the key titles which relate to ISSN.

Although it was the feeling at LC that the "uniquing" type of uniform title was at least implied in chapter 25 of AACR2 (a chapter whose provisions are, in any case, optional for institutions applying AACR2), LC did present its RI 25.5B on the entry of serials with non-unique titles under a uniform title to a meeting of the national libraries of Australia, Great Britain, Canada, and the United States for comment and/or agreement, and held special meetings with NLC so that NLC, as another center of responsibility in the CONSER project, would be able to construct and authenticate CONSER records according to the same AACR2 guidelines.

As originally written and implemented, RI 25.5B called for the creation of a uniform title for a serial entered under title, whenever the title proper of the serial was identical to the title proper of another serial in the catalog. The uniform title was to consist of the title proper of the serial plus qualifying information such as corporate body or place, with preference given to corporate body qualification whenever the title proper consisted entirely of words indicating the type of publication, the periodicity of the publication, or the subject content of the publication. Since the corporate body qualifier was regarded as a "meaningful" qualifier that would cause confusion if it were not entirely up to date, the RI further stipulated that whenever the name of the corporate body used as a qualifier changed or the body's responsibilities for the serial were taken over by another body, a new entry with a new uniform title should be created for the serial.

The original RI 25.5B did not last long after AACR2 was implemented at LC because catalogers soon found difficulty in determining and agreeing on which titles consisted only of words indicating type of publication, periodicity, or subject matter, with the definition of "subject matter" causing the greatest concern. This was, of course, the same problem or type of problem generated by AACR's Rule 6, which called for entry of serial titles consisting only of a generic term under the issuing body, as no two catalogers ever defined "generic term" in exactly the same way. Additionally, since the RI gave preference to corporate body as qualifier and required a new entry when the body changed, many new title entries with no change in the title proper of the serial were being generated.

After a number of revisions over the years since 1981, this RI, as it presently reads, gives preference to qualification by place and requires qualification by corporate body in fairly limited instances. The present version also comes very close to reflecting the rules for qualification of a title proper given in the *ISDS Manual* for the formulation of the key title, thus allowing catalogers at LC and other institutions to "pick up" the key title and use it as a uniform title in instances in which they are using for their cataloging a CONSER record in which the key title is already present—surely a great saving of intellectual effort if nothing else.

With the exception of the RIs mentioned above (RI 1.0D on the level of record and RI 25.5B on uniform title entry for serials), LC did not prepare or issue much in the way of rule interpretations relating only to serials in advance of the implementation of AACR2, the thought being that an attempt would be made to follow AACR2 as written and see then where guidance was needed for LC's serials catalogers and CONSER participants. It was recognized that chapter 12 of AACR2, which deals with the description of printed serials, gave fewer explicit instructions in some areas than chapter 7 of AACR and that it introduced a number of concepts, such as statement of responsibility and a rigid order of preference for the selection of a title page substitute, that were entirely new to serials catalogers. It was also recognized at LC that although AACR2 seemed to allow a great deal of latitude for cataloger's judgment, in many instances RIs for serials might be needed in order that CONSER participants, including LC, would all be able to fashion their records in the same way and use one another's records with a minimum amount of changing or "second guessing" by catalogers at the different institutions. It was hoped that by eventually providing RIs explaining how LC would handle certain matters of description of serials, the other CONSER participants, who had promised to follow LC's RIs for AACR2 (as they had promised for AACR), would be able to prepare records that would not only be of use, without change, to LC but that would also be acceptable to other participants and institutions.

The actual implementation and application of AACR2 to the descriptive cataloging of serials at LC (and in CONSER) can be best discussed perhaps by an examination of some of the rule interpretations for serials LC has issued over the years as well as by some brief indication of the reasoning that lay behind these interpretations.

Before going into specific rule interpretations, however, it might be well to mention that although most of LC's rule interpretations are originated by the Office for Descriptive Cataloging Policy, those relating to serials are frequently drafted in the Serial Record Division, as it is that division that is aware of the problems LC's serials catalogers and CONSER participants are having with specific serials rules. After a rule interpretation is drafted, it is usually sent for comment to a number of individuals in LC, such as heads of cataloging sections, chiefs of cataloging divisions, the Director for Cataloging, etc., the actual list of "commenters" depending very much on the topic of the RI (e.g., heads of sections that work only with books may not be asked to comment on RIs relating specifically to serials). After comments have been received, the Office for Descriptive Cataloging Policy revises the RI as necessary and issues it in its new form to all catalogers at LC with instructions to begin application of the RI upon receipt. The Name Authority Cooperative Project (NACO) sees that all NACO participants get copies of the RI at this point, and the Serial Record Division supplies CONSER participants with copies. The RI is then published in *Cataloging Service Bulletin* (CSB). In cases in which an RI is changed, the revised version generally follows the same review procedure, and is issued afterwards to catalogers and others. The RI is published in such instances *in toto* (i.e., both the revised and unrevised portions are included) in CSB.

Unfortunately, the preparing and issuing of RIs at LC is a time consuming process, if for no other reason than the greath length of time it sometimes takes to prepare the hundreds of copies for all of LC's catalogers plus CONSER and NACO participants. It is unfortunate, too, that since CSB is a quarterly publication, catalogers at other institutions may not hear about a new practice documented in an RI until after they have observed its appearance in LC's MARC records.

To return to an exploration of specific RIs for serials, it is impossible to try to discuss them in the order in which they were formulated or published, and so they will be taken up for the most part in "rule number." An exception is made in the case of RIs that are related. These are discussed together.

When AACR2 was implemented, serials catalogers quickly realized that information in 12.0B1 was contradictory, as the rule required the use of the title page or title page substitute of the first issue of the serial as the chief source for the description, yet indicated also that a title page published later, presumably to cover several issues, should be used. LC documented in an RI its decision always to use the chief source on the first issue and not to recatalog or change the entry thus prepared if a title page came along later with different information. In a further interpretation of this rule, LC indicated that when a serial lacked a title page, the title page substitute was to be chosen according to the order of sources listed in the rule (i.e., first the cover, then the caption, etc.). It stated further that in cases in which a title from a less preferred source was known to be stable, that less preferred source could be used as the title page substitute. Although this RI was written originally to handle problems in dealing with comic books, which often have a slightly different title on the cover of each issue but a stable title inside on the masthead, it has proven useful in preventing the proliferation of many different entries for many popular "newsstand" serials that frequently use varying cover titles to attract purchasers.

AACR2 provides little guidance about how to catalog reprinted editions of serials except that the whole concept of the code is to "describe" what is in hand. Presumably then, the reprint edition is to be described with the title page of that edition being used as the chief source. However, chapter 12 (12.3B1) indicates that the numeric designations of the original issues are to be used on the entry for the reprint but other details of the original (including the title of the original if different from the title of the reprint) are to be given in a note (12.7B7g). After staff in the Serial Record Division at LC prepared a number of entries for reprinted editions of serials according to a variety of approaches (description based on the title page of the reprinted edition, description based on the original with details of the reprint in a note, description based partly on the original and partly on the reprinted edition), it was concluded at LC that for reasons of filing, searching, and identification the description of the reprint should match as much as possible the description of the original. In order to achieve this match it was obvious that the title page of the reprinted edition could not be used most of the time as the chief source for the description. In cases, for example, in which the original serial had changed title, the title page of the reprint might carry only one of the titles. Basing the description on that title page would mean, therefore, that one would end up with perhaps three records for the original serial but only one for the reprinted edition. LC eventually decided that the title, edition, and designation of the issues should be derived from the issues reprinted rather than from the title page of the reprint, thus ensuring that the description of the reproduction resembles and files with the original. The imprint information (place, publisher, date) would come from the title page of the reprinted edition. There would be a single note giving details about the original, and all other notes would be concerned with the reprinted edition. These decisions are documented in another RI for 12.0B1.

Early in the implementation of AACR2 serials catalogers realized that the rules gave no guidance in regard to whether an initialism representing the words of the title or the title in full should be recorded as the title proper when both appeared on the chief source, although rule 12.1E1 did indicate that whenever the initialism was selected as the title proper, the full form of the title should be recorded as other title information. Since initialisms most often appear on the covers of periodicals and in that position are frequently regarded by publishers as decoration, LC decided to use, whenever possible, the full form of the title as the title proper. Consequently LC issued an RI to 12.1B1 indicating that the initialism should be selected as the title proper only in cases in which the initialism was the sole form in which the title was expressed elsewhere in the publication. A related RI, to 12.1E1, then indicated that when the initialism was not recorded as the title proper, it should be recorded as other title information. These RIs have worked well in resolving to everyone's satisfaction the whole problem of initialism, and it is probable that AACR2 will eventually incorporate the criteria for selection of an initialism as the title proper as given in LC's rule interpretation.

Somewhat related to the question of what should be recorded as the title proper when two possibilities (initialism and full title) are given on the chief source is the question of how much of what is on the chief source should be recorded as the title proper, i.e., where the title proper begins and ends. Rule 12.1B2 addresses this question in a very limited way by indicating that when there is doubt as to whether a corporate body's name or an abbreviation of its name is part of the title proper, the name or abbreviation is so treated only if it is consistently presented as such in various locations in the serial. LC decided to use the same guidelines in determining whether words, phrases or other statements on the chief source should be treated as part of the title proper, and issued an RI to 12.1B2 to this effect. This RI has been successful in cutting down the number of times LC serials catalogers and catalogers at CONSER participating institutions disagree on the "extent" of the title proper.

Another concern that appeared soon after the adoption of AACR2 was how, in a linking note, to refer to another serial that had been cataloged according to pre-AACR2 rules. In an effort to keep the record for the serial being cataloged as "pure" AACR2, LC issued a rule interpretation to as 12.7B that required that the linking note give the entry of the serial referred to as it would be had it been cataloged according to AACR2 and that, if the serial referred to was in the CONSER data base, its entry, but nothing else in the record, should be changed to AACR2. It was assumed that it would be possible by looking at a serial record prepared under pre-AACR2 cataloging rules to determine what its entry should be under AACR2, but this proved not to be the case, and catalogers often had to search for issues of the related serial in order to make the entry determination. It was also assumed that having a record with an AACR2 entry (often a "uniquing" type of uniform title) and an AACR description, would bother no one. But it did. So LC eventually changed its RI to 12.7B to indicate that the linking note would cite the serial according to whatever entry it had in the catalog (i.e., the CONSER data base) except that name headings used as main entries would be given in AACR2 form.

Since AACR2 did not provide guidelines for determining when an index or a supplement to a serial should be noted on the record for the serial and when the index or supplement should be cataloged separately, LC issued rule interpretations to 12.7B7k, 12.7B17, and 21.28B. These interpretations indicated that indexes published by the publisher of the serial were to be noted on the record for the serial, as were supplements that in some manner updated the serial. All other indexes and supplements were to be cataloged separately, as monographs or serials, as appropriate. These RIs, by setting rather arbitrary but easily recognized parameters for which indexes and supplements are added to an existing serial record, have done much to settle the "one record or two" controversy for these types of publication.

Turning to the question of entry for serials, catalogers had some difficulty in determining when a serial should be entered under a personal author's name. In order to clarify this situation LC issued a rule interpretation to 21.1A2, in which guidance was given to the effect that an entire run of a serial needed to be considered when a decision was being made about entry under personal author, and that in instances in which it was known that different issues of the serial were created by different persons, entry should not be under a personal name. This RI went on to specify that a serial might often be considered to be of "enduring" personal authorship, and should be entered under the name of the person when the person is named as both author and publisher, the whole name or part of the name of the person is carried in the title, or the serial does not emanate from a corporate body that might see that it was continued if the person involved were no longer available. The RI then indicated that in cases of doubt, preference should be given to an entry for the serial other than under personal name. This RI reflects, rather well, the general feeling among those who catalog serials that in the present day few "true" serials are written by one person and that by using entry under a personal name one is in effect opening the door to an infinite number of related records for the serial, as there is little doubt that in time the person responsible for the publication will change.

Although LC and the CONSER participants made a serious attempt over several years to follow strictly the provisions of rule 21.2 concerning changes in the title proper that would require a new entry for the serial, it was apparent that new entries were proliferating with great rapidity and that users of the serial records, reference staff, and even catalogers were having a hard time determining quickly what the "change" in title had been, since the earlier and later titles looked so much alike. Consequently LC issued a series of rule interpretations indicating that certain changes in the representation of a word or words (e.g., words connected with a hyphen versus the same words given separately), and certain changes in title that occurred very late in the title and did not affect the meaning of the title would not be considered changes in the title proper and would not require a new entry to be made for the serial. LC also documented in an RI its earlier practice under AACR's successive entry rules of not maintaining and continuing to create separate records when a serial title fluctuated back and forth a number of times. Another rule interpretation indicated that LC would not make a new record for a serial because the order of the titles in different languages had changed and a title different from that selected from an earlier piece as the title proper would now be appropriate.

In regard to the cataloging of serials under AACR2, it seems likely that rule 21.2A has created more difficulty than most because of its total lack of a listing of reasonable exceptions. The rigidity of the first statement in 21.2A that "*any* change in the first five words" is to be regarded as a change in the title proper (and requires a new entry for the serial) has been particularly worrisome. In general, 21.2A marks also the place where AACR2 is most at variance with accepted international standards for serials. The *ISDS Manual* and the soon to be forthcoming second edition of the *ISBD(S): International Bibliographic Description for Serials*, for example, identify a number of "minor" title changes that do not require that a new ISSN/key title be assigned or a new bibliographic description be prepared, but few of these are "minor" under 21.2A. Fortunately efforts are underway to have this rule revised.

On the whole, LC's (and CONSER's) application of AACR2 to the new form of descriptive cataloging of serials has gone very well. The AACR2 provision that the description of the serial (i.e., the body of the record) be based on the earliest issue of the serial works extremely well in a cooperative cataloging environment such as that of CONSER, as it is possible for institutions to maintain and update AACR2 records by adding information on later pieces in the notes areas and it is not necessary for them to constantly redo the "body" of the record, as was true under AACR, where description was based on latest issue.

The major problems encountered at LC and in CONSER in the application of AACR2 were those associated with the need to apply it in the case of an existing data base, one already containing records done according to at least two earlier sets of rules. Such application has made recataloging the only way in some instances to achieve correct and meaningful records, and recataloging to AACR2 can only be done with a piece of the serial in hand. The very provision in AACR2 that makes it a most satisfactory set of rules to use for new records in a cooperative cataloging environment, i.e., the provision that description be based on the earliest issue, is what makes it such a difficult set to superimpose on existing records.

NOTES

1. *Anglo-American Cataloging Rules*. North American Text. Prepared by the American Library Association, et al. Chicago, American Library Association, 1967.
2. *Anglo-American Cataloguing Rules*. 2nd ed. Prepared by the American Library Association, et al. Edited by Michael Gorman and Paul W. Winkler. Chicago, American Library Association, 1978.
3. *Cataloging Service Bulletin* no. 1 (Summer 1978)-Washington, Library of Congress, Processing Services, 1978-.
4. *ISDS Manual*. Prepared by the ISDS International Centre. Edited by A.A. Mullis. Paris, ISDS International Centre, 1983.

Bilingual Serial Cataloguing at the National Library of Canada

Wayne Jones, BA (Hons), MA, MLS
John Clark, BA, MLS

SUMMARY. A description is presented of bilingual serial cataloguing at the National Library of Canada. In this, detailed discussions are undertaken of NLC policies regarding: creation of English and French bibliographic descriptions for bilingual serials and for serials issued in separate language editions; creation of English and French authority headings for personal, corporate and conference names, and for uniform title headings and conventional uniform titles; and use of bilingual subject headings on bibliographic descriptions.

I. BACKGROUND

Canada, like many other countries in the world, is made up of divergent ethnic groups. The two principal groups in Canada speak either English or French, and both languages are recognized legally as official languages.

Linguistically, the three major types of libraries in Canada are:

1. unilingual English libraries,
2. unilingual French libraries, and
3. bilingual libraries.

Unilingual English Libraries

A unilingual English library's bibliographic files are in English only. Bibliographic descriptions are provided in English only, regardless of the publication's language of text.

For authorities, where a personal, corporate or conference name has a form in both official languages, e.g., National Library of Canada or Bibliothèque nationale du Canada, a unilingual English library uses the English form of name as the accepted heading with a "seen from" cross reference from the French form of name.

Wayne Jones and John Clark are serial cataloguers at the National Library of Canada, 395 Wellington St., Ottawa, Ontario K1A 0N4.

Subject headings in a unilingual English library are provided only in English.

Unilingual French Libraries

A unilingual French library's bibliographic files are simply a reversal of the situation described above for a unilingual English library.

Bilingual Libraries

A bilingual library's bibliographic files are, where applicable, in both official languages. Most libraries, however, do not have the resources to provide both English and French descriptions for all materials received and some restrictions are imposed. While it varies from institution to institution, the restriction is usually based on the language of text. An English publication is described in English only; a French publication is described in French only; and a publication containing text in both English and French is described twice, a description being provided in each official language.

For authorities, where a personal, corporate or conference name has a form in both official languages, a bilingual library normally uses both forms of name as accepted headings.

Subject headings are provided in English and French although again, practices vary among bilingual institutions.

The National Library of Canada (NLC), as an agency of the federal government, is a bilingual library and bibliographic products are provided in both official languages.

II. DESCRIPTIVE CATALOGUING AT NLC

The following chart illustrates the basic descriptive cataloguing policy for most types of materials received at the NLC.

Language of text; sound recording; contents; etc.	*Language and number of bibliographic descriptions*
1. English only	1. 1 English record
2. French only	2. 1 French record
3. English and French in a single physical item	3. 1 English record; 1 French record

Note: in case 3 above, two descriptions are created only when the publication contains substantial text in both official languages. Substantial is considered to be a 50/50 or 60/40 English/French or French/English ratio. Ratios of greater than 60/40 are individually judged;

an English/French ratio of 90/10 would result in the creation of only one English record.

Language of text; sound recording; contents; etc.	Language and number of bibliographic descriptions
4. English and any other language(s) excluding French	4. 1 English record
5. French and any other language(s) excluding English	5. 1 French record
6. Any other language(s), excluding English and French	6. 1 English record

Bilingual Serials (English and French Text in a Single Physical Item)

The NLC policy for bilingual (and multilingual) serials is as follows: "If a serial, during any period of its publication, is issued in a bilingual English/French format, two separate records, one in English and one in French, will be created to describe that period of its publication history."[1]

The simple case is a serial which starts publication with text in English and French and maintains this bilingual format throughout its publication history. These serials are described in English and French and what is called an equivalence relationship is made between the two records. The equivalence relationship is a field created for internal use in DOBIS and does not appear in national products. DOBIS (Dortmurder Bibliothekssystem) is a data base which NLC contributes to, generates products from and shares with other libraries in Canada.

There are, however, more complicated cases than this. For example, a serial may start publication unilingually then switch to a bilingual format, or may start publication bilingually and switch to a unilingual format, or may change language format several times during its publication history.

In these cases NLC creates two records, one in English and one in French, and the specific nature of the language of text is explained in a language note (MARC tag 546) on each record: e.g., Text in English only, 1950-1960; text in English and French, 1961-1978 or Texte en anglais seulement, 1950-1960; texte en anglais et en français, 1961-1978.

Serials in Separate Language Editions (English and French)

While a bilingual format (English and French text in the same physical item) is common in Canada, many authors and corporations publish the same work in separate English and French editions (two physical items).

In these cases NLC breaks away from its policy of describing unilingual works in only one language. The reason is that while records describing different language editions of the same work should be linked together with the "Other editions available" relationship (MARC tag 775), it is an important principle at NLC not to create relationships between English and French descriptions, except for the equivalence relationship. As a result, four records must be created in the case of a serial issued in separate English and French editions. The English edition is described in English and French, as is the separate French edition. The following diagram illustrates what is done at NLC.

FIGURE 1

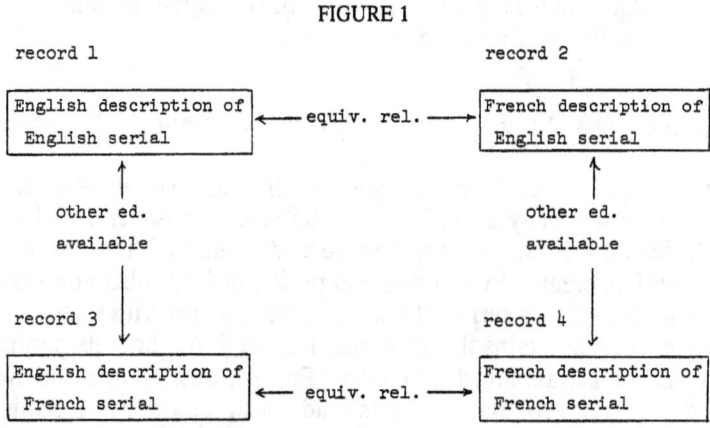

It would not be correct in the above example to create the "Other edition available" relationship between record 1 and record 4.

At the present time only records 1 *and* 4 appear in NLC's national products and in CONSER. Records 1 *through* 4 appear in NLC's local products and in DOBIS.

III. AUTHORITIES AT NLC

Authorities at the NLC are created in English and/or French according to the *Anglo-American Cataloguing Rules* (2nd ed.) and an authorized French translation entitled *Règles de catalogage anglo-américaines* (2e éd.).

There is an important rule in AACR2 upon which the authorities' policy of any bilingual library must be based. Rule 0.12 says in part:

> The rules contain some instances in which a decision is made on the basis of languages and in which English is preferred. It is expected

that users of the rules who do not use English as their working language will replace the specified preference for English by a preference for their working language. Authorized translations will be allowed to do the same.[2]

In the authorized French translation (RCAA2), a preference for French is therefore specified in rule 24.3,[3] whereas a preference for English is specified in the same rule in AACR2.[4] As NLC uses both sets of rules, one of the results of rule 0.12 is that authority headings can be in bilingual form.

The basic policy for establishing bilingual authorities at NLC is as follows:

> Headings [i.e., personal, corporate or conference names; uniform title headings and conventional uniform titles] required for use as either main or added entries created for *Canadiana* [the national bibliography], plus headings authenticated by the National Library for the Library of Congress, for CONSER, or for the SHARAF project will be established in both an English and a French form (i.e., according to both the *Anglo-American Cataloguing Rules*, second edition and the *Règles de catalogage anglo-américaines*, deuxième édition), provided they fall into one or more of [twenty-eight designated categories]. All other headings will be established in one form only, but that [unilingual] form, in most cases will be equally valid for use in both English and French catalogues . . . .[5]

Space constraints do not allow the authors to list all twenty-eight categories describing the various situations in which a heading should be established in a bilingual form. An example of one of the categories is provided below:

> e.g., Headings for corporate bodies that include as an addition to its name, a place name or the name of an institution, where the name used as an addition has been established in both an English and French language form:
>
> Sociedad Nacional de Minería (Peru)
> Sociedad Nacional de Minería (Pérou)
>
> Loyola University (New Orleans, La.)
> Loyola University (Nouvelle-Orléans, Louisiane)

In all cases where bilingual forms of a heading are established, an equivalence reference (analogous to the equivalence relationship between bibliographic records) is made between the English and French headings. For example, National Library of Canada and Bibliothèque nationale du Canada are designated as equivalent headings and an equivalence reference is made in authority products between the English heading and the French.

Where a bilingual authority exists, the English form of heading, when required, is provided on English descriptions and the French form of heading, when required, is provided on French descriptions. The equivalent heading appears on each description in certain products in what are called equivalence fields (9XX MARC tags).

IV. SUBJECT HEADINGS AT NLC

All subject headings used by NLC have an equivalent form in the other official language.[6] Where English and French descriptions exist for the same bibliographic item (i.e., equivalent records), English subject headings are provided on the English description and French subject headings are provided on the French description.

Where a bibliographic item has been described only once, in English or French, both English and French subject headings are provided on the bibliographic description.

As a result of resource limitations, some bibliographic descriptions appearing in *Canadiana* (i.e., records describing most government documents) are not provided with subject headings.

V. BILINGUAL DESCRIPTIVE CATALOGUING FOR SERIALS – CHARTS

It was explained earlier in this discussion that many serials have a tendency to change language content and/or format during their publication history. English and French text presented in a parallel column format could change to what is referred to as a tête-bêche format, which is the English text followed by French text on inverted pages or vice versa depending on which title page one is viewing. Unilingual serials can become bilingual. Separate language editions can merge to become a single bilingual publication, etc. What is worse is that often these format changes are accompanied by title changes.

In order to achieve consistency of practice by serial cataloguers at NLC and to preserve mental health, it was decided to create a comprehensive set of charts and examples that would illustrate what records and revisions would be required when language formats changed. At the same time, it was decided that these charts, in addition to illustrating format changes, would illustrate format changes in conjunction with title changes, again in order to achieve consistency and to save wear and tear on serial cataloguers.

This procedure document is called *Bilingual Cataloguing for Serials* and runs some eighty pages. It contains nine specific cases, each case being divided into part A and part B.

Part A of each case illustrates what revisions and new records are required in a bilingual situation where a publication's language format changes. Part B of each case outlines the exact same format change, with a title change thrown in.

The following example replicates part B of case 8 where a bilingual publication with a single title page splits to become separate language editions and the English title proper changes.

FIGURE 2

B-8   Bilingual publication with single title page splits to become separate publications with change in title proper.

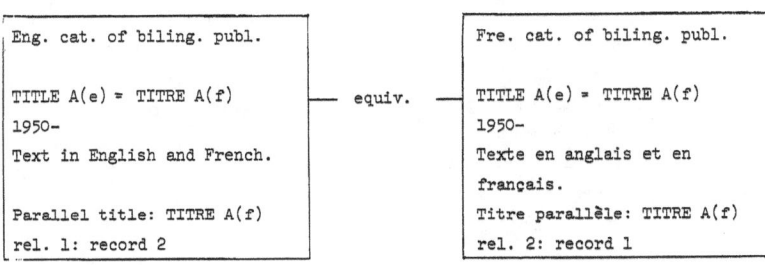

Prior to the format change, two DOBIS records are required to describe the bilingual publication.

```
        Language of                        Language of
     cataloguing: English              cataloguing: French

record 1                            record 2
```

Eng. cat. of biling. publ.		Fre. cat. of biling. publ.
TITLE A(e) = TITRE A(f) 1950– Text in English and French. Parallel title: TITRE A(f) rel. 1: record 2	— equiv. —	TITLE A(e) = TITRE A(f) 1950– Texte en anglais et en français. Titre parallèle: TITRE A(f) rel. 2: record 1

After the format and title proper change, records 1 and 2 are closed. Four new records are created for the new titles. Record 3 describes in English the unilingual English publication with the new title. Record 4 describes in French the unilingual English publication with the new title. Record 5 describes in English the unilingual French publication. Record 6 describes in French the unilingual French publication.

Revisions are as follows:

FIGURE 2 (continued)

```
record 1                              record 2

  i) Close formatted date:              i) Close formatted date:
     1950-1960.                            1950-1960.
 ii) Add Split into (rel. 43):         ii) Add Scindé en (rel. 43):
     record 3                              record 4
iii) Add Split into (rel. 43):        iii) Add Scindé en (rel. 43):
     record 5                              record 6

create record 3                    create record 4

  i) Descriptive title:                 i) Descriptive title:
     TITLE B(e)                            TITLE B(e)
 ii) Add formatted date: 1961-         ii) Add formatted date: 1961-
iii) Add Equiv. (rel. 1):             iii) Add language note: Texte
     record 4                              en anglais seulement.
 iv) Add Continues in part             iv) Add Equiv. (rel. 2):
     (rel. 25): record 1                   record 3
  v) Add Other lang. ed. (rel.          v) Add Fait suite après scission
     8): record 5                          (rel. 25): record 2
                                       vi) Add Éd. dans une autre langue
                                           (rel. 8): record 6

create record 5                    create record 6

  i) Descriptive title:                 i) Descriptive title: TITRE A(f)
     TITRE A(f)                        ii) Add formatted date: 1961-
 ii) Add formatted date: 1961-        iii) Add Éd. dans une autre langue
iii) Add language note: Text in            (rel. 8): record 4
     French only.                      iv) Add Fait suite après scission
 iv) Add Other lang. ed. (rel. 8):         (rel. 25): record 2
     record 3                           v) Add Equiv. (rel. 2):
  v) Add Continues in part (rel.           record 5
     25): record 1
 vi) Add Equiv. (rel. 1):
     record 6
```

FIGURE 2 (continued)

Revised and new records will appear as follows:

```
record 1                                    record 2
┌─────────────────────────────┐             ┌─────────────────────────────┐
│ Eng. cat. of biling. publ.  │             │ Fre. cat. of biling. publ.  │
│                             │             │                             │
│ TITLE A(e) = TITRE A(f)     │── equiv. ──│ TITLE A(e) = TITRE A(f)     │
│ 1950-1960.                  │             │ 1950-1960.                  │
│ Text in English and French. │             │ Texte en anglais et en      │
│                             │             │ français.                   │
│ Parallel title: TITRE A(f)  │             │ Titre parallèle: TITRE A(f) │
│ rel. 1: record 2            │             │ rel. 2: record 1            │
│ rel. 43: record 3           │             │ rel. 43: record 4           │
│ rel. 43: record 5           │             │ rel. 43: record 6           │
└─────────────────────────────┘             └─────────────────────────────┘

record 3                                    record 4
┌─────────────────────────────┐             ┌─────────────────────────────┐
│ Eng. cat. of Eng. publ.     │             │ Fre. cat. of Eng. publ.     │
│                             │             │                             │
│ TITLE B(e)                  │── equiv. ──│ TITLE B(e)                  │
│ 1961-                       │             │ 1961-                       │
│ rel. 1: record 4            │             │ Texte en anglais seulement. │
│ rel. 8: record 5            │             │ rel. 2: record 3            │
│ rel. 25: record 1           │             │ rel. 8: record 6            │
│                             │             │ rel. 25: record 2           │
└─────────────────────────────┘             └─────────────────────────────┘

record 5                                    record 6
┌─────────────────────────────┐             ┌─────────────────────────────┐
│ Eng. cat. of Fre. publ.     │             │ Fre. cat. of Fre. publ.     │
│                             │             │                             │
│ TITRE A(f)                  │             │ TITRE A(f)                  │
│ 1961-                       │             │ 1961-                       │
│ Text in French only.        │             │ rel. 2: record 5            │
│ rel. 1: record 6            │             │ rel. 8: record 4            │
│ rel. 8: record 3            │── equiv. ──│ rel. 25: record 2           │
│ rel. 25: record 1           │             │                             │
└─────────────────────────────┘             └─────────────────────────────┘
```

N.B. a) The following scenarios would be handled as in case B-8 with appropriate alterations to language of cataloguing, language of text codes and bibliographic notes:

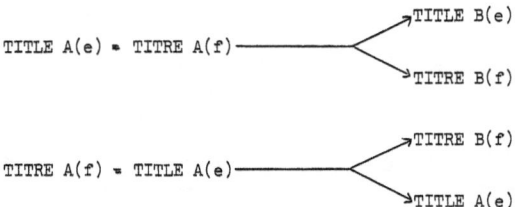

FIGURE 2 (continued)

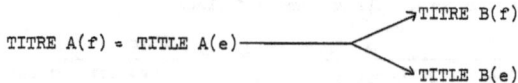

b) For same situation with no change in title proper, see no. A-8.

VI. CONCLUSION

This ends the brief overview of bilingual serial cataloguing at the National Library of Canada. The authors hope it has been informative and illustrative of the unique difficulties a library faces when cataloguing in two languages.

NOTES

1. National Library of Canada, Cataloguing Branch, *Cataloguing Manual* ([Ottawa]: NLC, [1981]-   ), part I, section 2.2, p. 2.
2. *Anglo-American Cataloguing Rules*, 2nd ed., edited by Michael Gorman and Paul W. Winkler (Chicago: American Library Association, 1978), p. 3.
3. *Règles de catalogage anglo-américaines*, 2e éd., rédigées par Michael Gorman and Paul W. Winkler, version française établie par Paule Rolland-Thomas avec la collaboration de Pierre Deslauriers (Montréal: ASTED, 1980), p. 612.
4. *AACR2*, p. 406.
5. *Cataloguing Manual*, part I, section 2.1, p. 1.
6. English subject headings are taken from: Library of Congress, Subject Cataloging Divison, *Library of Congress Subject Headings*, 10th ed. (Washington: LC, 1986) and from: National Library of Canada, *Canadian Subject Headings*, 2nd ed. (Ottawa: NLC, 1985); French subject headings are taken from: *Répertoire de vedettes-matière*, 9e éd. (Québec: Bibliothèque de l'Université Laval, 1983).
7. The letters A(e) in titles indicate the first occurrence of a title in English. The letters B(e) indicate a title change in English. The letters A(f) indicate the first occurrence of a title in French. The letters B(f) indicate a title change in French.

POTENTIAL FOR CHANGE

Multiplication of Serial Titles Forever?

Günter Franzmeier

SUMMARY. Starting from the observation that certain serial titles nowadays, besides having an ISDS key-title, which already is a de facto uniform title, get an AACR2 uniform title as a heading, the necessity and usefulness of such uniform titles are questioned. The advantages and disadvantages of the different types of uniform titles are compared and evaluated, and are in particular contrasted with the traditional principle of corporate body main entry abandoned by AACR2. As a result, a return to author/title entry is recommended for all (generic) serial titles containing the name of the issuing body or needing to be supplemented by that name to be distinctive. The ISDS key-title should be kept as an additional element, but no other uniform titles should be created because they create more problems than they solve.

When I wrote an article with a similar title in 1981,[1] I had been alarmed by the appearance of two new, or at least new-style, union lists of serials used worldwide, *Serials in the British Library* and *New Serial Titles*, showing, for the first time, examples of the AACR2-like "uniform" serial titles used as headings.

What alarmed me in particular at that time was the fact that after having had to accept, during the seventies, ISDS "key-titles" as de facto uniform titles for serials which were to be applied internationally, and which are in fact also given in the two union lists mentioned above, another—similar but different—type of uniform title for the same serials seemed to establish itself, also internationally, in the early eighties.

Competition may be a good thing, even in cataloguing, if it leads to a

---

Günter Franzmeier is Executive Director fo the German National Serials Data System "Zeitschriftendatenbank (ZDB)" at the Staatsbibliothek Preussischer Kulturbesitz, Postfach 1407, D-1000 Berlin 30. Franzmeier was Chairman of IFLA's Section of Serial Publications from 1981 to 1985.

gradual recognition that one of the solutions is better than the other, and if only the better one survives. Perhaps four or five years are indeed too short a period for the situation to clarify itself in that sense. Or perhaps there is no "better" solution, and each system has its merits and should survive!? The normal situation, however, would then be that each solution would be applied under different circumstances, in different countries, or for different purposes. But this is not the case: the two types of uniform titles are continuously used *together*, for the same serials, catalogued by the same cataloguers, applying the same rules. So many serials, all of which have their title as it appears on the piece, of course, keep on being rebaptised, first by ISDS, then additionally by AACR2, and therefore end up with three names which, as I pointed out in my earlier article, sometimes may differ in nothing else but slashes, dashes, or brackets, if at all, and at other times may differ very significantly.

My main concern, therefore, still is the duplication of effort and the unnecessary creation of additional titles which do not help anybody and serve no purpose. If the construction of uniform titles is inevitable, then, definitely, there should be only *one* international system. But which? And are uniform titles for serials really inevitable? These questions shall be dealt with in some greater detail on the following pages.

Based on the principles of ISBD, a serial can be described bibliographically like any other publication. If that bibliographic description is sufficiently complete, correct identification is also possible: by looking at the statement of responsibility, the place of publication, the year of publication or at other elements of the description, a reader will always be able to distinguish the serial from any other serial with a similar or even identical title! It is important to state this because in discussing serials problems a distinction is sometimes made between "description" and "identification," pretending that these are completely different things. Judgments can also be heard that one is more or less art for art's sake, and the other is the thing that really matters. More seriously, one could say that identification may have its particular problems, but that it must be based on, and should always start from, a sufficiently complete and correct description. So the people responsible for ISBD(S), in my view, were perfectly right when they resisted, in the mid-seventies, a tendency somehow to skip the descriptive stage for serials and to go to identification right away. Since it may not be remembered nowadays, let me explain that the first text of ISBD(S), published in 1974, had as one of its major recommendations the creation of a "distinctive title" instead of the "title proper" used in other ISBDs. If the title proper consisted of a generic term only, this distinctive title was to include the name of the issuing body "transcribed exactly as to wording" from the title page, even if there was no grammatical link to the generic term. This first attempt to establish uniform titles within the descriptive part of a serials record failed, and the revised text, called the "first standard edition" and published in 1977, reverted to the concept of "title proper" and "statement of responsibility" without deciding a priori whether one needs to be supplemented by the other. So, fortunately, today we have the "neutral" description of serials upon which everything else, and in particular any uniform titles, can be based, in whatever form they are deemed necessary, useful, or desirable. But we are also free to do without, if we like and if we can.

On the other hand, the revised ISBD(S) was unable to ignore the International Serials Data System (ISDS) already well established at that time, and admitted not only the ISSN, but also the corresponding ISDS "key-title," to the record. So, although the body of the description remained purely descriptive, area 8 incorporated what might well be called a uniform title. Admittedly, this contributes directly nowadays to the duplication of uniform titles in many AACR2 records.

But let us come back to the fundamental question: are uniform titles as additional elements really necessary, when there is a complete description? Under which conditions? And how should they be constructed?

If uniform titles are needed, they will, first of all, be needed for the correct filing of bibliographic records in a large catalogue. It is to be admitted that this may no longer be much of a problem in online catalogues, but for the time being we still have large traditional catalogues. Furthermore, filing is and always has been more than just arranging things alphabetically; it includes elements of access. If, for instance, a corporate body in its authoritative form is used as a heading, it serves access by collocating publications of one and the same body irrespective of the form of the name of that body used in the various publications, and thus found in the bibliographic descriptions. At least this element of filing will remain valid even in an online environment.

Having made these general observations, what about serials?

Every ISBD of a serial begins, rightly, with the title proper. There would be no problems if all these titles proper were distinctive and could be taken as the primary access point and as the one and only filing element. Unfortunately, we have to distinguish at least the following types of serial titles (proper):

1. Non-generic titles not containing the name of the issuing body, e.g., Journal of computer science.
2. Non-generic titles containing the name of the issuing body, e.g., IEEE transactions on electronics.
3. Generic titles containing the name of the issuing body, e.g., Bulletin of the Society . . .
4. Generic titles not containing the name of the issuing body, e.g., Bulletin / . . .
5. Generic and non-generic titles containing only parts of the name of the issuing body, e.g., Monthly bulletin of the Statistics Division / . . .

Statistically speaking, types 1 and 3 are, of course, far more numerous than the other types, followed at some distance by type 4. Filing problems, on the other hand, are most likely to occur among type 1 and, above all, type 4 titles.

Type 1 titles, if they are identical, are usually filed by place of publication. This choice is hardly controversial internationally, and is also favoured by the Library of Congress rule interpretation (LCRI) 25.5B,[2] although with certain exceptions. The rule interpretation, however, does not simply recommend filing by place of publication, but stipulates the creation of a uniform title (in addition to the title proper) where the place of publication is to be added as a qualifier in parentheses. Is this inevitable? I would say no. Manual as well as computer filing can easily be based directly on the place name contained in the imprint (field). The catalogue user can be expected to look up identical titles in the very same way; at least he was expected to do so for many decades when there were no uniform titles. The German Union Catalogue of Serials (ZDB) does this sort of filing and has never met any problems with it.

A slight problem arises, perhaps, when reference is to be made to such a title from other parts of the catalogue, e.g., from the successor title to the predecessor. In manual systems, the place name could be added as a qualifier to the title cited, but with the inconvenience that main entry and citation of the same serial would not correspond exactly. In automated systems, on the other hand, it would be almost impossible for the programme to know whether the title cited needs a qualifier when the main record of that title does not have one. My recommendation is to dispense with a qualifier even in this case and leave it to the user to find the title cited. In Germany it has been our experience that this works well enough when the user is offered full bibliographic records as main entries. It works even better in our online version where, for instance, marking a predecessor title cited in the notes area switches the user directly to the desired record.[3] Under these conditions, looking through identical titles is not necessary any more.

To summarize: there is no real need to create uniform titles for this type of serial just for the sake of filing (and distinguishing) identical titles. The place of publication can be taken directly as it appears in the imprint and serves the same purpose there.

Types 2 and 3 serials offer no substantial differences to type 1. The number of identical titles will even be lower here.

The main problems are obviously posed by *type 4*, since there will always be lots of identical generic titles even in smaller catalogues. Although not as numerous, the same problems are met with *type 5* serials. Two solutions seem to be possible, and have been used at different times and in different places. One is to add something as a qualifier and create a uniform title, the solution chosen by AACR2. The other is to put this sort of title under the heading for the issuing body, a solution with a long-standing tradition in earlier Anglo-American cataloguing.

The first solution, viz. to add a qualifier, will always prefer the corporate body for this type of title, not the place of publication. This is hardly controversial internationally and is applied by ISDS as well as by LCRI 25.5B. But the form in which that corporate body shall be given as a qualifier is already controversial. While paragraph 1.1.2 of the ISBD(S) of 1974 wanted to have the statement of authorship transcribed from the title page or title page substitute "exactly as to wording but not necessarily as to capitalization or punctuation" and linked to the title proper by space-dash-space, and the ISDS manual stipulates (in paragraph 3.2.2.3) that the name of the issuing body be transcribed "in the sequence and form given on the title source," separated from the generic term by a space-hyphen-space, LCRI 25.5B requires that the *heading* for the body (copied "from the name authority record exactly, with no deletions, rearrangements, changes in punctuation etc.") be added as a parenthetical qualifier.[4]

To make confusion perfect, ISDS, under the impact of AACR2 and its world-wide acceptance, offers an alternative for ISDS "Centres subject to the bibliographic agreements of the CONSER . . . Project [to] transcribe the name of the issuing body in the form established by national cataloguing practice for use in headings and other access points" (3.2.2.3, Note).[5]

Even if there were no alternatives to uniform titles in general, such as taking the issuing body as the primary heading, the situation described is obviously far from being satisfactory internationally, as was already stated at the beginning of this article, merely because of this co-existence, and overlapping, of two international systems used by the same people. But let us try to forget that for a while and examine the pros and cons of the two solutions, ISDS key-titles and AACR2 uniform titles, and also a third solution described in a paper by Jim Cole (in this work) suggesting, among other things, still another arrangement of hierarchical corporate bodies to follow the title proper: from lowest to highest in ascending order.

As I have written on the topic before,[6] and since Cole, in the article mentioned, deals very aptly and very knowledgeably with similar aspects, I shall concentrate on describing very briefly the advantages and the disadvantages of the different solutions.

ISDS Key-Titles (Advantages)

— Avoid changing certain corporate bodies, saving intellectual effort and time otherwise needed to construct the desired form;

— Avoid changes which lead to a sometimes fargoing deviation from what a user might expect.

ISDS Key-Titles (Disadvantages)

— Have to accept the vagaries of title pages, where the same title or similar titles appear in all sorts of variants, e.g., Special report — Northern Illinois University, Center for Southeast Asian Studies. *But:*
Special report — Center for African Studies of Northern Illinois University.
— If this disadvantage seems unacceptable, because users may not know the sequence of the parts and not find the title, a lot of cross-references are needed just for safety.
— Have to accept the other frequent vagary, that the same title or similar titles partly have a link, a preposition or something like it, between the generic term and the issuing body, partly they don't have.
— If this disadvantage seems unacceptable, too, because users may not know whether there is a link or not, and not find the title (if filed alphabetically word by word, or even, as in ISDS, letter by letter), a lot of cross-references are needed, also just for safety.

AACR2 Uniform Titles (Advantages)

— Avoid the vagaries of title pages, and probably have the two Special reports mentioned under ISDS treated alike, as Special report (Northern Illinois University. Center . . .).
— Profit from existing authority files by avoiding intellectual effort to construct the form of name in many cases and thereby fostering consistency between titles and name authorities.

AACR2 Uniform Titles (Disadvantages)

— Move away, in many cases, from the form of name in the title source, creating "artificial" titles which a user may not expect. Consistently applied, a title like "Bulletin / Société internationale . . . " would get the uniform title "Bulletin (International Society . . .)" since the English form of name would be the preferred form for international bodies, whereas "Bulletin de la Société Internationale . . . " would stay as it is, merely because the corporate body is linked and not a qualifier.
— Depend completely upon certain (national or international) rules for the form of headings and the respective authority files. When something is changed there, the change will most probably not be trans-

ferrable automatically to the uniform titles where these names appear in context (in contrast to what is possible for other headings).
— Have to accept the other vagaries already mentioned under ISDS, i.e., the same title or similar titles partly having a link with the corporate body, partly not, with the corresponding problems for filing and finding.

Uniform Titles, as Proposed by Cole (Advantages)

— Avoid the vagaries of title sources by giving the corporate body in a uniform way from the lowest hierarchical part ascending to the highest, which at least for me, makes more sense than from highest to lowest, since in most cases the lowest is the directly responsible part.
— Avoid the vagaries of title sources in particular by giving *every* corporate body as a qualifier in its nominative case, even when the source (and the descriptive part of the entry) has that body grammatically linked to the generic term. Once the user knows this, he will no longer search, perhaps in vain, under "Bulletin of the Society . . . ," but will instantly look under "Bulletin Society . . . ."

Uniform Titles as Proposed by Cole (Disadvantages)

— Intellectual effort and time are necessary to establish the "lowest to highest" order, to establish the nominative case for all parts (which may be difficult in the case of foreign languages).
— Profit only very partially from existing authority files, e.g., for getting the nominative cases.
— Give the corporate body yet another form besides the form found in the title source and the form found in the authority file, which is all the more unsatisfactory as the authority file headings have to be established in any case, if they are not already in the file, for other main and added entries.

When comparing and assessing all these advantages and disadvantages, one solution seems — partially — better than the other. For instance, the possibility of AACR2 to use one and the same heading, which has to be established in any case, for various purposes, seems to be an advantage over Cole's proposal. On the other hand, Cole's proposal would avoid completely artificial constructions such as the "Bulletin (International Society . . .) instead of the original title "Bulletin / Société Internationale . . . ," while ISDS has the advantage of keeping the original form of the corporate name even in cases where this is lowest to highest here and highest to lowest there. From the filing (and finding) aspect,

Cole's proposal looks better than the other solutions. It is scarcely possible to say which solution is to be preferred in total when compared to the other solutions. Two statements, however, can be made:

- If one solution is not far better than the other, it is even worse that two of them are being applied at the same time!
- In my view, all three of the solutions have more disadvantages than advantages, and all of them are far worse than avoiding uniform titles altogether and sticking to the long-standing practice of using the name of the corporate body, in a standardized form, as a heading preceding the bibliographic description, at least for types 4 and 5 serial titles (but also for type 3)!

Many arguments for preferring this solution have been explained in my earlier articles,[7] so I shall confine myself to a summary and some additional aspects.

Advantages of Author/Title Entries

- The vagaries found in title sources, in particular the arbitrary differences between linked and unlinked bodies and the change from one form to the other even within the same serial publication, become irrelevant because the title is only second in filing after the corporate heading.
- No new, additional, and sometimes artificial titles have to be constructed. Instead, filing, identification, and citation are by author/title, a mode every user is well acquainted with since this is also used for works of personal authors and occurs over and again in the catalogue anyway, in the form of added entries, also for corporate bodies.
- The authority headings existing in the authority file or to be input in that file anyway, be it for added or other entries, can be directly used for the main entry, too.
- The cross-reference structure for names of corporate bodies contained in the authority entries and so eminently necessary, can also be used directly for the title entries. One name reference, e.g., from "IFLA" to the "International Federation of Library Associations and Institutions," will be sufficient to direct the user to all IFLA publications listed. The use of uniform titles, on the contrary, would necessitate the same cross-reference, but leave some titles under IFLA, e.g., "IFLA journal," others under the full name, and others again under, e.g., "Transactions of IFLA." Collocation would be possible, but only at the cost of multiple references and/or added entries. And a user looking under "Transactions International Fed-

eration . . . " would probably not find anything, if this variant were not cross-referenced, too!
— Any changes in the authority file, perhaps due to changes of the rules, can be transferred, at least in automated systems, to the headings of all pertinent bibliographic records, which they cannot be when the heading is part of a uniform title, hence a title field.
— The author/title entry type is not only used in other places of the catalogue: it has a long-standing tradition in the Anglo-American countries especially when applied to serials with generic titles. Thousands of cataloguers knew and know how to use it and have to learn and to apply *additional* rules now, the usefulness of which is very doubtful.

Disadvantages of Author/Title Entries

— The serial receives its main entry not under its title, but under the issuing body, the heading for which may be different from what appears in the title source. (On the other hand, a user will be much less surprised to find a standardized form of name *preceding* the title proper than following it, because this is what he is used to in author/title catalogues).
— If reference is made to such entries from other entries, e.g., from a predecessor title, the serial has to be cited in this author/title form.
— Since the form and structure of corporate headings may vary from country to country and from cataloguing code to cataloguing code, the author/title form will look different in different countries, and in the case of the exchange of machine-readable records, the notes may contain the citation of, e.g., a predecessor in an author/title form which may not be acceptable for the receiving institution.
— In short title catalogues where there are no extensive descriptions of the serials, and perhaps no cross-references, added entries, etc., many titles will not be found by the user, because, e.g., certain "Bulletins" will not be registered at all under that word, but under the issuing body which may even have an unexpected heading.

All this is certainly true, but most of the disadvantages are the same that are encountered with uniform titles:

— If, for uniform titles, the official heading is preferred over the form as it appears in the title source, as stipulated by AACR2, a search for a certain "Bulletin" may be equally difficult.
— National differences, therefore, also affect uniform titles.
— Short title catalogues of serials which contain larger numbers of generic titles, but no descriptive elements and no cross-references,

e.g., from "IFLA" to the "International Federation . . . ," are difficult to use anyway and cannot be recommended, neither for author/title catalogues nor for uniform titles.

To summarize: there is, of course, no perfect cataloguing of serials. Every solution has also certain disadvantages. The disadvantages of putting generic titles under the headings of their issuing bodies, however, are not very different from the disadvantages encountered for uniform titles. But uniform titles have *many additional and serious disadvantages*, as I have tried to show. But even if it were not so they could be called superfluous in an environment such as AACR2 where headings for corporate bodies are being used as entries anyway, even for the same serial; and they are the more superfluous if two systems, AACR2 and ISDS, are used at the same time, both of which can be called international in scope. Since certain serial titles, admittedly, do not lend themselves easily to identification, filing, and retrieval, and *something* must be done, something artificial has to be introduced by cataloguers whether we like it or not; in my view this should not be additional titles, and certainly not two of them, but author/title entries which have worked well for such a long time before AACR2.

ISDS, on the other hand, is a very particular aspect of the problem: ISDS key-titles may perhaps be inevitable and should be carried in any serials record. The more the creation of additional uniform titles should be avoided!

NOTES

1. Günter Franzmeier, "The Miraculous Multiplication of Serial Titles," *International Cataloguing* 11 (1982):9.
2. *Cataloging Service Bulletin*, no. 25 (summer 1984):70-77.
3. In our system, by simply asterisking that title in the notes, before the first title word, and then depressing the SEND key, the program switches the user to the respective record.
4. *Cataloging Service Bulletin*, no. 25 (summer 1984):72.
5. This means nothing less than: certain ISDS Centres can construct key-titles as if they were AACR2 uniform titles, except for the parentheses. But as a national ISDS centre they can only do this for titles of their national imprint, whereas, as CONSER participants, they are responsible for titles from all over the world for which they have to accept "ordinary" key-titles.
6. Günter Franzmeier, "Serials Cataloging in the Federal Republic of Germany," *Serials Review* 11, no. 2 (summer 1985):71-72.
7. Franzmeier, "Miraculous Multiplication," p. 9. See also my "Can ISDS Replace ISBD(S)?" *International Cataloguing* 12 (1983):41-44.

Corporate Names as Qualifiers in Uniform Titles

Jim E. Cole

SUMMARY. The currently accepted guidelines for the creation of uniform titles for serials cause certain difficulties when the title proper, exclusive of the name of the issuing body, consists of an initial generic term. Among these difficulties are (1) the need to predict the existence and form of a grammatical link between the generic term and the corporate name; (2) the use of the catalog heading for the issuing body as the qualifier, which may reverse the "natural" order of hierarchical elements or be in a language different from the title proper; and (3) the usual placement of the qualifier after the title proper when the title proper consists of a common title and section title. Alternative guidelines intended to rectify these problems are proposed.

INTRODUCTION

In 1982 Andrew Clarke of the Australian National Library published an article in *Catalogue & Index* proposing a restructuring of uniform titles for serials with generic titles (with or without a grammatical link to the name of the issuing body) that was based on the practice then found in the *British Union Catalogue of Periodicals*.[1] This paper will attempt to refine and develop further the concept advanced by Clarke and will discuss both his and the present author's reasons for such a change.

SOME PROBLEMS TO CONSIDER

One of the oldest cataloging traditions in this country—and one of which we should all be proud—is the organization of our catalogs. The 1968 edition of the *ALA Rules for Filing Catalog Cards* states that "the basic order [of the catalog] is alphabetical, word by word, except in certain areas where a numerical or chronological arrangement is preferable."[2] This basic order is accepted today, as it was in the past, when the

---

Jim E. Cole is Assistant Professor and Serials Cataloger, 204 Parks Library, Iowa State University, Ames, IA 50011. Cole was the American Library Association Serials Section liaison to the Committee on Cataloging: Description and Access, from 1983 to 1985.

cataloging rules prescribed corporate main entry too frequently, at times frustrating rather than helping the user by requiring its use even though the title was distinctive and did not include the name of the issuing body.

Today, however, AACR2 greatly restricts corporate main entry for all publications, including serials. The title proper has by default become the primary access point; if it is itself not unique, then a uniform title is constructed, following the policies established by the Library of Congress.[3] Clarke aptly points out the problem title main entry introduces, given our word-by-word filing:

> The identification of a . . . title . . . depends on a user's prior knowledge of whether a preposition appears on the chief source of information of a serial which he or she might not yet have seen, and which may in fact have no chief source of information.[4]

Franzmeier earlier discussed this same problem in 1978 at a colloquium on the German cataloging code, saying that title main entry accompanied by strict word-by-word filing places too great an emphasis on the various particles (articles, prepositions, and conjunctions) by creating split files or clusters of titles.[5] His and Clarke's assertions are adequately verified in the 1981-84 cumulation of *New Serial Titles,* where of the titles beginning with the word "Bulletin," one encounters two separate files—the first consisting of 132 serials having uniform titles "Bulletin ([Corporate name])" and the second consisting of 137 serials having unique titles proper of the form "Bulletin . . . [Corporate name]." The latter group is, of course, interspersed with other titles beginning "Bulletin . . . ," for example "Bulletin of research in the humanities." One not only needs to predict the existence of a grammatical link between the generic term and corporate name, but also the form of it, which may be difficult in even a commonly known foreign language. In English itself, as Franzmeier knew, subclusters are already developing within the group "Bulletin . . . [Corporate name]," caused by (1) variant prepositions being used (The . . . Bulletin from the Norwegian Music Information Centre), and (2) articles being omitted before the corporate name (Bulletin of Mathematical Association of India). This entire situation will continue to worsen and the catalog will become so difficult to search by title, that the corporate name, now an added entry, will re-emerge as the most valid access point. To solve this problem, one must either reconsider corporate main entry for these titles, as outlined by Howard in his "Alternative 2,"[6] or devise some method whereby the necessity of predicting the existence of the grammatical link (preposition and/or article) is eliminated.

The other problem Clarke discusses pertaining to generic titles is the fact that according to the present guidelines for uniform titles for serials, if a corporate hierarchy is involved, the qualifier is given in catalog entry form in descending order, beginning with the highest element. Unfortunately titles are most often grammatically linked to the lowest element instead. This is demonstrated by the 1981-84 cumulation of *New Serial Titles*, where, of the forty-two titles beginning "Bulletin," "Journal," or "Publications" that were grammatically linked to an element of a corporate hierarchy, thirty-nine were directly linked to the lowest element, while only three had the name of the higher body intervening. The same cumulation of *New Serial Titles* lists another forty serials with uniform titles consisting of these same generic terms and qualifiers of the form "Geographic and/or parent body name. Subordinate or related body name," reversing the more "natural" lower-to-higher order of the hierarchical elements. To use Clarke's example, if the title of the "Bulletin of the Institute of Historical Research" were merely "Bulletin," the uniform title "Bulletin (University of London. Institute of Historical Research)" would then be assigned—an entry the patron may well overlook, knowing that it is the institute's, and not the university's, bulletin. Perhaps a lower-to-higher order of hierarchical elements would be preferable, since this would less frequently violate the order of elements found in a title proper with grammatical link, and thus less frequently force the patron to predict whether that grammatical link indeed exists.

Because corporate names are given in catalog heading form when used as qualifiers in uniform titles, the qualifier may well be in a different language than the title which is being qualified. For example, "Bulletin/Centre de recherches anthropologiques préhistoriques et ethnographiques" is published in Algiers and therefore has a uniform title of "Bulletin (Markaz al Buhūth . . .)." A system of cross references to the uniform title must be established in such cases (here, "Bulletin (Centre . . .) *search under* Bulletin (Markaz . . .)." If it is not, in order to locate the serial by title, the user has to (1) find the correct catalog heading for the body, and then (2) search under the title, using that heading as a qualifier. It would seem simpler for both the cataloger and user either to apply Howard's "Alternative 2" and use a corporate main entry or to derive the qualifier from data on the item being cataloged.

A related problem is concerned with the rules for title changes as found in AACR2 and the *ISDS Manual*. After 1980, when catalogers began applying the AACR2 guidelines for title changes, they rapidly discovered that many changes in title which were considered minor under AACR1 necessitated the creation of separate records under AACR2. Even accord ing to the 1984 Library of Congress rule interpretation regarding title changes,[7] the addition, deletion, or change in the grammatical link between the name of the issuing body and a generic term is usually considered a change in title proper, especially if the grammatical link occurs within the first five words of the title. The *ISDS Manual*, however, treats this as a minor title change.[8] Catalogers could be spared a great deal of work if AACR2 were brought into conformity with the *Manual*, either by rule revision or rule interpretation. But if the present guidelines for the formulation of uniform titles were applied to these variant titles (this is not now done), they could, if involving a corporate hierarchy, be obscured in the catalog. This would be possible even if particles were disregarded in the filing. As shown above, the qualifiers now used in uniform titles often reverse the order of the elements of the hierarchy from that given in the title proper when a grammatical link exists. Thus, for example, a user looking for "Bulletin Institute . . . " may be required to search under "Bulletin University . . . " instead. Qualifiers in a language different from that of the title proper would present similar difficulties for the patron; for example, "Bulletin du Centre . . . " vs. "Bulletin (Markaz . . .)."

Most of the problems discussed above apply equally well to titles in the form "Common title. Section number and/or title." The user encounters the same difficulty regarding a grammatical link between a generic common title and a corporate name. The problem is worsened here, however, by the fact that if the common title/section title combination is unique, as it often is, no uniform title is generally assigned, even if the common title is solely a generic term. Is the title "Proceedings of the Indian Academy of Sciences. Animal sciences" or merely "Proceedings. Animal sciences"? The user, often not having previously seen the item, must predict. When a uniform title is indeed assigned, the qualifier normally follows the section title; hence, the catalog records for the various sections of a serial with a generic common title may easily become interspersed with records for sections of still other serials having the same common title. One can envision over the years other titles filing among those of the five sections of the "Proceedings" of the Indian Academy of Sciences, which begin with "Proceedings. Animal sciences" and end with "Proceedings. Plant sciences." It is interesting, too, that since the common title is not qualified, one now finds *three* distinct clusters of entries beginning with "Proceedings" in the 1981-84 cumulation of *New Serial Titles*: "Proceedings. [Section number and/or title]," "Proceedings ([Corporate name])," and "Proceedings . . . [Corporate name]." Perhaps some method of qualifying the common title could reduce this clustering effect.

Many librarians may wonder if these problems will not resolve themselves in the online setting, where all of the 245 field—including the other title information and statements of responsibility—may be searched by keyword. If, for example, one may find the name of the issuing body in the language of the title proper in subfield c, does it matter that the uniform title contains the name in a different language? Perhaps, in such a case, it doesn't matter a great deal. But all too often there is no formal statement of responsibility in the record; the issuing body is named in the

260 (Publication, Distribution, Etc.) field or in a 550 (Issuing Body Note) field instead. Moreover, as Franzmeier has said, printed/microform catalogs will continue to be produced for some time, and their requirements must be taken into account.[9]

A POSSIBLE SOLUTION

The following guidelines are proposed as a possible solution to the problems discussed above.

1. If the title proper of a serial consists solely of (*a*) a generic term, or (*b*) a generic term followed by the name of the issuing body, assign the serial a uniform title in the form of

Generic term (Corporate name)

If in the title proper a grammatical link exists between the generic term and the name of the issuing body, include in the record an added entry for the title proper.

2. Transcribe the corporate name as it appears (*a*) in the title proper, or (*b*) on the title source (in that order of preference). When the name of an issuing body not included in the title proper appears in more than one form on the title source, choose the form which is given typographical prominence, or, if that does not apply, choose the briefest form (not an acronym or initialism) which adequately identifies the issuing body. When the name of an issuing body not included in the title proper also does not appear on the title source, take the name from elsewhere in the piece. If a corporate name appears in an inflected form, use the form in the nominative case. Omit an initial article from a corporate name unless the intent is to file on the article.

The parenthetical qualifier may be an initialism or acronym for a corporate name if it is so given in the title proper or is the sole form on the title source. In such instances, however, make a reference to the uniform title from the generic term followed, in parentheses, by the full form of the name in the nominative case. (See Figure 1.)

3. If a corporate hierarchy appears on the item, use as the parenthetical qualifier the name of the *lowest* element of the hierarchy. If further elements of the hierarchy are needed to make the uniform title unique, include, in ascending order, those elements required for adequate identification of the *body*; omit intermediate elements that are not essential. Record each element of the hierarchy as it appears on the item. Omit grammatical links between elements of the hierarchy; if the name of an element appears in an inflected form, use the name in the nominative case. Omit an initial article from the name of an element unless the intent is to file on the article. Separate elements by a comma-space.

An initialism or acronym for the superior body may be considered an

EXAMPLES:

Title page	Uniform title	Added entry for title proper?
Bulletin / International Federation of Surveyors	Bulletin (International Federation of Surveyors)	No
Bulletin / Research Institute of Geodesy, Topography and Cartography in Prague	Bulletin (Research Institute of Geodesy, Topography and Cartography in Prague) <u>not</u> Bulletin (Výzkumný ústav geodetický, topografický a kartografický (Prague, Czechoslovakia))	No
Journal of the Optical Society of America	Journal (Optical Society of America)	Yes
Transactions of the Japan Society for Composite Materials	Transactions (Japan Society for Composite Materials) <u>not</u> Transactions (Nihon Fukugō Zairyō Gakkai)	Yes
Jahrbuch der Deutschen Bücherei	Jahrbuch (Deutsche Bücherei) <u>not</u> Jahrbuch (Deutschen Bücherei) <u>not</u> Jahrbuch (Deutsche Bücherei (Germany))	Yes
Bulletin of JSME	Bulletin (JSME) <u>with reference from</u> Bulletin (Japan Society of Mechanical Engineers)	Yes

FIGURE 1

integral part of the name of the subordinate or related body. Similarly, a geographic name may be considered an integral part of the name of a governmental body. If in such instances, however, the initialism/acronym or geographic name begins the name of the subordinate body, make a reference to the uniform title from the generic term, followed, in parentheses, by the name of the subordinate/related body or governmental body, omitting the initialism/acronym or geographic name, respectively. (See Figure 2.)

4. If the title proper of a serial is in the form "Common title. Section designation and/or title," and the common title consists of (*a*) a generic term, or (*b*) a generic term followed by the name of the issuing body, assign the serial a uniform title in the form of

Generic term (Corporate name). Section designation and/or title.

Follow the instructions in 2.–3. above for recording the corporate name. Precede the section designation and/or title by a period and two spaces.

Include in the record an added entry for the title proper if the section title includes a subject term (see also 1. above). (See Figure 3.)

5. Do not consider the title proper of a serial to have changed if (*a*) the title proper or common title, exclusive of the name of the issuing body, consists of a generic term, and (*b*) the grammatical link with the name of the issuing body following the generic term is added, deleted, or changed.
For example,
Bulletin of the Society . . .
later becomes
Bulletin / Society . . .
Include in the record a specific note regarding the variant title(s), in the form "Published as: . . . , dates." Include added entries for the variant title(s) as necessary (see 1. and 4. above).

If the title proper or common title, exclusive of the name of the issuing body, consists of a generic term and a corporate hierarchy is involved,

EXAMPLES:

Title page	Uniform title	Added entry for title proper?
Journal of the Engineering Mechanics Division	Journal (Engineering Mechanics Division)	Yes
Veröffentlichungen des Instituts für Forstpolitik und Forstliche Betriebswirtschaftslehre der Forstlichen Forschungsanstalt München	Veröffentlichungen (Institut für Forstpolitik und Forstliche Betriebswirtschaftslehre)	Yes
Memoirs of the Faculty of Agriculture, University of Miyazaki	Memoirs (Faculty of Agriculture, University of Miyazaki)	Yes
Memoirs of the Faculty of Agriculture, Kagoshima University	Memoirs (Faculty of Agriculture, Kagoshima University)	Yes

FIGURE 2

EXAMPLES:

Title page	Uniform title	Added entry for title proper?
Proceedings of the Royal Society of Edinburgh. Section B, Biology	Proceedings (Royal Society of Edinburgh). Section B, Biology.	Yes
Proceedings. Plant sciences / Indian Academy of Sciences	Proceedings (Indian Academy of Sciences). Plant sciences.	Yes

FIGURE 3

also do not consider the title proper to have changed if (*a*) grammatical links with all or parts of the hierarchy following the generic term are added, deleted, or changed; or (*b*) names of elements of the hierarchy, included in the title proper but not in the uniform title, are added, deleted, or changed.
For example,
   Bulletin of the Section . . . of the Society . . .
later becomes
   Bulletin of the Section . . .
or
   Bulletin / Section . . .
In these instances include in the record a specific note regarding the variant title(s), in the form "Published as: . . . , dates." Include added entries for the variant title(s) as necessary (see 1. and 4. above).

DISCUSSION

The first section of the above proposal incorporates Clarke's suggestion that generic titles proper with or without a prepositional link to the name of the issuing body be qualified by the name of the body. According to both his suggestion and this proposal, a uniform title would be assigned to any serial whose title proper, exclusive of the name of the issuing body, consists of an initial generic term. Uniqueness of any corporate main entry/title proper combination would no longer be a consideration. This section could have two effects: (1) it would remove the need to predict the existence and form of any grammatical link with the name of the issuing body; and (2) if the uniform title rather than a non-unique title proper were traced, it would impose a filing order on those non-unique titles proper that at present do not require a uniform title because a corporate main entry is present. (For example, the 1981-84 cumulation of *New Serial Titles* contains twenty-four pages of randomly arranged references from just "Annual report.") The entire proposal moreover assures user access by exact title proper, since it requires an added entry if the title is distinctive.

The second section of this proposal requires that the name used as the qualifier be taken from the item being cataloged. The qualifier consequently may not agree with the catalog heading for the same body (for instance, the qualifier may be in English and the heading in another language). The user therefore need not first establish the correct catalog heading in order to access the publication by title. Provisions for choice among varying forms of the name of the body on the item are taken from the *ISDS Manual*.[10] The name used as qualifier is recorded in the nominative case because other case endings may be governed by the preceding preposition, which was eliminated. It must be admitted that this contradicts the practice in lists of serials such as *Gesamtverzeichnis ausländischer Zeitschriften und Serien* (GAZS), where the linking prepositions and articles are recorded but ignored in the filing.[11] Both the second and third sections of this proposal require certain references to the uniform title because of difficulties in predicting the form of the corporate name. These difficulties do not originate with the proposal, however, since they already exist for unique titles proper with a grammatical link (for instance, is the title "Bulletin of JSME" or "Bulletin of the Japan Society of Mechanical Engineers"?).

Clarke suggests that a lower-to-higher arrangement of the various elements of a corporate hierarchy be used in uniform titles, and that elements of the hierarchy unnecessary for the identification of the serial be omitted. He took this idea from the arrangement of entries in the *British Union Catalogue of Periodicals*. This same basic arrangement has been incorporated into other union lists of serials, of which GAZS is a good example. A somewhat similar provision was for decades found in the *Instruktionen für die alphabetischen Kataloge der preussischen Bibliotheken*, the catalog code in effect in many parts of Germany until the mid-1970s.[12] Clarke's suggestion has formed the basis for the third section of the above proposal.

Serial titles of the form "Common title. Section number and/or title" are not often generic, since the section title itself frequently contains a subject designation. The fourth section of the above proposal therefore separately addresses the problem of the common title, allowing a corporate qualifier to precede the section title in a uniform title. This would eliminate the clustering effect now found in *New Serial Titles*. It would also group together all the sections of a serial having a common title, as was done in GAZS and *Deutsches Bücherverzeichnis*, both of which employed a type of multilevel description for such publications (disallowed by AACR2).

If these guidelines were employed, it would become somewhat more difficult to detect the addition, deletion, or change of a grammatical link between a generic title and the name of the issuing body. Consequently, the fifth section refines the concept of change in title proper of a serial and instructs the cataloger how to treat such a change in wording. This would align AACR2 with the *ISDS Manual* and reduce the number of new serial records created. The American Library Association Committee to Study Serials Cataloging has already agreed in principle to a similar change and is drafting a rule revision to that effect. The present proposal, however, provides similar treatment for changes in the elements of a corporate hierarchy when those elements are not needed to identify the serial, here going beyond the provisions of the *ISDS Manual* in reducing title changes.

CONCLUSION

Several problems are associated with the present guidelines for uniform titles for serials. These problems vary in nature and degree of consequence, but they will all continue to compound themselves with time unless something is done. The proposal presented here is a reasonable solution to these problems. Another solution would be the adoption of Howard's "Alternative 2."

NOTES

1. Andrew Clarke, "Borge's Rules for Series, Serials and Supplements: The New Uniform Titles Reconsidered," *Catalogue & Index*, no. 66 (winter 1982):2-3.
2. American Library Association, Subcommittee on the ALA Rules for Filing Catalog Cards, *ALA Rules for Filing Catalog Cards*, 2nd ed. (Chicago: American Library Association, 1968), p. 1.
3. *Cataloging Service Bulletin*, no. 25 (summer 1984):70-77.
4. Clarke, "Borge's Rules," p. 2.
5. Günter Franzmeier, "Die Katalogisierung fortlaufender Sammelwerke unter besonderer Berücksichtigung der Zeitschriftendatenbank," *Zeitschrift für Bibliothekswesen und Bibliographie* 26 (1979):305-315. See also his "Can ISDS Replace ISBD(S)?" *International Cataloguing* 12 (1983):41-44.
6. Joseph H. Howard, "Main Entry for Serials," *Drexel Library Quarterly* 11, no. 3 (July 1975):14-15.
7. *Cataloging Service Bulletin*, no. 25 (summer 1984):55-57.
8. ISDS International Centre, *ISDS Manual*(Paris: ISDS International Centre, 1983), p. 59.
9. Günter Franzmeier, "Serials Cataloging in the Federal Republic of Germany: Main Features and Main Differences from AACR II," *Serials Review* 11, no. 2 (summer 1985):72.
10. ISDS International Centre, *ISDS Manual*, p. 42-43.
11. *Gesamtverzeichnis ausländischer Zeitschriften und Serien*, 5 vols. (Wiesbaden: Harrassowitz, 1959-1968), 1:xiii-xvi.
12. *Instruktionen für die alphabetischen Kataloge der preussischen Bibliotheken vom 10. Mai 1899*, 2. Ausg., in der Fassung vom 10. Aug., 1908 (1909; reprint ed., Wiesbaden: Otto Harrassowitz, 1970), p. 72. For explanation see Hermann Fuchs, *Kommentar zu den Instruktionen für die alphabetischen Kataloge der preussischen Bibliotheken*, 5., unveränderte Aufl. (Wiesbaden: Otto Harrassowitz, 1973), p. 240.

The First Shall Be Last: Earliest Entry Cataloging

Jim E. Cole

SUMMARY. Librarians are again beginning to discuss latest entry cataloging of serials. If, however, the description of a serial is based on the first issue as specified by AACR2, then earliest entry cataloging is an alternative to be considered seriously. Here the change is handled through a note and added entry, leaving the older record basically intact. Because of the computer's Boolean search capabilities, this method does not impair the user's access to the record. At a time of escalating technical services costs, libraries would find this to be an economical solution to the problems of changes in entry of serials.

For more than a decade, institutions adhering to the cataloging practices of the Library of Congress have cataloged serials that changed their titles under successive entries. This practice, now well familiar to the library community, is prescribed by both editions of the *Anglo-American Cataloging Rules.* Some librarians, however, are now beginning to reconsider this basic AACR principle. For instance, Northwestern University Library announced in April that it is beginning an experiment using latest entry cataloging for selected serials.[1] This paper will examine the various methods of cataloging serials that have been used recently in the United States and will advance the principle of earliest entry cataloging as a viable option.

HISTORICAL OVERVIEW

Two distinct methods of describing a serial—one based on the latest issue, one on the earliest—have been used in the United States in the latter half of the twentieth century. Similarly, two different principles have governed the treatment of serials that

---

Jim E. Cole is Assistant Professor and Serials Cataloger, 204 Parks Library, Iowa State University, Ames, IA 50011. Cole was the American Library Association's Serials Section liaison to the Committee on Cataloging: Description and Access, from 1983 to 1985.

Reprinted from The Serials Librarian, Vol. 11(1), September 1986.

© 1986 by The Haworth Press, Inc. All rights reserved.

changed title, the former being the latest entry principle, and the latter, successive entry. Various codes have contained various combinations of rules for description and entry.

A.L.A. Cataloging Rules and the Library of Congress Rules

The second edition of the *A.L.A. Cataloging Rules for Author and Title Entries*[2] was published in 1949, the same year that the *Rules For Descriptive Cataloging in the Library of Congress*[3] appeared. The two works together constituted a cohesive whole, with the Library of Congress rules replacing Part II, "Description of Book," of the first edition of the *A.L.A. Catalog Rules*. ALA rule 5C(1) specified that a currently published periodical was to be entered under its latest title; a periodical that had ceased publication could be entered under its earlier title if it had been used for a "much longer period." Special attention was given to the numbering of the periodical: if the title changed and the newer title continued the numbering of the previous title, the two were considered one bibliographic unit; if the newer title did not continue the numbering, it was considered a new periodical and would be given a separate entry. At the same time, Library of Congress rule 7:2 stated that "a serial publication in several volumes with varying bibliographical details is described from the latest volume, with the variations from that volume noted."

In general, a catalog record constructed according to the ALA/LC 1949 rules—with the descriptive paragraph (including the title) reflecting the latest volume, and earlier details being given in notes—could be characterized as one based upon retrospect. (See Figure 1.) This method enjoyed the advantage of gathering together in one location the entire bibliographic history of the serial, regardless of title changes. Since the serial was described as a unit, one could ascertain the library's holdings for the entire serial by checking in a single place in the catalog, not under as many successive headings as the serial had title changes. Also, the descriptive paragraph contained in theory the latest imprint, which was helpful to acquisitions librarians and others wishing to obtain the serial.

While the ALA/LC 1949 rules did offer certain advantages, they nevertheless also brought with them disadvantages. One of these was caused by the context in which the rules were originally applied: the card catalog, which lacks the Boolean search capability that the computer offers. Henderson points out that the user of the card catalog may search for specific titles under subject or added entries; when the title of the serial has changed, the person may overlook the desired serial, since the subject and added entries file

```
Monatshefte für Chemie. Chemical monthly. 1.-    Bd.;
   1880-      Wien, New York [etc.] Springer-Verlag [etc.]
     v.    illus.   21 cm.

   At head of title: 1916-46, Akademie der Wissenschaften in
Wien (1916-17 have "Kaiserliche Akademie") Mathematisch-Natur-
wissenschaftliche Klasse; 1947-       Österreichische Akademie
der Wissenschaften, Mathematisch-Naturwissenschaftliche Klasse
(and, 1954-    , Verein Österreichischer Chemiker)
   Vols. for 1880-1927 "gesammelte Abhandlungen aus den
Sitzungsberichten der Akademie der Wissenschaften" (varies
slightly)
   Title varies: 1880-1967, Monatshefte für Chemie und ver-
wandte Teile anderer Wissenschaften (varies slightly)
   Vols. for 1880-1981 lack English title.

   1. Chemistry--Periodicals.   I. Kaiserl. Akademie der Wissen-
schaften in Wien. Mathematisch-Naturwissenschaftliche Klasse.
II. Akademie der Wissenschaften in Wien. Mathematisch-Natur-
wissenschaftliche Klasse.   III. Österreichische Akademie der
Wissenschaften. Mathematisch-Naturwissenschaftliche Klasse.
IV. Verein Österreichischer Chemiker.   V. Title: Chemical
monthly.   VI. Title: Monatshefte für Chemie und verwandte
Teile anderer Wissenschaften.
```

FIGURE 1

Example of latest entry cataloging according to the ALA/LC 1949 rules. (Corporate added entries given in AACR2 form.)

to the current title, not an earlier one.[4] For example, under the subject heading "Physical therapy—Periodicals" in a card catalog using the ALA/LC 1949 rules, one would find the title "American journal of physical medicine" but not "Archives of occupational therapy" or "Occupational therapy and rehabilitation," earlier titles of the journal.

Another less serious but annoying disadvantage was caused by entry under the *latest* title. In a card catalog, holdings are generally listed only once, at the main entry. As a consequence, a patron using the same catalog over the course of years would be directed to different points in the catalog to find the holdings—first to "Archives of occupational therapy," then to "Occupational therapy and rehabilitation," and still later to "American journal of physical medicine"—depending upon the latest title at the time the catalog was used. Unlike the online situation, the patron here would have to make a conscious effort to find the correct entry to determine the holdings.

A third and minor difficulty arose from the fact that the descriptive paragraph lacked stability. In theory based upon the latest volume published, the data contained in the paragraph were in practice checked each time the serial was recataloged, and changes were made as necessary. For instance, during its first hundred years of publication "Monatshefte für Chemie" had five different imprints; as other bibliographically significant changes occurred, the imprint was also updated. Thus for an ongoing serial, the description was actually based upon an intermediate—and not the latest—volume, which was not specified in the cataloging.

ANGLO-AMERICAN CATALOGING RULES

The first edition of the *Anglo-American Cataloging Rules* (AACR1)[5] was published in 1967. In keeping with paragraph 11.5 of the "Statement of Principles" of the International Conference on Cataloging Principles, rule 6D1 of AACR1 stated

> if the title of a serial changes, if the corporate body under which it is entered changes or undergoes a change of name, or if the person under whom it is entered ceases to be its author, make a separate entry for the issues appearing after the change.

The rule also originally contained an exception for very short-lasting or minor title changes that could be noted on the existing record; eventually, as a result of other considerations, the exception was limited to minor title changes.[6] Rules 167G and 167Q specified the use of notes to link the various entries, with rule 167G including directions for the use of the terms *continues* and *supersedes*. As did the LC 1949 rules, rule 160B specified that the description be based upon the latest volume of the serial. The second edition of AACR (AACR2)[7] continues the practice of successive entry, rule 12.0B1 requiring, however, a description based upon the first issue (or first issue available) of the serial, and rule 12.7B7 discontinuing the use of the term *supersedes* in linking notes. (See Figures 2–3.) Rule 21.2 defines a title change; the Library of Congress subsequently issued a rule interpretation for this in *Cataloging Service Bulletin*.[8]

The AACR concept of successive entry allows multiple titles to be accessed under a subject or added entry in a card catalog; for example, "Archives of occupational therapy" and "Occupational therapy and rehabilitation" as well as "American journal of physical medicine" can now be found under the subject heading "Physical therapy—Periodicals." The patron with a citation containing the serial title at the time of publication is more likely to find the title directly in the card catalog, not via an added entry brought

```
Monatshefte für Chemie und verwandte Theile anderer Wissen-
   schaften : gesammelte Abhandlungen aus den Sitzungsberichten
   der Kaiserlichen Akademie der Wissenschaften. -- 1. Bd.
   (Jahrg. 1880)-98. Bd., 6. Heft (Dez. 1967). -- Wien : In
   Commission bei K. Gerold, 1881-1967.
   98 v. : ill. ; 21 cm.

   Title varies slightly, 1903-1967.
   Vols. for 1918-1927 have subtitle: Gesammelte Abhandlungen
aus den Sitzungsberichten der Akademie der Wissenschaften; vols.
for 1928-1967 lack subtitle.
   Issued 1916-1967 by the Mathematisch-Naturwissenschaftliche
Klasse of the Kaiserliche Akademie der Wissenschaften (called,
1918-1946, Akademie der Wissenschaften in Wien; 1947-1967,
Österreichische Akademie der Wissenschaften); with the Verein
Österreichischer Chemiker, 1954-1967.
   Continued by: Monatshefte für Chemie, Jan./Feb. 1968.
   Imprint varies: Wien : In Kommission bei A. Hölder, 1905-
1919; Wien : Hölder-Pichler-Tempsky, Kommissionsverleger, 1920-
1927; Leipzig : Akademische Verlagsgesellschaft, 1928-1944;
Wien (and New York, 1965-1967) : Springer-Verlag, 1946-1967.

   1. Chemistry--Periodicals. I. Kaiserl. Akademie der Wissen-
schaften in Wien. Mathematisch-Naturwissenschaftliche Klasse.
II. Akademie der Wissenschaften in Wien. Mathematisch-Natur-
wissenschaftliche Klasse. III. Österreichische Akademie der
Wissenschaften. Mathematisch-Naturwissenschaftliche Klasse.
IV. Verein Österreichischer Chemiker.
```

FIGURE 2

AACR2 cataloging for earlier title.

```
Monatshefte für Chemie / Österreichische Akademie der Wissen-
   schaften, Mathematisch-Naturwissenschaftliche Klasse und
   Verein Österreichischer Chemiker. -- 99. Bd., 1. Heft
   (Jan./Feb. 1968)-      . -- Wien ; New York : Springer-Verlag,
   [1968-
      v. : ill. ; 21 cm.

   Other title: Chemical monthly, 1982-
   Continues: Monatshefte für Chemie und verwandte Theile
anderer Wissenschaften.

   1. Chemistry--Periodicals. I. Österreichische Akademie der
Wissenschaften. Mathematisch-Naturwissenschaftliche Klasse.
II. Verein Österreichischer Chemiker. III. Title: Chemical
monthly.
```

FIGURE 3

AACR2 cataloging for later title.

about by a title change. Moreover, the Library of Congress in its 1970/71 *Annual Report* stated that successive entry "eliminated the double cataloging of serials, i.e., establishing an entry in the serial record and subsequently cataloging the same serial for printed cards."[9]

In its decision to describe a serial from the first issue (or the first available), AACR2 has established a more permanent descriptive paragraph, one which is revised only if earlier issues become available. Thus in the context of a bibliographic utility, the AACR2 descriptive paragraph is even relatively stable from library to library. Later variations are recorded as needed in notes, and, while from the point of view of the acquisitions librarian this may obscure current data such as the imprint, this saves precious cataloging time: it is no longer necessary both to update the descriptive paragraph and to transfer important previous data to the note area.

Although successive entry is based upon an international statement of principles, it nevertheless has at least two interrelated and negative aspects for the user of the catalog. The first is its "explosive" effect, causing one to search in as many points in a card catalog as the serial has had title changes. This may impact the acquisitions librarian most, but it affects anyone from a cataloger to a patron who is interested in the entire serial. The second negative aspect is the corresponding proliferation of "hits" in an online catalog where the 780 and 785 MARC linking fields are searchable.

For the cataloger using a bibliographic utility, successive entry means having to "close out" the pertinent elements in the record for the older title—fixed fields, imprint, collation, numbering/data area, dates in the note area—and adding a linking entry field; having the record modified online; and proofreading the modifications. It also means either creating an entirely new record or modifying an existing one (anything from a pre-publication record to full cataloging) for the later title, having the record input or modified online, and then proofreading it. This must be viewed as a great expenditure of effort at a time when one is constantly trying to cut the costs of technical services.

EARLIEST ENTRY CATALOGING

The fact that an AACR2 description of a serial is based on the first issue allows one to consider an option long neglected in this country—earliest entry cataloging, as opposed to latest entry or successive entry. The ALA/LC 1949 rules were consistent in their treatment of serials: both the description and the entry were derived from the latest volume. If one were to apply earliest entry cataloging in the context of AACR2, the same consistency would be maintained—both the description and entry would be derived from the first issue. (See Figure 4.) Formally stated, a proposal for earliest entry cataloging would be as follows:

1. If the title proper of a serial with continuous numbering changes, give the title proper of the first issue as the title of the whole serial. Record the later title(s) in a conventional note beginning "Title varies": and include the inclusive dates or numbering of the issues having each title. Make an added entry for each later title.
2. If the corporate body under which a serial with continuous numbering is entered changes or undergoes a change of name, or if the person under whom such a serial is entered ceases to be its author, retain the main entry appropriate to the first issue. Record the changes in responsibility in the note area (see 12.7B6) and make added entries for the persons or bodies.
3. Treat the issues of a serial that are identified solely by chronological designations as being continuously numbered.

Such a proposal once enjoyed some favor in this country. In his *Rules for a Dictionary Catalog,* Charles Cutter recommends successive title cataloging, but adds "or the periodical may be cataloged in full under the first title with a note of the changes."[10] Dunkin similarly states that "both logic as to what the user may need and practical consideration of what the cataloguer will find possible to do seem to indicate that . . . serials entered under title should be entered under successive titles or possibly under first title."[11] Moreover, precedent for earliest entry cataloging may be found in international practice. Rule 121 of *Catalog Rules—Author and Title Entries* says that "(British) Library Association Rule calls for entry of periodicals which have changed their names under the earliest form with brief entries under the later forms."[12] Also, the *Instruktionen für die alphabetischen Kataloge der preussischen Bibliotheken,* in force in many German libraries until the last decade, provided similar treatment.[13]

In AACR2 serials cataloging, the subtitle, statement of responsibility, place of publication, and publisher as found in the descriptive paragraph may all become obsolete without a new record's being required. Only the title proper (and perhaps the numbering) may not noticeably change. Earliest entry cataloging treats the title

> Monatshefte für Chemie und verwandte Theile anderer Wissen-
> schaften : gesammelte Abhandlungen aus den Sitzungsberichten
> der Kaiserlichen Akademie der Wissenschaften. -- 1. Bd.
> (Jahrg. 1880)-   . -- Wien : In Commission bei K. Gerold,
> 1881-
>   v. : ill. ; 21 cm.
>
>   Title varies: 1968-   , Monatshefte für Chemie. Other
> slight variations in title, 1903-1967.
>   Other title: Chemical monthly, 1982-
>   Vols. for 1918-1927 have subtitle: Gesammelte Abhandlungen
> aus den Sitzungsberichten der Akademie der Wissenschaften; vols.
> for 1928-1967 lack subtitle.
>   Issued 1916-   by the Mathematisch-Naturwissenschaftliche
> Klasse of the Kaiserliche Akademie der Wissenschaften (called,
> 1918-1946, Akademie der Wissenschaften in Wien; 1947-   ,
> Österreichische Akademie der Wissenschaften); with the Verein
> Österreichischer Chemiker, 1954-
>   Imprint varies: Wien : In Kommission bei A. Hölder, 1905-
> 1919; Wien : Hölder-Pichler-Tempsky, Kommissionsverleger, 1920-
> 1927; Leipzig : Akademische Verlagsgesellschaft, 1928-1944;
> Wien (and New York, 1965-   ) : Springer-Verlag, 1946-
>
>   1. Chemistry--Periodicals. I. Kaiserl. Akademie der Wissen-
> schaften in Wien. Mathematisch-Naturwissenschaftliche Klasse.
> II. Akademie der Wissenschaften in Wien. Mathematisch-Natur-
> wissenschaftliche Klasse. III. Österreichische Akademie der
> Wissenschaften. Mathematisch-Naturwissenschaftliche Klasse.
> IV. Verein Österreichischer Chemiker. V. Title: Monatshefte
> für Chemie. VI. Title: Chemical monthly.

FIGURE 4

Example of proposed earliest entry cataloging.

proper consistently with the other elements, and thereby more closely standardizes the treatment of serials and multi-volume monographs, which are cataloged as a single unit (under earliest or latest title, depending upon which predominates).

Because of the Boolean capabilities of the computer, both the latest and earliest entry methods of cataloging have overcome the searching problems encountered in the card catalog. One may search by any combination of subject heading and corporate heading or title, or corporate heading and title. Certain combinations—latest form of corporate name used on the serial, and earlier title, for example—are possible only if latest or earliest cataloging techniques are employed. Both methods also greatly limit the multiple "hits" online because of searchable MARC 780 and 785 fields.

Earliest entry cataloging would save the cataloger considerable time and effort. As compared to latest title cataloging, the descriptive paragraph is virtually static; all changes are recorded in the note area. Thus one need not totally recatalog the serial with each change of title. Unlike AACR2 successive entry cataloging, where several elements in the record for the older title must be "closed out" and the new title cataloged separately, under the earliest entry method the cataloging changes may be as simple as adding a MARC 247 (Title varies) field. (Compare examples 2 and 3 to example 4.) This is no more difficult than adding just the 785 field, only one of the steps in closing out the older title under the AACR2 successive entry method.

CONCLUSION

In 1973 Judith Proctor Cannan wrote that "for years librarians have argued which of the three possible ways of cataloging a serial—earliest, successive, or latest title—is the most efficient, informative, and economical. To my knowledge no one has arrived at a definitive answer."[14] Earliest entry cataloging is indeed an efficient and economical method, since thereby one can avoid both the total recataloging of the older title and also the creation of separate records, one for each title change of the serial. It is also informative, because one is able to find in a single place the bibliographic history of the entire serial, and also, with the searching capabilities of the computer, one can access the record in as many—and perhaps more—ways than the records created by successive entry. Earliest entry cataloging is thus a viable form of serials cataloging and should be viewed as such.

NOTES

1. "Latest Entry Cataloging Experiment Using NOTIS," *RTSD Newsletter* 10, no. 4 (1985):44.
2. American Library Association. Division of Cataloging and Classification. *A.L.A. Cataloging Rules for Author and Title Entries*. 2nd ed. Chicago: American Library Association, 1949.
3. Library of Congress. Descriptive Cataloging Division. *Rules for Descriptive Cataloging in the Library of Congress*. Washington: Library of Congress, Descriptive Cataloging Division, 1949.
4. Henderson, Kathryn Luther. "Serial Cataloging Revisited—A Long Search for a Little Theory and a Lot of Cooperation." In *Serial Publications in Large Libraries*, edited by Walter C. Allen. Urbana: University of Illinois, Graduate School of Library Science, [1970], p. 68.
5. *Anglo-American Cataloging Rules*. North American text. Chicago: American Library Association, 1967.
6. *Cataloging Service* 120 (Winter 1977):8.
7. *Anglo-American Cataloguing Rules*. 2nd ed. Chicago: American Library Association, 1978.
8. *Cataloging Service Bulletin* 25 (Summer 1984):55–57.

9. Library of Congress. *Annual Report of the Librarian of Congress for the Fiscal Year Ending June 30, 1971.* Washington: Library of Congress, 1972, p. 30.

10. Cutter, Charles A. *Rules for a Dictionary Catalog.* 4th ed., rewritten. U.S. Bureau of Education, Special Report on Public Libraries, pt. 2. Washington: Government Printing Office, 1904, p. 62.

11. Dunkin, Paul S. "Problems in the Cataloguing of Serial Publications." In International Conference on Cataloguing Principles, Paris, 1961, *Report.* London: International Federation of Library Associations, 1963, p. 198.

12. *Catalog Rules—Author and Titles Entries.* American ed. Chicago: American Library Association, Publishing Board, 1908, p. 36.

13. *Instruktionen für die alphabetischen Kataloge der preussischen Bibliotheken.* 2. Ausg., in der Fassung vom 10. August 1908. Unveränderter Nachdruck. Wiesbaden: O. Harrassowitz, 1970, p. 89–90.

14. Cannan, Judith Proctor. "Serials Cataloging: Successive Entry," *Library Resources & Technical Services* 17, no. 1 (Winter 1973):73.

Title Changes in an Automated Environment: The Last Shall Be First

Jackie Zajanc

SUMMARY. The application of successive entry cataloging in an automated environment impairs the efficiency of both accessing and processing a library's serials collection. A return to either earliest or latest entry cataloging would eliminate difficulties caused by adherence to successive cataloging principles. Of earliest and latest, however, the latter offers greater flexibility in all aspects of serials processing and is therefore preferable.

COPING WITH TITLE CHANGES

"Serials need not be frightening . . . they are a challenge to those who will accept the taunts they give."—Lynn Smith[1]

One of the most common taunts that serials hurl is: "Hey! I've changed my title again. What are you going to do about it?!" Three techniques have gained acceptance over the past 100 years to cope with this particular challenge. Briefly, they are:

1. Earliest entry cataloging (proposed by Cutter in 1876; incorporated into the 1908 British Rules) calls for a single bibliographic record containing in the notes area the full history of the serial. That is, the title statement (245 field) contains the earliest title used by the serial, with notes recording any subsequent variations in the title. Added entries (247 field) for these subsequent titles provide access from them to the bibliographic record. (See Figure 1.)
2. Latest entry cataloging (incorporated into the 1908 American and 1949 ALA Rules) also prescribes a single bibliographic record with notes providing the full history of the serial. Here, however, the title statement contains the latest title used by the serial and the notes record earlier variations. Added en-

---

Jackie Zajanc is Associate Professor and Head of the Serials Cataloging Unit at the Washington State University Libraries, Washington State University, Pullman, WA 99164-5610.
Reprinted from The Serials Librarian, Vol. 11(1), September 1986.

tries for these earlier titles provide access from them to the bibliographic record. (See Figure 2.)
3. Successive entry cataloging (proposed by Cutter also in 1876; incorporated into 1967's AACR) calls for the creation of separate bibliographic records for each title of a serial. Notes in each record "link" it to bibliographic records for the immediate earlier and/or later title only. (See Figure 3.)

WHICH IS BEST?

None of the above is inherently better than the other two. Rather than asking which is better, it is more appropriate to ask which one today has the potential for greatest success in achieving the major goals of serials cataloging. Specifically these goals are:

1. to provide the most efficient, economical access to the serials represented in the catalog ("access" applies not only to searching by users but also to processing by staff since if material is not cataloged/processed in a timely manner, that material is not accessible), and;
2. to provide the most comprehensive, and comprehensible, bibliographic description for each serial represented in the catalog.

```
Graduate and Professional Students Association newsletter. -- Vol. 1, no. 1

    (Jan. 1970)-      -- Pullman, Wash. : GPSA, 1970-

    v. ; 28 cm.


Title varies: GPSA newsletter, Vol. 12, no. 1 (Oct.-Nov. 1981)-v. 13, no. 5

(Apr.-May 1983)

Title varies: GPSA overview, Vol. 14, no. 1 (Sept.-Oct. 1983)


    1. Washington State University--Graduate students.  I. Graduate and Professional

Students Association (Washington State University).  II. Title: GPSA newsletter.

III. Title: GPSA overview.
```

Figure 1: Earliest Entry Cataloging (Numeric Designation, etc. According to AACR2)

```
The GPSA overview.  -- Vol. 1, no. 1 (Jan. 1970)-    -- Pullman, Wash. :
   GPSA, 1970-
     v. ; 28 cm.


   Title varies: Graduate and Professional Students Association newsletter,
   Vol. 1, no. 1 (Jan. 1970)-v. 11, no. 5 (Apr.-May 1981)
   Title varies: GPSA newsletter, Vol. 12, no. 1 (Oct.-Nov. 1981)-v. 13,
   no. 5 (Apr.-May 1983)


     1. Washington State University--Graduate students.  I. Graduate and Professional
   Students Association (Washington State University).  II. Title: Graduate and
   Professional Students Association newsletter.  III. Title: GPSA newsletter.
```

Figure 2: Latest Entry Cataloging (Numeric Designation, etc.
According to AACR2)

Latest and earliest entry cataloging both provide a single source for bibliographic information for a serial. Both consequently achieve a high measure of success in terms of access by users and comprehensive bibliographic description. Unfortunately in manual cataloging systems both are very labor intensive in terms of processing: each title change requires that cards be pulled from the local card catalog and then either extensively modified or (more usually) replaced by new cards. Furthermore, any new title acquired by an individual library must be researched by catalogers in an attempt to uncover the full history of the serial, in addition to describing bibliographically any earlier titles discovered. It was not surprising then that with the information explosion of the 50s and 60s to find libraries falling further and further behind in the cataloging of serials. The Library of Congress, in April of 1971, expressed the situation quite succinctly:

> We were losing the serial battle at LC and something had to be done. We have an average of approximately 30,000 titles backlogged and it was growing rapidly. Successive Entry Cataloging allows us to work from the piece in hand and to limit the amount of bibliographic searching done since we no longer need [to provide] the complete history of a particular title.[2]

Graduate and Professional Students Association newsletter. -- Vol. 1, no. 1 (Jan. 1970)-v. 11, no. 5 (Apr.-May 1981) -- Pullman, Wash. : GPSA, 1970-1981.
11 v. ; 28 cm.

Continued by: GPSA newsletter.

1. Washington State University--Graduate students. II. Graduate and Professional Students Association (Washington State University).

GPSA newsletter. -- Vol. 12, no. 1 (Oct.-Nov. 1981)-v. 13, no. 5 (Apr.-May 1983) -- Pullman, Wash. : GPSA, 1981-1983.
2 v. ; 28 cm.

Continues: Graduate and Professional Students Association newsletter.
Continued by: GPSA overview.

1. Washington State University--Graduate students. I. Graduate and Professional Students Association (Washington State University).

The GPSA overview. -- Vol. 14, no. 1 (Sept.-Oct. 1983)-   -- Pullman, Wash. : GPSA, 1983-
v. ; 28 cm.

Continues: GPSA newsletter.

1. Washington State University--Graduate students. I. Graduate and Professional Students Association (Washington State University).

Figure 3: Successive Entry Cataloging (Numeric Designation, etc. According to AACR2)

To summarize, the rationale for adoption of successive entry cataloging was: in a manual environment successive entry cataloging enables materials to be more quickly and economically made available to users than with either earliest or latest entry cataloging. This advantage was so compelling that it overrode three significant disadvantages:

1. Access to and description of the entire run of the serial is fragmented;
2. With broken runs, the continuity of the linking notes is lost and bibliographic records are left dangling;
3. If the search is made for one of the titles not owned, no record will be found; yet perhaps an earlier or later segment of the serials would have satisified the searcher.

IMPACT OF SHARED ONLINE CATALOGING

In today's automated environment, and with shared online cataloging of serials, the amount of staff effort devoted to cataloging in individual libraries has been greatly reduced. It is now quite common to discover in a bibliographic utility all relevant historical data for serials in publication for more than one year. And in those instances where the serial's history cannot be fixed at the time of initial cataloging, notes alert users of the record to the uncertainty. Once the record is in the utility, it can be updated by other participants—adding new or previously unknown information. In the Western Library Network (WLN), serial bibliographic records are regularly updated by WLN participants, CONSER participants, the Library of Congress, and the Superintendent of Documents. These updated records automatically replace superseded records in all the individual participant's COM and/or online catalogs—if the participant had previously flagged the record with its own unique identifier, generally its local call number. Furthermore it is now simpler to update only a single bibliographic record to reflect a title change (earliest and latest entry) rather than update one record *and* create a new one (successive entry).

Thus the prevailing rationale for the use of successive entry cataloging is no longer valid. In the automated environment both earliest and latest entry cataloging are now efficient and economical. Since a single bibliographic record represents the entire serial, the user is freed from the requirement of multiple searches when title changes have occurred. Broken runs have no negative effect on retrieval with earliest or latest entry cataloging. The result of a valid title search for any serial represented in the catalog is a display of a single bibliographic record (assuming of course that the 247 field—title variations note/added entry—is included in the parameters for the title search); this single bibliographic record includes a history of the title variations of the serial. This history statement can then be compared with relevant summary/detailed holdings statements to determine which specific titles are available.

EARLIEST VS. LATEST ENTRY CATALOGING

If both earliest and latest entry cataloging provide the potential for greater success in achieving the major goals of serials cataloging, i.e., the most efficient, economical access and most comprehensive, comprehensible bibliographic description, which of these two is preferable? The argument can be made that earliest is preferable since fewer fields in the record require modification with each title change. For a simple, first-time title change earliest requires only the addition of one note while latest requires (at a minimum) the modification of the title statement and the addition of a note. With latest entry the imprint will probably require updating as well since the description is for the first issue of the latest title, not the first issue of the earliest title.

However, in any evaluation of the advantages of earliest vs. latest entry cataloging in an automated environment, consideration must also be given to other aspects of serials processing. Serial bibliographic records have commonly supported a variety of complementary files—notably checkin and acquisitions. And this continues to be true in an automated environment. Let us examine the impact of both techniques on these two major Files:

1. Checkin. For access in an automated checkin file, the most current title need not be listed in the title statement (again as long as the 247 field is included in any title search). However, if the title statement does contain the most current title (latest entry) changes in title can be more quickly and easily detected by checkers. Also, verification that the correct record has been retrieved is more quickly and easily made with the current title in the title statement. Checkin files are often the basis for auxiliary listings (for collection development, statistical, and reference uses); this implies that the listings contain only the institution's current acquisitions—it is then desirable for the titles listed to be the most current ones used by the serials.
2. Acquisitions. With the bibliographic record supplying the title for purchase orders and payment records in an automated system, confusion can fairly confidently be predicted if the title statement contains anything other than the most current title.

In terms of overall serials processing then, latest entry cataloging offers the potential for greater efficiencies and flexibility than does earliest entry cataloging.

CONCLUSION

In an automated environment the continued use of successive entry cataloging as a means of coping with title changes is costly to libraries and confusing to users. An evaluation of earliest and latest entry cataloging in the context of an automated environment indicates that latest offers greater overall efficiencies and flexibility than does earliest. However, before latest entry cataloging can be widely reimplemented, the 247 field (title variation note/added entry) must be universally included in the parameters of any title search. There is also the issue of mutual exclusivity between latest and successive bibliographic records: should use of both techniques be sanctioned by AACR3 in order to accommodate libraries not involved in the online sharing of bibliographic data? This is obviously a question that will receive close, careful scrutiny during the next few years.

NOTES

1. Smith, Lynn S. *A Practical Approach to Serials Cataloging.* Greenwich, Conn.: JAI Press, 1978.
2. Library of Congress. *Information Bulletin,* 30:215 (Apr. 15, 1971). Washington, D.C.

SPECIAL APPLICATIONS OF SERIALS CATALOGING

Serials Cataloging from the Union List Standpoint

Lori L. Osmus, BA, MSLS

SUMMARY. Union lists of serials share many elements in common with catalogs of serials, and so are similarly affected by serials cataloging practices. However, since a union list is a consolidation of serials data from a number of libraries, more cataloging discrepancies will require resolving in it than in any one library's catalog. In this article, various serials cataloging issues are described as they affect union lists, such as fullness of bibliographic description, choice and form of entry, successive versus latest entry cataloging, and microform reproductions. In particular, the problems of OCLC-produced union lists are described.

INTRODUCTION

Not only do serials change, but the rules by which they are cataloged change. Some stubborn serials have been known to outlive several sets of cataloging rules, challenging generations of ambitious librarians to recatalog them time and again. As recataloging the entire serials collection every time the rules change is not, however, practical for most libraries, librarians have had to develop methods of integrating new records with old, while minimizing confusion for library users. The catalogs of most libraries consequently consist of an amalgamation of records created according to various rules.

Lori L. Osmus is Assistant Professor and Head, Serials Cataloging Section, Iowa State University, 204 Parks Library, Ames, IA 50011. Since 1982 she has been a member of the Iowa Union List of Serials Standards/Verification Committee. For the past three years she has also served as Vice-Chair/Secretary of the Serials Control Section of the Iowa OCLC Users Group.

For those with responsibility for editing a union list of serials, the problems posed by various cataloging codes and their local application is multiplied by the number of participants contributing to the union list project. The union list editor is faced with consolidating reports reflecting every possible choice and form of entry for a given serial publication, including various interpretations as to when title changes have occurred. The resulting union list records will not necessarily match those in all reporting libraries' catalogs.

The creation of union lists has been revolutionized in recent years with the development of online union lists with offline products. The major support for this development has come from OCLC, the chosen utility for the creation and maintenance of a national serials data base via the CONSER project. By utilizing OCLC's union listing capability, libraries in a union listing group may attach their holdings to any of OCLC's hundreds of thousands of serial bibliographic records. However, the union list record will reflect any flaws in the bibliographic record in the OCLC data base, since only CONSER participants have the power to modify the master OCLC records used in the union list. Although the vast majority of OCLC records are of high quality, OCLC union lists afford "no opportunity for the 'fine tuning' that local editing control provides."[1] As a result, the consequences of cataloging discrepancies are more obvious in OCLC-produced union lists than in most other kinds. Records from an OCLC union list printed product[2] will be used as a basis to illustrate the cataloging differences that might be found in any union list produced without control by an editor.

BIBLIOGRAPHIC DESCRIPTION

Most union lists are not intended to serve the same functions as catalogs, although some libraries that do not otherwise catalog or classify their periodicals or other serials may use a union list as a substitute catalog for these items. The purpose of a list actually determines the amount of bibliographic data needed, and thus how close it comes to being a catalog, as opposed to the "title a line" type of publication. By definition, a union list of serials at its simplest is considered to be a list of serial holdings of two or more libraries, indicating which library has what. Most union lists are intended primarily as finding tools, and important information, like the holdings, may be obscured by a full bibliographic description in the union list. On the other hand, if a union list is large, more bibliographic data may be needed in order to fully distinguish titles, although physical limitations on the size of the list and financial considerations may prevent inclusion of all elements considered desirable.

Jean Whiffin, in her work for the IFLA/UNESCO project to develop international guidelines for union lists of serials, recommended a record "at a mid-point between a full bibliographic record and a finding list . . . consisting of a practical subset of essential bibliographic data elements."[3] The American Library Association's *Guidelines for Union Lists of Serials*, edited by Marjorie Bloss, also recommended a specific set of data elements.

In union lists produced from online bibliographic data bases, computerized manipulation of data allows great flexibility in the choice of elements to be displayed from the full bibliographic record. As part of the OCLC *Union List Offline Products Order Profile Form*, OCLC union list groups may choose to print from an extensive list as many fields as they can afford. Figure 1 shows the minimum bibliographic data element set

DATA ELEMENT	MARC TAG
Main entry, if other than title	100, 110, 111
Issuing or sponsoring corporate bodies	710, 711
Uniform title	130, 240
Title proper	245
General material designation	245, subfield h
Edition statement	250
Numerical/chronological designation	362
Place of publication, and Publisher/distributor	260
Notes:	
Other title information	246
Numbering peculiarities, etc.	515
Microform/reprint description	533, 580
Preceding and succeeding titles	580, or generated from 780, 785
ISSN and key title	022 and 222
National bibliography numbers	015

Figure 1.

Recommended minimum union list bibliographic data elements.

recommended by both the national and international guidelines, along with the corresponding MARC tags of each element as it would appear in an OCLC record.

Since a union list is mainly a finding tool, the impact of different cataloging rules on bibliographic description is not as serious as it is for choice and form of entry. Differences may occur in the format of the 362 field and in punctuation, and place and publisher may differ if description is based on different issues. The differences will only be obvious in cases where a union list includes multiple records for the same serial, as in the case of separate records for print and microform editions. Some of these differences are illustrated in Figures 2a-d.

ACCESS POINTS

In its role as a finding tool, a union list should provide access by all titles, issuing bodies, or other elements under which each serial may be sought. If complete records under both author and title cannot be provided, then at least cross-references might be made from one to the other, as appropriate. Ideally, an authority system should be established for names and uniform titles, to ensure consistency in the union list.

The reality in union lists may be far from these ideals. To save money, many lists contain only one entry per record. Usually single-entry lists are by title, because title main entry often simplifies union list procedures by resolving the wide variations in cataloging practices among participating libraries. One rule for organizing the list is also easier on the user.

Title entry is not foolproof, because of numerous generic titles like "Bulletin" or "Proceedings," or other non-unique titles like "Science," which need additional identification in order to be filed in an orderly manner in the union list. Methods for making serial titles unique have varied over time as the cataloging rules and their interpretations have changed. AACR Rule 6A stated that "If an added entry is required for a serial that is entered under title, and if the title of the serial is identical with that of another serial that is entered under title, add in parentheses the city of publication. If this addition is insufficient, add also the years of publication." Examples of this are shown in Figure 3.

The International Serials Data System began to have an impact after 1973, with its purpose of registering the world's serials and creating the unique identifiers of key title and ISSN for each. This caused the Library of Congress to write a rule interpretation in its *Cataloging Service*, bulletin 110, for the creation of distinctive titles as follows: "If the title of a serial consists solely of a generic term, the generic term is followed by the author statement. The two elements are separated by a space-hyphen-space (-). The author statement is transcribed as it appears on the publication."[4] Examples of this are also shown in Figure 3.

AAUP bulletin.   Cross-reference

  See: from 245

  American Association of University Professors.   of print ed.

  AAUP bulletin.   in Fig. 2b.

AAUP bulletin   microform   Washington, D.C. :   AACR2.

American Association of University Professors,

Began with: Vol. 42, no. 1 (spring 1956);   Print ed. in

ceased with: Vol. 64, no. 4 (Dec. 1978).   Fig. 2b under

OCLC   5022365;**ISSN** 0001-026X.   corporate body.

Continues: Bulletin (American Association of

University Professors)

Academe.   Washington   American Association of   AACR.

University Professors.

v. 65-   Feb. 1979-   Microform in

OCLC   4688683;**ISSN** 0190-2946.   Fig. 2b under

Continues: American Association of University   uniform title.

Professors. AAUP bulletin

Absorbed: Academe (Washington)   1979

Figures 2a-d.

Bibliographic records from an OCLC off-line union list

in OCLC filing order.

Discrepancies result from differences in OCLC records.

Figure 2a.

Key titles continue to be assigned by national ISDS centers, including the National Serials Data Program, the ISDS center for the United States, which is based at the Library of Congress. However, non-ISDS centers are no longer supposed to create distinctive titles that resemble key titles. With the adoption of AACR2, the Library of Congress offered a new means of making serial titles unique with its concept of uniform titles for

Academe microform	Cross-reference
See:	from 245
Academe (Washington, D.C. : 1979) Academe microform	of record below.
Academe (Washington, D.C. : 1979) Academe microform Washington, D.C. : American Association of University Professors, Began with: Vol. 65, no. 1 (Feb. 1979). **OCLC** 6374570;**ISSN** 0190-2946.	AACR2. Print ed. in Fig. 2a under title proper. Notes missing.
American Association of University Professors. AAUP bulletin. Washington, etc. American Association of University Professors. v. 42-64; spring 1956-Dec. 1978. **OCLC** 1846776;**ISSN** 0001-026X. **Continues:** Bulletin (American Association of University Professors)	AACR. Microform in Fig. 2a under title proper.

Figure 2b.

serials. Terms used to qualify a non-unique title to make it a uniform title may be place or corporate body name, in catalog entry form; beginning date of publication; edition; or other information, carefully selected according to guidelines in the Library of Congress rule interpretation of AACR2 Rule 25.2A. Figure 3 provides examples of each of these methods of making a title unique.

The form chosen for even an already unique title may also be affected by several factors. Variations in choice of the issue on which the description is based and the choice of the chief source of information within that issue may affect titles as well as the points of title changes. Variations in rules will determine whether an initialism is considered part of the title. When serials are in non-roman scripts, changes in romanization schemes or the use of local, non-standard schemes can result in discrepancies.

The differences between title entries is not significantly reduced by opting for corporate body main entry where called for in the latest rules. AACR2 Rule 21.1B restricts entry under corporate body to those items that are primarily an expression of corporate thought or activity, such as a company's annual report, or the proceedings of a conference. AACR Rule 6 went further by allowing corporate body main entry for serials issued under the authority of a corporate body "if the title (exclusive of

Bulletin (American Association of University Professors) Bulletin / American Association of University Professors. Easton, Pa. : The Association, 1943-1955. Vol. 29, no. 1 (Feb. 1943)-v. 41, no. 4 (winter 1955) **OCLC** 6867358; **ISSN** 0083-1491 **Continues:** Bulletin of the American Association of University Professors **Continued by:** American Association of University Professors. AAUP bulletin	AACR2. Microform below.
Bulletin (American Association of University Professors) Bulletin microform / American Association of University Professors. Easton, Pa. : The Association, [1943-1955] Vol. 29, no. 1 (Feb. 1943)-v. 41, no. 4 (winter 1955) **OCLC** 13113162; **ISSN** 0083-1491 **Continues:** Bulletin of the American Association of University Professors **Continued by:** American Association of University Professors. AAUP bulletin	AACR2. Print ed. above.

Figure 2c.

Bulletin of the American Association of　　　　　AACR2.
University Professors.　Easton, Pa : The
Association, 1915-1942.　　　　　　　　　　　　　Microform
Vol. 1, pt. 1 (Dec. 1915)-v. 28, no. 5 (Dec.　　below.
1942).
OCLC　3335476;ISSN 0083-1610
Continued by: Bulletin (American Association
of University Professors)

Bulletin of the American Association of　　　　　AACR2
University Professors.　MICROFILM
[Washington, D.C.] : The Association,　　　　　　Print ed.
1915-1942.　　　　　　　　　　　　　　　　　　　　above.
Vol. 1 (Dec. 1915)-v. 28, no. 5 (Dec. 1942)
OCLC　7309556　　　　　　　　　　　　　　　　　　Lacked GMD;
Continued by: Bulletin (American Association　　MICROFILM from
of University Professors)　　　　　　　　　　　　Repr code

Figure 2d.

the subtitle) includes the name or the abbreviation of the name of the corporate body, or consists solely of a generic term that requires the name of the body for adequate identification."

The form of corporate body names has also changed over time. While AACR2 prefers entry of bodies directly under their names in most cases, earlier rules often preferred entry under a place name or other higher body. In addition to corporate body main entry, entry under personal author is another possibility, but occurs only rarely for serials.

Most library catalogs contain records created according to more than one cataloging code, and libraries will probably report their serials to a union list editor in the variety of choice and form of entry existing in their catalogs. The union list editor will be faced with bringing some consistency to the differing reports. However, if the union list itself was begun before the last cataloging code change in 1981, the union list editor will also need to decide whether to change entries in the list to conform to the new rules, or, if not, how to integrate the new entries with the old. The OCLC data base contains records cataloged according to several

<u>AACR 6A</u>

International review (New York, 1874-83)

International review (Zurich)

<u>Cataloging Service, bulletin 110</u>

Information series - Geological Survey of Alabama.

Circular - Dept. of Fish and Game, California.

Yale University. Art Gallery.

    Bulletin - Yale University Art Gallery.

<u>Cataloging Service Bulletin 25</u>
<u>Interpretation of AACR2 25.2B</u>

Place of publication:

    Arrow (Montreal, Quebec)

Corporate body:

    Bulletin (California. Dept. of Water Resources)

Place and date or corporate body and date:

    Science bulletin (Akron, Ohio : 1921)

    Bulletin (Canadian Association of Medical Record Librarians : 1944)

Date:

    San Francisco journal (1980)

Edition statement, other title information, etc.:

    Progressive farmer (Southeast edition)

Figure 3.

Methods used to make serial titles unique.

different codes, and OCLC union list participants have no power to change OCLC records to follow consistent rules before the records are printed in an offline union list. The choices of OCLC union list groups consist of selecting a primary list arrangement from the following:

> 100, 110, 111, 130/245
> 130/245
> 245
> 752

and they may optionally choose additional fields by which records may be arranged. Another option is to have cross-references generated from some fields, such as the 246 field, which contain alternative titles that might be useful access points. The usefulness of the union list generated depends a great deal on the cataloging consistency between the OCLC records included. The great variations in choice and form of entry that inevitably result, as well as the effect of cross-references, are illustrated in Figures 2a-d.

Filing rules also affect the accessibility of a union list. The filing rules in OCLC offline lists reflect the machine-generated nature of the products, and what may seem to be filing errors result from the way a record appears in the data base, another important influence of the cataloging. Among the problematic OCLC filing rules is the fact that all subfields within a field are filed upon, including subfields c and h in the 245 field, which contain the statement of responsibility and the general material designation, respectively. Another problem is that initial articles are ignored according to the language code in the fixed field, which means that if the text is in a different language from that of the title, an article in the title might not be ignored as one might expect. These filing rules may place records in unexpected places, making titles difficult to find. Even the most consistent cataloging and wide choice of access points are useless, if hidden by an unintelligible filing arrangement.

SUCCESSIVE VERSUS LATEST ENTRY CATALOGING

One of the major characteristics of serials is that their titles often change. When a title changes, how should this be shown in the union list? Prior to AACR in 1967, the generally accepted practice was latest entry cataloging, which involved recataloging the serial under its latest entry, with a title varies note or other notes about its earlier entries. The Library of Congress announced that it would stop following this practice in 1971, but that still leaves countless records in existence that were cataloged according to latest entry.

Successive entry cataloging gained momentum after 1971, and continues to be the accepted practice under AACR2. It means that each time a serial's entry changes, a new record is created under the new entry, the record under the previous entry is closed, and linking notes are made between the two entries. The result is more direct access to serials records, since the serial will appear in the catalog or union list under the entry actually used on the issues at the time of publication.

Although it is unrealistic to expect individual libraries to recatalog all of their serials according to successive entry, union lists must follow a consistent pattern if duplication of records and the scattering of holdings is to be avoided. OCLC allows only successive entry records to be used for union listing, and expects CONSER participants to break latest entry records into successive entries. Both national and international union listing guidelines also recommend the use of successive entry records.

Union lists of serials that contain only successive entry records are easier to use. However, since many libraries have a number of their titles under latest entry, they may unwittingly report some of their serial titles under latest entry, leaving the union list editor to sort out the various titles involved. There will be discrepancies in the point at which different libraries consider a title change to have taken place, and some minor or brief title changes may not seem to justify the effort needed to create new records. The linking notes themselves must be checked diligently to assure that they match the choice and form of entry of the serials to which reference is made.

MICROFORM REPRODUCTIONS

The handling of microform reproductions is one of the greatest sources of difficulty both in cataloging and in union listing. The principle of creating a separate bibliographic record for each manifestation of a work, whether it is a new edition, a reprint, or a microform reproduction, is one of the foundations of cataloging, and has received greater emphasis under AACR2. If various producers have brought out reproductions of a serial, a strict application of the cataloging rules would require a separate record for each reproduction. The result would be several records for a serial even when the same physical format occurred in each reproduction. As long as a reproduction is an exact duplicate of the original, the average library user does not care whether the photocopied pages he receives through interlibrary loan came from microfilm, microfiche, or microopaque, or which company was responsible for the filming, as long as he or she gets the needed information. If a reproduction is not an exact duplicate of the original, separate records may be justified, but to aid the user, linkage should be made between the various records for the same serial.

When a union list contains multiple records for a title because of variations in physical format and producer, the purpose of the list of bringing together all holdings of a title in one place is defeated. Separate records also increase the size of the list and the expense of producing it.

One solution to this problem is to represent microforms in a union list as a function of the holdings statement on a "master record" for the serial title. *American National Standard Z39.44, Serials Holdings Statements*, as well as the summary standard it recently replaced, both provide for situations when different physical formats of an item are not separately described or identified. These standards for holdings are intended to be independent of any cataloging system. AACR2 and Library of Congress policies, along with OCLC support for the policies combine to make separate records necessary for microform reproductions. This requirement does not come about as a result of any technical difficulty in the holdings standard itself. The holdings standard requires only that if a bibliographic record describes a serial in a specific physical format, then holdings of the serial in that format alone may be attached to the record.

Despite this, OCLC has agreed to allow participants in the United States Newspaper project to use the record of the original print edition of a newspaper as a "master record" to which holdings of all physical formats of that newspaper title must be attached. This agreement came about because most of the newspapers being cataloged as part of the project will be microfilmed later as a means of preservation, and having to create a record for the microfilmed version of each newspaper would have doubled the project's workload. For serials other than newspapers, however, OCLC strongly recommends compliance with the holdings standard. OCLC's *Serials Control Training Manual* cautions that union list groups that do not follow the standard "will have to accept any consequences that such a departure from the standard may involve. . . . If Union List agencies deviate from this standard, they may find that future OCLC software modifications could cause problems."[5]

While the policies for microform reproductions are in transition, union list developers must deal with these ambiguous practices. Within the same union listing group, all members should agree to the same method in order to ensure consistency. OCLC union listing groups that heed OCLC's warnings, however, will encounter more problems than those that do not. Following the recommended practices means more work, because if there is no bibliographic record on OCLC for a microform edition a library holds, the library or its agent must create an original bibliographic record for the microform before the library can add its holdings to the union list. New records added to the OCLC data base must be cataloged according to AACR2, even though the OCLC record for the original print edition of the serial may have been created according to earlier cataloging rules. This could cause a problem because cataloging the microform according to AACR2 could result in a different choice and form of entry for the same serial. The print edition record may even be latest entry cataloging, while AACR2 would require the microform edition cataloging to be input as two or more successive entry records. OCLC's filing rules, which use the general material designation as a filing word, provide no guarantee that records for the print and microform editions of the same serial will file near each other, even when the choice and form of entry are the same. Finally, despite a union list group's best efforts to follow OCLC's requirements for microform reproductions, the group will nevertheless find a different standard being used for any newspapers they may wish to include in their lists. Figures 2a-d also illustrate some consequences of separate bibliographic records for microform reproductions in a union list.

ONLINE UNION LISTING

The development of rules and standards for machine-readable records and requirements by major bibliographic utilities that users adhere to them have, on the whole, increased ease of cooperation and encouraged the development of online union lists. There are several advantages to online union listing:

- Changes can be recorded in a timely manner, making maintenance easier.
- Information can be provided at a number of locations without the cost of multiple printed lists.
- Creation of bibliographic descriptions and holdings data can be shared by participants.
- Holdings can be simultaneously part of several union lists, such as by subject or by geographic location of libraries.
- Computerized manipulation of data can allow flexibility in display of data to meet specific needs.
- Choice of main entry becomes less important, if the same data can be found through searches on a variety of access points.

OCLC RECORD SELECTION

OCLC's online union listing capability, available to its members since the fall of 1980 as a feature of its serials control subsystem, has all the advantages described above for online union lists, with the added advantage of the ability to generate offline products. However, the actual contents of the union list, either online or offline, is only as good as the

OCLC data base and the records selected from it. Record selection is almost the only control OCLC union list participants can exert over the quality of their union lists.

Ideally, there would be only one bibliographic record in OCLC for each serial title, but this is not the case. There may be several records to choose from because of such things as inadequate searching by a member library before inputting a record that duplicates one already in the data base; the existence of both successive entry and latest entry records for the same title in the data base; or differing opinions as to whether a title changed and thus justified a new entry. If members of a union listing group choose different records for the same title, their holdings will be scattered, and the resulting union list will be more difficult to use.

It is clear that one of the most important tasks facing a library is determining to which bibliographic record it should attach its holdings. OCLC's criteria for selecting records for union listing suggests choosing the record that meets the following requirements:

1. Is in serials format.
2. Uses successive entry, and if more than one,
   a) Is authenticated.
   b) Most closely adheres to AACR2.
   c) Has the most information.

If still in doubt, OCLC advises to select the record with the greatest number of holding institutions, and if equal, the lowest OCLC record number.[6] Johanna Bowen reported that in a decentralized union list project, there was a 3.1 percent difference in record selection, which is actually quite low.[7] Since the quality of the union list depends heavily on the consistent identification of the "best" record for each title, union list groups are wise if they choose to have record selection performed centrally, or if they utilize the work of other union list groups that have already compiled lists of recommended OCLC numbers.

CONCLUSION

A union list of serials may have the rather simple goal of being a compilation of the serial holdings in two or more libraries, and may serve a variety of purposes, such as resource sharing or cooperative collection development. However, to organize a union list in an effective manner, the union list developers will soon find that they need some guidelines to follow. Libraries contributing their serial records may have followed a variety of cataloging practices, and some may not have cataloged their serials at all. Usually a union list editor is needed to resolve the numerous discrepancies that arise.

The decisions that must be made in creating a union list are similar to those needed in creating a catalog: What common elements will be included in each record? What will be the method of organizing the list— by title, author/title, or by some other element? What additional access points will be provided? Will cross-references be used? How will similar titles be distinguished? How will title changes be shown? How will different physical formats of the same serial be handled? A knowledge of serials cataloging is indispensible for a union list editor to make sound judgements on these matters.

Discrepancies in the application of cataloging rules in a union list will lessen its usefulness as a finding tool. OCLC-produced union lists suffer from this problem, but as the OCLC data base changes and improves daily as a result of the efforts of the CONSER participants, it is expected that over time the problems will diminish. Overall, OCLC union lists meet the needs of their users, allowing libraries to participate in a union list for less cost and effort than a home-grown, non-automated union list would necessitate. The bottom line in both union listing and cataloging is the same — to organize information about bibliographic materials in a way that best serves the needs of its users.

NOTES

1. Susan Fayad and Charlene D. Wecker, "The OCLC Union List Product: Michigan's Recommendations for Design Options," *Serials Review* 10, no. 4 (Winter 1984):86.
2. *Iowa Union List of Serials*. [2nd ed.] ([Dublin, Ohio]: OCLC, Inc., [1985]), contains bibliographic records printed according to the following options:
    List arrangement: 100, 110, 111, 130/245
    Bibliographic record elements:
        Provided by OCLC: 1xx, 245, Repr, 250, 260, 362,
        OCLC number, 022, 030
        Options chosen in addition: 770, 772, 780, 785
        Cross references: 245, 246, 770.
3. Jean Whiffin, "Union Catalogues of Serials: Guidelines for Creation and Maintenance, with Recommended Standards for Bibliographic and Holdings Control," *Serials Librarian* 8, no. 1 (Fall 1983):45.
4. *Cataloging Service* 110 (Summer 1974):3.
5. OCLC, Inc., *Serials Control Training Manual*. 2nd ed. (Dublin, Ohio: OCLC, Inc., 1981), p. 154.
6. OCLC, Inc., *Serials Control Training Manual*, p. 152.
7. Johanna Bowen, et al., "Quality Control: Centralized and Decentralized Union Lists," *Serials Review* 8, no. 3 (Fall 1982):87.

REFERENCES

American National Standard Z39.44: Serials Holdings Statements. (New York: American National Standards Institute, 1986).
Anglo-American Cataloging Rules. North American text. (Chicago: American Library Association, 1967).
Anglo-American Cataloguing Rules. 2nd ed. (Chicago: American Library Association, 1978).
Marjorie E. Bloss et al., *Guidelines for Union Lists of Serials*. (Chicago: American Library Association, Resources and Technical Services Division, Serials Section, 1982).

Marjorie E. Bloss, "The Impact of AACR2 on Union Lists of Serials," *Cataloging and Classification Quarterly* 3, no. 2/3 (Winter 1982/Spring 1983):97-109.

Marjorie E. Bloss, "In Order to Form a More Perfect Union . . . List of Serials," in: Peter Gellatly, ed., *The Management of Serials Automation*(New York: Haworth Press, 1982), p. 191-197.

Marjorie E. Bloss, "Uniformity in Union Lists of Serials: Measuring Up to Standards," in: Nancy Jean Melin, ed., *Library Serials Standards: Development, Implementation, Impact* (Westport, Conn.: Meckler Publishing, 1984), p. 61-70.

Ruth C. Carter, "Cataloging Decisions on Pre-AACR2 Serial Records from a Union List Viewpoint," in: Dianne Ellsworth, ed., *Union Lists: Issues and Answers* (Ann Arbor: Pierian Press, 1982), p. 77-80.

Ruth C. Carter and Scott Bruntjen, "The Pennsylvania Union List of Serials: From Development to Maintenance," *The Serials Librarian* 8, no. 4 (Summer 1984):55-67.

Cataloging Service Bulletin 25 (Summer 1984):70-74.

Jean A. Conochie, "Has Serials Union Listing Come of Age?: A Review of Four Recent Works on Union Listing," *The Serials Librarian* 9, no. 4 (Summer 1985):67-72.

Anne-Marie Hartman, "The Implications of AACR2 on Serials Management and Union Listing," in: Dianne Ellsworth, ed., *Union Lists: Issues and Answers* (Ann Arbor: Pierian Press, 1982), p. 71-76.

Terrence J. O'Malley, "Union Listing Via OCLC's Serials Control Subsystem," *Special Libraries* 75, no. 2 (April 1984):131-150.

Bonnie Postlethwaite, "The Impact of AACR2 on Serials Processing: Beyond Cataloging," in: *AACR2 Goes Public* (Tucson: Art Libraries Society of North America, 1982), p. 54-62.

"A Serials Discussion Group: Form of Entry," in: Dianne Ellsworth, ed., *Union Lists: Issues and Answers* (Ann Arbor: Pierian Press, 1982), p. 53-67.

Debora Shaw, "A Review of Developments Leading to On-line Union Listing of Serials," in: Peter Gellatly, ed., *The Management of Serials Automation* (New York: Haworth Press, 1982), p. 185-190.

Charlene D. Wecker and Susan Fayad, "The OCLC Union List Product: Evaluation and Critique of Michigan's Statewide Product," *Serials Review* 11, no. 3 (Fall 1985):73-84.

The Iowa Newspaper Project: A Field Report

Nancy Kraft

SUMMARY. The goal of the Iowa Newspaper Project is to inventory, catalog, and microfilm the state's newspapers. This paper discusses the planning process and implementation of the project. The project is partially funded by the National Endowment for the Humanities.

I. BACKGROUND

The Iowa Newspaper Project is a pioneer in the 20-year, $50-million United States Newspaper Project, an undertaking created to locate, catalog, and microfilm all of the 300,000 newspapers published in the country since 1690. The project originated in 1973 when the Organization of American Historians (OAH) requested and received funding from the National Endowment for the Humanities (NEH) to update the national newspaper bibliography, *American Newspapers, 1821-1936*, which had been compiled by Winifred Gregory. Results of a study conducted by OAH changed that aim. Project planners decided to compile a national computer data base rather than to update the printed bibliography, and Iowa was selected to test the feasibility of the new plan.

In 1976, the State Historical Society of Iowa received funding from NEH to conduct a two-year pilot project for the purpose of creating an online newspaper bibliography and union list. A historian, a librarian, and several student assistants worked on the project. The staff conducted letter and telephone surveys and did extensive in-house research, compiling bibliographic information on 6,500 Iowa newspaper titles as well as holdings information for approximately half of them. Of the one thousand potential newspaper repositories surveyed, seven hundred replied that they retained newspaper files. All the survey information was processed by the University of Iowa's Weeg Computing Center and resulted in a searchable data base and a printed Iowa newspaper guide, *A Bibliography of Iowa Newspapers, 1836-1976*.

Nancy Kraft is Director of the Iowa Newspaper Project and Acting Director for Library and Archives, State Historical Society of Iowa. Her office is at 402 Iowa Avenue, Iowa City, IA 52240.

© 1987 by The Haworth Press, Inc. All rights reserved.

The successes and failures of the Iowa pilot project convinced the Library of Congress and NEH that newspaper cataloging guidelines, a national computer data base, and a master plan for collecting information on United States newspapers were needed. Over the next few years the Library of Congress developed cataloging guidelines, OCLC agreed to act as the national bibliographic center, and NEH developed a plan to fund newspaper projects in all fifty states and in seven territories. One very important element—the preservation of still extant newspapers—was added to the original concept of bibliographic control.

In 1982, NEH launched its United States Newspaper Program (USNP) by awarding two-year grants to six national repositories and inviting submission of grant proposals for planning statewide newspaper projects. In order to make the ambitious program to inventory, catalog, and microfilm U.S. newspapers manageable, NEH divided the plan into three phases: planning, bibliographic work, and microfilming. Each phase usually requires a separate application for funding. The State Historical Society of Iowa applied for and received funding for planning a statewide newspaper project in 1983.

II. PLANNING PHASE

During the planning phase, the Iowa Newspaper Project staff conducted on-site visits in fourteen eastern Iowa repositories, including colleges, public libraries, and newspaper offices. We conducted the on-site visits for two reasons: to verify the accuracy of the bibliography produced during the pilot project, and to test the forms and procedures we had developed for the bibliographic phase.

We discovered that the 1976 newspaper guide contained incomplete data and misinformation. When comparing our findings with the pilot project's survey results, we discovered that reporting institutions had overlooked many small collections and that many respondents had relied on memory or out-of-date files to answer the questionnaire. The pilot project staff had also relied heavily on county histories, newspaper centennial editions, and newspaper bibliographies to collect information which was useful, but often not detailed enough for cataloging purposes. The accuracy of information input into the automated system at that time was uneven due to reliance on part-time data entry clerks and inadequate quality control procedures. Our findings pointed to the need for quality control, a professional staff, and on-site visits in order to catalog from the actual piece.

The decision to plan for on-site visits created a substantial problem for the Iowa Newspaper Project staff. In Iowa, about one-third of the 6,500 newspaper titles are housed in the Society's libraries in Des Moines and

Iowa City, while the remaining two-thirds are scattered in seven hundred repositories throughout the state. Over half of the seven hundred repositories are in newspaper offices; one-third are in small town public libraries, with the remainder in college and university libraries, local historical societies, museums, and courthouses. Iowa newspaper repositories generally hold titles of local interest and often contain extensive runs covering 100 years or more. Most repositories have fewer than five titles each. Given this situation, how could a project located in eastern Iowa, with limited staff, space, and budget, inventory and catalog newspapers for the entire state?

At first, the solution to the problem appeared to be a plan that would divide the state into several regions, each with a cataloging center. But we discovered that although Iowa has over five hundred public libraries, ninety-four percent of them serve populations of less than ten thousand and are most often staffed by paraprofessionals. Although the six percent serving larger populations employ professional librarians, none of them have serials cataloging expertise.[1] The fifty-nine smaller academic libraries employ an average of fewer than three full-time professional librarians and often face chronic staff and budget shortages.[2] We therefore abandoned the idea of several regional centers and invited the Iowa State University Library (central Iowa) to join our project. Their acceptance of our invitation solved staff, space, distance, and budget problems to a significant degree, and increased the number of professional serials catalogers and OCLC terminals available to the project. (See Map 1.)

Once we had confirmed ISU's participation in the project, we turned our attention to how the actual cataloging would be done. Should we catalog the holdings of the two major repositories first and then conduct on-site visits, or should we combine the two? To test different cataloging procedures, we searched OCLC records for the town of Dubuque which had been input by one of the six participating U.S. newspaper repositories. We discovered that even having an OCLC record input by a member library and information from our in-house collections did not always ensure enough information to create or edit a bibliographic record with confidence. The missing piece to the cataloging puzzle was often still in Dubuque, especially in the case of very early titles. The exercise was frustrating because we could see from the holdings information in our 1976 newspaper guide that an on-site visit to Dubuque would answer our questions.

We were also concerned that if we cataloged the Society's two repositories first and then made the on-site visits, the catalogers would spend one and a half years in-house and then spend a year and a half in constant travel. We feared losing our cataloging staff as the project became more travel intensive. Our solution was to model our project after the state-by-state concept of the USNP. We decided to catalog on a county-by-county

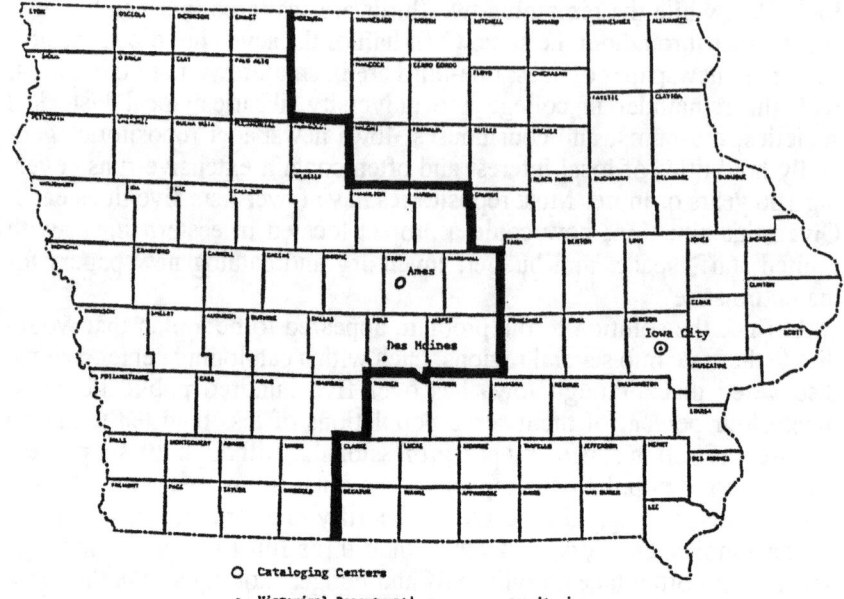

O Cataloging Centers
• Historical Department's newspaper repositories

MAP 1

basis, mixing travel and in-house work and allowing a cataloger to work with a newspaper run to its completion. In-house work would precede travel to the repositories in a given county.

The budgeting process for the Iowa Newspaper Project proved to be quite complex. We knew that we had about 6,500 titles to catalog and needed to visit seven hundred repositories in three hundred towns. Experience showed that we could expect an original serials cataloger to catalog between eighty and one hundred titles a month. We needed to factor in time for the on-site visits, so we divided the towns into three categories: those with one repository, those with two to three repositories, and those with four or more. A chart was drawn for each county indicating towns requiring a visit, the number of repositories, and distance from Ames or Iowa City. From these charts we estimated the amount of time a cataloger would need for travel and for important public relations activities. We calculated that a traveling cataloger would be able to do only half the normal workload, or forty to fifty titles a month. With this knowledge, our needs became a matter of simple arithmetic. NEH grants funds for a three year bibliographic phase, and we had 6,500 titles to be cataloged; therefore, four catalogers would be required to process the two hundred titles a month necessary to complete the project within three years.

Hiring four entry-level, professional catalogers for three years at Iowa salaries would have cost the project $240,000 — a price we felt the project could not afford. Since the Society and the University of Iowa are both located in Iowa City, we invited the UI library school to participate in the Iowa Newspaper Project by establishing a cataloging internship in place of one of the professional cataloging positions. We decided to trim costs at the ISU center by substituting a library assistant for one professional serials cataloger. This reduced the budget request by $35,000. To determine travel costs we went back to our county charts which indicated towns, number of repositories, and mileage. Based on our experiences with the trial on-site visits, we estimated that a visit would average four hours. We added travel and on-site time to our charts, and the completed charts had enough information to estimate mileage, lodging, and meal costs.

Example:

Dubuque County

Cascade — 1 repository — 120 miles round trip
2-1/2 hours travel time — 4 hours on-site visit time =
6-1/2 hour work day — 1 meal — no overnight

Dubuque — 5 repositories — 175 miles round trip
3-1/2 hours travel time — 20 hours on-site visit time =
3-days — 7-8 meals — 2 overnights

After travel and personnel costs, the third major budget consideration in a newspaper project is the fees for OCLC services. The fees are in two categories: fixed costs for access and variable charges for using different subsystems. The monthly fixed fees include telecommunication charges, system service fee, and maintenance fees for terminals and modems. OCLC also charges users for monthly activity on the cataloging and union listing subsystems.

Union listing fees are charged for input, modification, and storage of a record. Based on information from our 1976 newspaper guide, we assumed three union list records per title. Currently, if no cards are ordered and the union listing work to a record is done first, there is no charge for using the bibliographic record in the cataloging subsystem. In fact, projects receive credit for the input of new bibliographic records. (About seventy percent of the records we input are new.) Profiling charges for union listing and cataloging also need to be included when budgeting for OCLC services. Because OCLC is constantly revising its fee structure and each network varies slightly in its charges, projects need to work closely with both OCLC and their network during the budgeting process.

During the planning phase, we called upon our advisory committee to assist us several times. Quite frankly, the group was formed only because it was required by NEH, and our first impulse was to set up a token committee. A token committee would have been a disaster. We very quickly discovered why a project needed an advisory group. Formation of the committee guaranteed that the Iowa Newspaper Project became a *statewide* project and not just the Society's project. Cooperation throughout the state became the key to implementation of the Iowa Newspaper Project. Advisory committee members contributed the following elements during the planning process:

- all participated in some way to the writing of the bibliographic grant proposal—some wrote sections, all participated in the review, another edited to insure consistency
- no purchase of OCLC computer terminals was necessary—Iowa State University Library, State Library of Iowa, and the Society agreed to share computer terminals with the project
- no hiring of cataloging supervisors was necessary—Iowa State University Library and the Society agreed to contribute staff time
- all assisted with publicity efforts.

The advisory committee was largely responsible for the success of the planning phase.

The planning phase is crucial to the success of a statewide newspaper project. I strongly recommend taking a full year for this process. Time to try out ideas, to test work procedures and forms, and to develop time lines is vital. The planning process should allow enough time to fully formulate a plan, to lay all the groundwork, to develop a working committee, and to rewrite the bibliographic grant proposal if necessary. The more groundwork accomplished during the planning phase, the smoother the bibliographic phase will go.

III. BIBLIOGRAPHIC PHASE: IMPLEMENTING THE PLAN

The table of organization delineates staffing for the bibliographic phase of the Iowa Newspaper Project and highlights the cooperative efforts of three institutions. The State Historical Society of Iowa is providing a director and cataloging supervisor. Iowa State University provides a cataloging supervisor and a coordinator between ISU and the Society. The University of Iowa provides a coordinator between the library school and the Society and a hiring mechanism for both cataloging and public relations interns. A serials cataloger was hired for each center, with a full-time paraprofessional cataloger and a part-time library clerk added in central Iowa. The staff working out of ISU is slightly larger to compensate for the time lost in a forty-five minute commute between ISU (Ames) and the Society's collection in Des Moines. (See Table of Organization.)

The project director, coordinator, and supervisors play an important

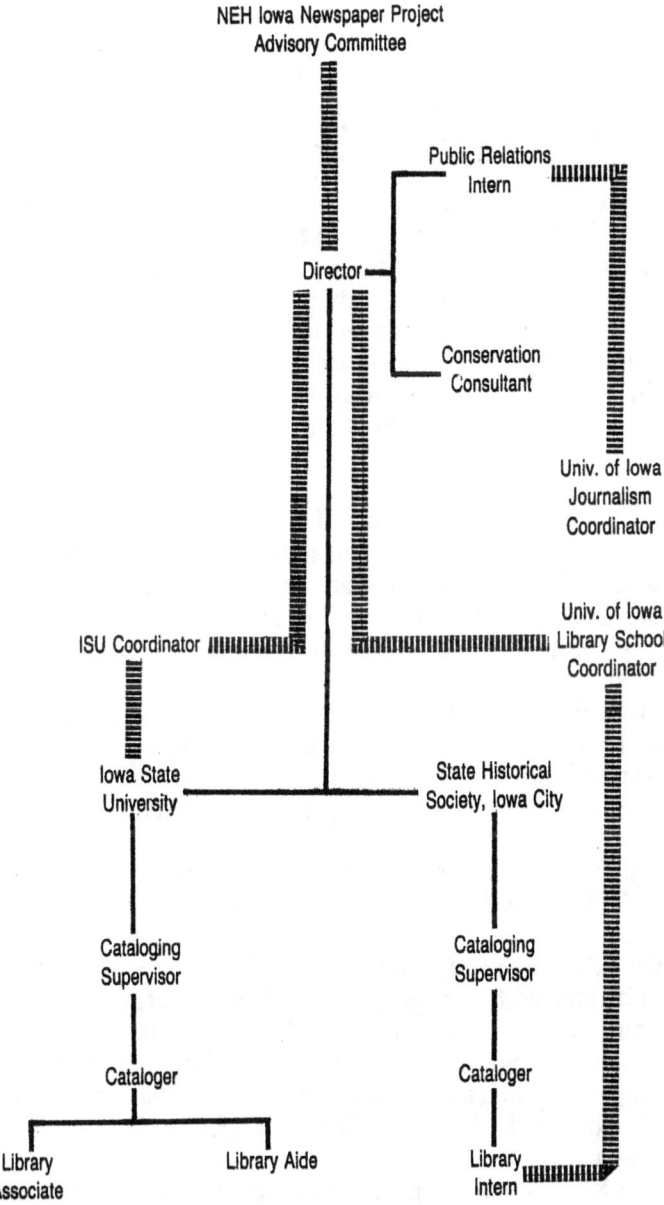

TABLE OF ORGANIZATION

role in managing the Iowa Newspaper Project. As director, I average ten hours a week with the project, monitoring the spending of funds, the onsite and in-house workflow, and standards for the bibliographic and holdings information. I train supervisors and sometimes the catalogers, conduct monthly staff meetings, meet with the advisory committee, act as a public relations officer, and raise funds. The cataloging supervisors contribute twenty-five percent of their time to the project. They train staff, monitor the workflow, participate in publicity activities as needed, contribute to the planning of monthly meetings, evaluate staff performance, and coordinate quality control efforts. The project coordinator serves as the link between the Iowa Newspaper Project and the administration of the ISU library and contributes five percent of her time. Her assistance as trouble shooter and advisor is invaluable. The project coordinator attends the monthly staff meetings, assists with problem solving, and participates in publicity activities.

A major concern for the Iowa Newspaper Project was how to structure the union list and disseminate holdings information. Three options were considered:

1. One three-character code could be assigned to the state with the fourth character designating the holding library. This is inexpensive and all holding institutions are arranged neatly under one filing code. The limitations are: OCLC printed directories only list the three-character codes, and institutions already on OCLC may want to retain their three-character symbols.
2. Each institution could receive its own unique three-character symbol. This allows the user of the OCLC system to determine the holding library in a one-step process. However, the profiling and storage charges make the cost prohibitive to states with many holding institutions.
3. The third option is a mixture of the above two and is recommended by OCLC. They recommend that 10-20 major newspaper repositories be identified throughout the state and given three-character codes. Clusters of repositories around the three-character code can then be created by assigning a fourth character. For states with numerous repositories holding few titles, the fourth-character code can represent a geographic area with the holdings statement indicating the repository in a note. These methods are intended for non-OCLC institutions in the U.S. Newspaper Project.
Examples:
   XXX   Major repository (State Historical Society)
   XXXA   Specific holdings location (public library)
   XXXB   Minor holdings locations (newspaper office)[3]

The disadvantage to this method is that it requires the user to look under several symbols. The advantage is that it is cost-effective and efficient. The Iowa Newspaper Project was fortunate to have John Miller of BCR as its advisor for creating a union listing code system. He had gained experience in the field while working with the Montana Newspaper Project. Miller's expertise and Iowa's seven hundred institutions to be coded led OCLC to use Iowa as its model for establishing a state newspaper union list. The new profiling guidelines for the U.S. Newspaper Project are based on the experience gained in profiling Iowa and other early state projects. Our profile is similar to the one now being recommended.

We chose to have the three-character code stand for east or west Iowa and not to be identified with any institution. Our three- and four-character codes stand for geographic entities rather than institutions. The holdings statement names the non-OCLC institution just before the holdings information.

Examples:

NEI — eastern Iowa
NEIC — Benton County
H1d lib: NEIC Copy: FM (microfilm)
SCHD #n Vinton Public Library, s = ‹1882-1887›.

This system is flexible. Because the framework has been established, we can add and delete institutions without further profiling. Researchers can identify the name of the institution without needing a directory. One disadvantage is that institutions' names must be manually input. In addition, several repositories may share the same four-character code, meaning that future deletions of holdings or participating institutions will also need to be done manually.

The above discussion is predicated on working within the limitations of the current OCLC system. All new state projects should be aware of that and consider what may be possible when the Oxford Project is implemented.

NEH has divided the U.S. Newspaper Project into state units; we have divided our project into county units. Managing the information on a geographic basis has many advantages. Title information often breaks into manageable units along geographic lines, allowing the cataloger to see a publication pattern. Like editors and publishers who frequently moved from town to town within a county or to the county next door, newspaper runs spanning a hundred years often changed titles, merged, or moved to the town down the road. Often the whole picture does not come into focus until the on-site visit. Following in-house work with the on-site visit allows a cataloger to tie up loose ends before moving on to another title. If we did not catalog on a county-by-county basis, much time would be lost trying to reconstruct bibliographic details based on incomplete information. Because both cataloging sites have titles from all the Iowa counties, the two centers need to keep pace with each other and stay in constant communication so that the fullest possible bibliographic information is available to the cataloger prior to the on-site visit.

County information is shared between sites in a packet with a cover sheet listing titles and a checklist to be initialed and dated as each step is completed. Once a county is completed, the packet is forwarded to the project director. In the past, no county packet was sent to the director unless all steps for all titles had been completed. However, some institutions have not been cooperative in allowing timely visits by catalogers. We are now pink-slipping these sites. The cataloger keeps the problem site on his/her calendar, but forwards the packet to the project director with the problem title(s) on a pink slip. The director can easily see that the county has not been completely cataloged and inventoried. These sites may need a personal call from the director or be put on hold until the site's holdings can be microfilmed.

We have established a policy that all titles requiring linking entries must be drawn out in a "newspaper family tree." Newspapers often change hands, proliferate when times are good and merge when times are bad, making them difficult to catalog. When a new link is discovered, we can immediately see the ramifications to the bibliographic records already established by looking at the family tree. During on-site visits, the family tree enables the cataloger to quickly see the relationships between titles without reviewing all the bibliographic records. This also makes it easier for a supervisor to review cataloging records. (See "Weekly Courier" figure and "Gazette" figure.)

We have developed several forms of communication to maintain workflow and quality control at the two sites. Our most important vehicle is monthly meetings which alternate between sites. Cataloging questions, difficulties with scheduling on-site visits, staffing problems, and upcoming publicity events are discussed. Resolutions to cataloging questions are written into a "Tech Memo" and distributed to staff. The technical memos insure uniformity of cataloging practices and procedures between

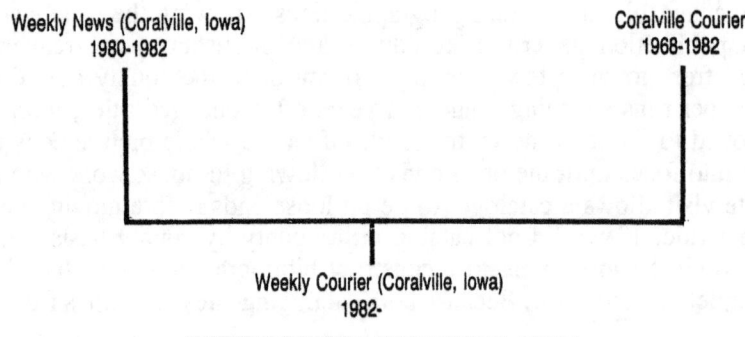

WEEKLY COURIER (CORALVILLE, IOWA)

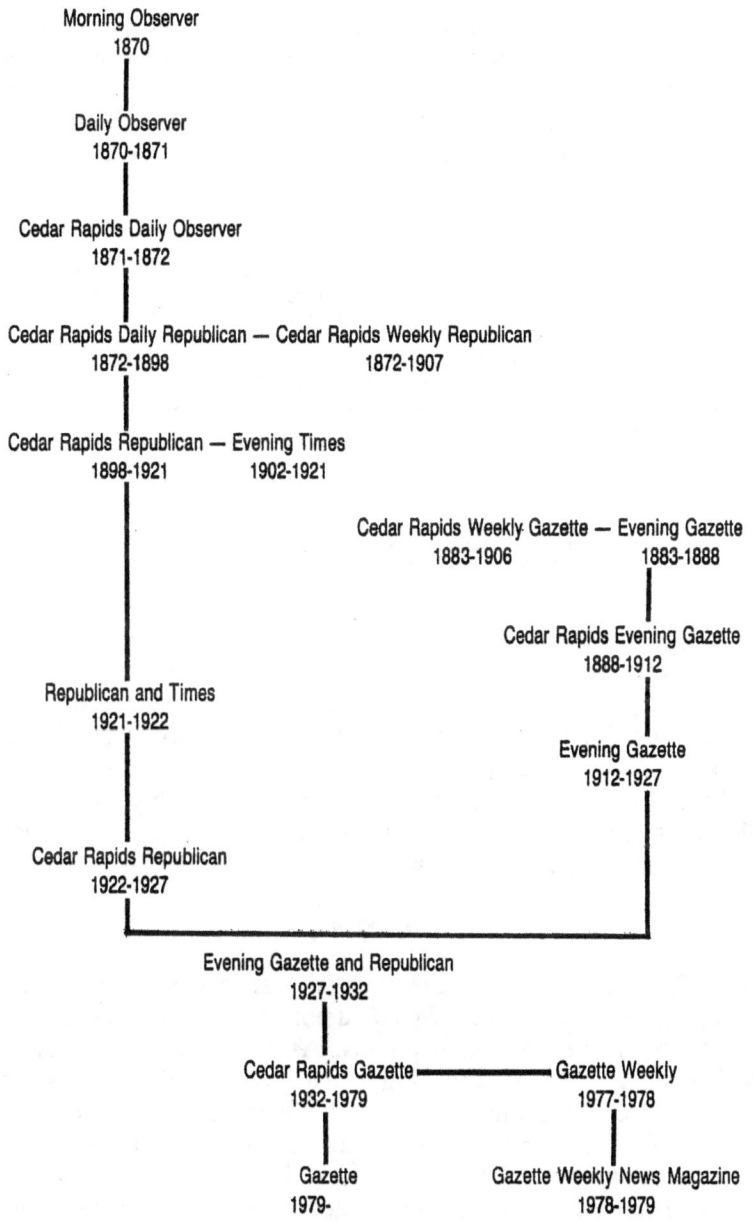

GAZETTE (CEDAR RAPIDS, IOWA)

the two cataloging sites. Weekly conference calls between catalogers and biweekly calls between supervisors supplement the monthly meetings.

The Iowa Newspaper Project also uses the OCLC computer system for daily communication. We have designated "Save 0" as our message center using field 590 of a "dummy" bibliographic record for the messages. The "dummy" record is used for verifying holdings or bibliographic information, and establishing times for telephone conferences or meetings. This information exchange not only encourages communication but saves time.

```
Screen 4 of 5
    19 590      KB--I want to get JEC's opinion (he is sick today) before I
answer above.  Perhaps a note about the different frequency would suffice?
JEC writes nifty notes, so I'll keep you posted, ok?  NL 5-22
    20 590      JEC/JC//NL--The State Archivist (Ed) has turned in his
resignation so I am extra busy right now (is it possible?) I can schedule a
meeting in Ames (or I.C. if you wish) May 29 or 30 or June 2-5. Let me know
what date, location, and times work for you.  JEC thanks for all the notes.
--NK 5/20/86
    21 590      NK--JEC was ill yesterday and today so I cannot get his input
on a mtg. date.  JC prefers June 2 and definitely not week of May 29 or 30 as
that is MALC at ISU.  I'll keep you posted and may call next week to get a
better idea of the agenda for everyone involved. NL 5-23
    22 730 02  Tempo (Iowa City, Iowa)
    23 752     United States 1b Iowa 1c Johnson 1d Iowa City.
    24 780 04  1t Iowa City daily press 1w (DLC)sn 85049504
```

The state of Iowa is in a recession. We have had to cope with budget cutbacks, a hiring freeze, and an absurd amount of paperwork to justify even the hiring of a fully federally funded position. When the supervisory staff, who work for the project part-time, are trying to cope with budget cutbacks and staff shortages in non-project areas, the temptation is to take shortcuts as we did when we suspended our monthly meetings. Our cataloging statistics immediately plummeted, which, of course, was not discovered until the end of the month.

IV. PUBLICITY

From the beginning, we have stressed that this is not the Society's project but a statewide effort. We could not have succeeded without help and encouragement from other groups. As mentioned earlier, the Iowa State University Library is making a major contribution to this project with staff, space, and computer time. The State Library of Iowa has also made their OCLC terminal available for project use. The University of Iowa set up a program allowing us to hire cataloging and public relations interns and waived certain fees connected with this. The student interns have been one of the most successful components of our work force.

Several organizations are helping us with publicity. The Iowa Newspaper Association waives fees for mailing press releases and provides conference space for us each spring. We are always assigned a choice location next to their display area and across from the wine and cheese! Many association members have written about the newspaper project and advertised for missing newspaper titles in their areas. One especially enthusiastic editor has offered a free coffee mug for anyone locating a missing newspaper.

The Iowa Library Association has provided numerous opportunities for project publicity. During the first year of our project, we prepared a slide-tape presentation for the seven ILA spring district meetings, which are usually attended by the librarians from small town libraries. We feel these librarians are a very important group because about a third of Iowa's newspapers are housed in their libraries. We have been program participants at the fall ILA conference since the project's beginning, filling a program slot one year and staffing a booth annually. Fall conference attendees tend to be from the larger public and academic libraries.

The Iowa Genealogical Society is another group important to the newspaper project. Its members are very enthusiastic about the project and have organized "hunts" for missing newspapers, raised funds for filming their county papers, and have publicized our activities in their newsletters. Several chapters have invited us to participate in their monthly meeting programs, which are well attended by the general public.

In addition to working with these groups, we prepare advance publicity packets that are sent to area newspapers prior to an on-site visit. After the cataloger has completed visits to a multi-county area, we send out a post-visit press release. We have also given occasional radio and television interviews.

Our biggest publicity success has been the map we prepared for display at conferences. On this map we have pinpointed all the towns in Iowa that have "lost" newspapers. We display it with clue forms for people to fill out with leads to missing papers. The map is quite impressive, graphically showing just how many Iowa towns have lost their newspapers, and has been remarkably effective in locating missing issues.

Publicizing the Iowa Newspaper Project is very satisfying because it sells itself. Rarely have we been asked to give the rationale for saving Iowa's newspapers, for pride of place and community are reflected in peoples' attachment to their local newspapers. In addition, the idea that someday researchers may be able to borrow microfilmed newspapers from anywhere in the United States and read them in their own local libraries is appealing and exciting.

NOTES

1. State Library of Iowa, *Iowa Public Library Statistics, 1981-1982*, 1983, pp. 114-137.
2. State Library of Iowa, "Summary data of Iowa's academic libraries, 1981", 1982.
3. Memorandum by Brian P. Moore (OCLC) to Serials Control Network/Service Center Coordinators, 22 January 1983.

AUTOMATION OF SERIALS CATALOGING

The CONSER Editing Guide

Linda K. Bartley
Jean L. Hirons

SUMMARY. The *CONSER Editing Guide* (CEG) gives extensive information about the nature of the CONSER Project, as well as comprehensive instructions and copious examples for content designation and input of serial records cataloged according to AACR2 and CONSER policy. The reasons for creating the guide, its method of preparation, and the basis for some of the decisions reflected in it are discussed. Part II of the CEG, to a great extent, replaces the *MARC Serials Editing Guide. Second CONSER Edition* (MSEG); a comparison is made with the MSEG to reveal what is new and different in the CEG. The contents of the yet to be published Part I, made up of current policies and procedures as applied in the project, are summarized.

INTRODUCTION

Two of the Library of Congress's roles in respect of the CONSER Project relate to training project participants in record creation and upkeep and monitoring the quality of CONSER records. Good training is fundamental to the creation of good records. Good documentation is fundamental to the offering of good training. It is therefore appropriate that a corollary LC role within CONSER is the documentation of project policies and procedures, notably as they relate to the preparation of the MARC serial record.

Linda K. Bartley is the CONSER Operations Coordinator, Serial Record Division, Library of Congress, Washington, D.C. 20540. Jean L. Hirons is the head of the CONSER Minimal Level Serials Cataloging Section at the Library of Congress and a technical assistant to the CONSER Operations Coordinator.

© 1987 by The Haworth Press, Inc. All rights reserved.

The overall objective in preparing the newest CONSER documentation, the *CONSER Editing Guide (CEG),* was to provide accurate documentation of what the CONSER Project is and does and how it is done. It is a mark of CONSER's vitality that such a guide is needed—certainly for use within the project—but also for the wider information community as well.

As its name implies, the *CONSER Editing Guide* is oriented to the CONSER Project. Also, some of the procedures described in the *CEG* of necessity have an OCLC slant, since OCLC is the common data base for creating and maintaining CONSER records. We know from experience with the two CONSER editions of the *MARC Serials Editing Guide (MSEG),* however, that documentation pertaining to CONSER has relevance to more than just the participants in the project. It is to that wider audience that this article is addressed.

In their report analyzing the current state of and future prospects for the CONSER Project, Jeff Heynen and Julia Blixrud made this statement:

> Despite existing data base inconsistencies, the significance of the agreement to abide by [standard] conventions cannot be overstated. The ability of a group of disparate institutions to create a common data base of records, to agree to abide by a certain set of rules, and to agree to interpret those rules in the same way underscores the historic nature of CONSER and of its landmark contribution to cooperative data base development. No project since CONSER can claim to have the same commonality of approach.[1]

The *CONSER Editing Guide* documents the "common approaches" followed within the project. The structure of the *CEG* has been designed to accommodate both lofty and mundane statements pertaining to CONSER, gathering in one publication those standards, policies, guidelines, admonitions, and interpretations that constitute the "agreed-upon practices."

WHY PREPARE A NEW GUIDE?

CONSER has had to contend with a variety of cataloging practices—those that predated the project and those implemented since the project's inception. Just as serial publications seem to be in a perpetual state of change, so are rules and procedures for their bibliographic handling. The goal of creating and keeping CONSER documentation up to date before the introduction of the *Anglo-American Cataloguing Rules. Second Edition (AACR2)* was one that could be reasonably achieved, albeit by cutting and pasting typed camera-ready master pages.

After the introduction of *AACR2*, however, much of the existing CONSER documentation became suspect, if not obsolete. Given the pervasiveness of the effects of implementation of *AACR2* (we in serials could not close the data base), all the policies and procedures expressed in the form of project documentation had to be reappraised. With the implementation of *AACR2*, examples became obsolete and many of the instructions were found to be incorrect, inadequate, or unnecessary. Piecemeal updating of examples and essential instructions was no longer tolerable.

In addition to cataloging changes, procedural changes related to record authentication and maintenance had been introduced to CONSER. CONSER participants now have the ability to perform authentication of their records and to make modifications to LC-authenticated records. These are among other CONSER practices and procedures that had not been documented outside of the project.

For all of the above reasons it was agreed among the CONSER participants that the indicated remedy for augmenting and revising CONSER documentation was to prepare a new guide.

Relationship to Former Documentation

Much of what is contained in the new guide had not been previously published; equally much is a revision of earlier published materials. Part I of the *CEG* completely replaces the unpublished *CONSER Manual*, updating and expanding on the policies and procedures that were set forth during the early years of the project. Part II of the *CEG* replaces the *MARC Serials Editing Guide. Second CONSER Edition* for purposes of current cataloging. The earlier editing guide has not been entirely superseded. Parts of it are still applicable for creating online records for existing retrospective cataloging. It is beginning to seem, however, that the usable parts of it that have not already been incorporated should be organized into a Part III of the *CEG* as a guide for retrospective conversion. That decision has yet to be made.

Preparation and Updating

An IBM personal computer (OCLC M300 Workstation) and Samna Word III, a "high-end" word processing package, were used to create the text. Upon discovering that the output of our near-letter quality printer was not of camera-ready quality, we turned to an alternative that gave the pages a typeset appearance. The page-perfect output was done using a Hewlitt Packard Laserjet printer and its Times Roman cartridge.

The print selections included ten-pitch proportional spacing and unjustified right margins. The print and page format selections permitted more characters to be printed per line than could be displayed on the PC monitor, causing the need to "rewrap" the text so that it would take full advantage of the 8-1/2 × 11 inch page upon printing. The reformatting of the text was added to the tasks included in one of many editorial passes through each file.

At one point in the preparation of Part II, 157 files were dispersed on 12 disks, with each file having to go through editing, reformatting, "laserizing," proofing, correcting, etc. stages. Happily, part way through the editorial production we were able to load the files, in publication order, to a hard disk. Only after we were immersed in our method of PC-assisted publication did it occur to us that we were involved in what is dubbed desktop publishing: conferring on us not only the role of author but also that of publisher and typesetter. Our equanimity had not seemed in as much jeopardy while performing similar roles using a self-correcting electric typewriter!

Updating the *CEG* will be much easier with the guide online (in a manner of speaking). Each field is separately paged. This not only allows easy addition or removal of pages, but also has the distinct advantage of allowing users to arrange parts of the guide as best suits their needs.

Structure of the Guide

The *CEG* is organized in two parts, each with three sections. Part I (sections A-C) is "Background, Policies, and Procedures." Most of Part I will be published in the first update to the *CEG*, with an expected publication date of fall 1986. Part II (sections D-F) is "Technical Guidelines." All of Part II was published in April 1986.

PART I

The objectives in preparing Part I were to set forth the tenets of the project and to provide guidance for the cooperative use of serial records on a shared data base. To that end, the organization of Part I allows for documenting the complete set of policies and procedures to be applied in the CONSER Project that will serve both as guidelines for participants and as information for others. Section A, "The CONSER Project: Background and Organization" provides general information on the project — its history, current members, and products. Also included is an extensive definition of authentication, a description of the various institutions currently authenticating records, and the elements required to identify these records. Other subsections, such as those on membership, will be drafted when the CONSER governing groups decide what the new policies will be.

Section B contains the agreed-upon policies, formerly contained in the *CONSER Manual* and in spoken lore about the project. Many of the policies have been expanded to reflect current cataloging and changes in the CONSER Project.

Also in Section B is a subsection on "Database Responsibilities," which states several of the tenets of the CONSER Project: that participants accept each others' records (long strings of codes in the 040 field notwithstanding) and that the data base be maintained. Changes to cataloging rules and interpretations, combined with changes in serials themselves, necessitate a certain amount of record modification, consolidating, and deleting. In Section B guidelines are given for what must, may, or may not be changed in existing records.

Perhaps most valuable to CONSER participants in a daily context, and of considerable interest to others, is Section C, "Procedures and Instructions." The procedures outlined there — modifying records, identifying duplicate records, converting or consolidating records, etc. — get to the core of cooperative data base management. It is the ability to perform these activities that makes CONSER participants different from other institutions creating and updating serial records on the OCLC data base.

Many of the procedures reflect recently assumed responsibilities of the CONSER participants that allow them to modify previously authenticated records and to authenticate their own records, shifting to them some of the responsibilities of record maintenance.

Of particular interest in Section C is the subsection on "Record Consolidation." One of the most troublesome areas since the implementation of *AACR2* has been determining to what extent pre-*AACR2* cataloging must be adjusted. With the introduction of new rules for entry, the number of records needed to cover a serial often differs from that needed under earlier rules. Most frequently what is required is a consolidation of several records entered under corporate body into one record entered under title. This would seem simple enough, but the presence of the authenticated records in LC's internal data base has necessitated detailed procedures specifying which record to retain, who can actually make the changes, and whom to notify about associated actions.

Also in Section C is a chapter giving procedures for the conversion of pre-*AACR2* records to *AACR2*, including a detailed listing of each descriptive area that must be considered with the proviso that a piece must be in hand before one can even attempt a conversion (a record cannot be converted to *AACR2* merely based on the addition of ISBD-S punctuation).

PART II

The objectives in preparing Part II, the "Technical Guidelines," were to provide a comprehensive guide for the content designation and input of serial records with clear instructions for complex, as well as routine, situations, and to define CONSER usage of USMARC data elements as they apply to current *AACR2* serials cataloging.

To explain how these objectives were attained, it is necessary to contrast the new guide with the *MSEG*. Such a comparison will illustrate differences in the overall structure, scope, and content of the MARC format as applied in CONSER, as well as highlight changes to CONSER practice that appear in specific fields.

Structure

Part II consists of three sections: D, E, and F. Section D, the "Introduction to Format," provides explanatory information and sources used for this part of the guide. Symbols, phrases, and codes used in Section E are defined. Abbreviations and acronyms are given in their spelled-out form, and a complete glossary is provided. Section E, the "USMARC Format for Serials as Applied within CONSER," is arranged numerically field-by-field, with general information sections for categories of interspersed fields (e.g., headings, series, subject headings, linking fields, etc.). Section F contains appendices, some of which were not available in the *MSEG*.

Each field has been structured to follow a pattern, beginning with the content designators defined for the field and their respective repeatability and requirement codes, followed by a definition of the field, editorial instructions, indicator and subfield usage, additional or special instructions where necessary, and finally, related fields. (See Figure 1.)

The inclusion of references to related fields was somewhat controversial. Some who reviewed draft pages felt references to related fields should be omitted, others wanted them to be far more comprehensive. The result is a listing of fields that are in some way related to the field being described, with those having a direct relationship also mentioned in the text.

To avoid repetitive instructions, the discussion of intimately related fields was combined, e.g., fields 310 and 321. General information sections were prepared for instructions that are common to a number of related fields. Preparation of general instructions of this nature had the advantage of avoiding repetition and presenting the instructions in a sensible and unified manner. Use of a general information section worked particularly well for the heading and linking entry fields, for which numerous subfields are defined.

Content Designators

Description of the content designation for each field consists of the following: (1) name of field or element and its tag; (2) names of all codes,

FIGURE 1

	Rep.	Full	Min.
260 PUBLICATION, DISTRIBUTION, ETC. (IMPRINT)	NR	M	M

First indicator

0 Publisher, distributor, etc. is present		M	M
1 Publisher, distributor, etc. is not present [CONSER practice: not used]			

Second indicator

0 Publisher, distributor, etc. is not the same as issuing body transcribed in added entry		M	M
1 Publisher, distributor, etc. is the same as issuing body transcribed in added entry [CONSER practice: not used]			

Subfields

a Place of publication, distribution, etc.	R	M	OD
b Name of publisher, distributor, etc.	R	M	M
c Date of publication, distribution, etc.	R	MA	MA
e Place of manufacture	NR	OD	OD
f Manufacturer	NR	OD	OD
g Date of manufacture	NR	OD	OD

Description/Instructions

Field 260 contains the place of publication, publisher and/or distributor, date of publication, as well as the place, name, and date of manufacture when necessary.

Editing instructions

1. Input a terminal period only when the field includes an ending date and no other terminal punctuation, such as a closing bracket, is present.

    260 00 $a New York, N.Y. : $b E. Steiger, $c 1878-1879.
    260 00 $a London : $b Howard League for Penal Reform, $c [c1965-c1983]

2. When subfield $c is not input, the field ends with a comma (unless subfields $e and $f are input).

    260 00 $a [New York] : $b American Statistical Association,

Indicators

Current practice (September 1984-)

Use value "0" for both indicators in all cases.

    260 00 $a [Nsukka, Nigeria : $b Institute of African Studies, University of Nigeria,
    260 00 $a Mexico : $b Fondo de Cultura Economica, $c 1982.
    260 00 $a Washington, D.C. : $b The Foundation,

Past practice (Pre-September 1984)

Prior to January 1981, first indicator value "1" was used in pre-AACR2 records when the publisher was omitted from the imprint because it was the same as the main entry.

    110 20 $a American Baptist Convention.
    260 10 $a Valley Forge, Pa.

Prior to September 1984, second indicator value "1" was used to enable the suppressing for printing of subfield $b for brief listings or union lists such as NST, and to provide instead the entry given in the 710-730 field with the second indicator set to value "0".

FIGURE 1 (continued)

```
250 00   $a Journal of social philosophy.
260 01   $a Chicago : $b Center for Business and Economic Research, University of Chicago.
710 20   $a University of Chicago. $b Center for Business and Economic Research.
```

Subfields

Apply the following conventions for the subfielding of data in field 260:

1. Enter each place name or publisher in a separate subfield.

2. Enter multiple occurrences of other components, such as dates, in separate subfields only when a different type of component intervenes.

3. Enter components of "real" imprints (carried in brackets and identified by the phrase "i.e.") in separate subfields only when a different type of component intervenes.

$a Place of publication. Input the place of publication and any additions to place names in subfield $a.

```
260 00   $a New York, N.Y. :
260 00   $a [Reston, Va.?] :
260 00   $a Rio [de Janeiro] :
260 00   $a Cambridge [Cambridgeshire] :
260 00   $a [New York] :
260 00   $a [United States] :
```

When two places are given, input each in a separate subfield $a. When repeated, the subsequent subfield $a is preceded by a space-semicolon-space (;).

```
260 00   $a Basel ; $a New York :
260 00   $a [Reston, Va.?] : $b U.S. Dept. of the Interior, Geological Survey ; $a
         Washington, D.C. : $b Supt. of Docs., U.S. G.P.O.,
```

When the place is unknown and the abbreviation "s.l." is given, capitalize the "S" only if it is the first subfield $a in the field.

```
260 00   $a [S.l. : $b s.n.,
260 00   $a [Philadelphia : $b United States Pharmacopeial Convention ; $a [s.l.] : $b
         Distributed by Mack Pub. Co., $c 1980-
```

$b Name of publisher, distributor, etc. Input in subfield $b the name of the publisher or distributor and any qualifying words. If both a publisher and a distributor are given, input each in a separate subfield $b. Subfield $b is always preceded by a space-colon-space (:).

```
260 00   $a [New York] : $b American Statistical Association,
260 00   $a Cambridge [Cambridgeshire] : $b Published for Medico-Legal Society by W.
         Heffer & Sons, $c 1947-
260 00   $a Washington, D.C. : $b U.S. Dept. of Agriculture, Forest Service : $b For sale
         by the Supt. of Docs., U.S. G.P.O.,
260 00   $a Victoria, B.C. : $b [s.n.], $c 1898-1945.
260 00   $a Berkeley : $b The Auditor, $c 1947-
```

$c Date of publication. The date of publication is given only when the first and/or last issues are in hand. (Angle brackets cannot be used in this field.) When cataloging from issues other than the first or last, leave this area blank but input the comma which precedes it. When inputting only an ending date leave 3 spaces before the closing date.

```
260 00   $a London : $b Howard League for Penal Reform, $c [c1965-c1983]
260 00   $a Berkeley : $b The Auditor, $c    -1936.
260 00   $a London : $b [s.n.,
260 00   $a London : $b H. Mulford, Oxford University Press, $c 1921-
260 00   $a Washington : The Board, $c    -[1982]
```

FIGURE 1 (continued)

$e, $f, $g Place, name and date of manufacture. When given, enclose in parentheses. Do not input additional punctuation between the preceding subfield and subfield $e. Subfield $f is preceded by a space-colon-space (:). Subfield $g is preceded by a comma. If subfield $g is not given in the record, do not input the comma.

    260 00 $a [Pennsylvania : $b s.n.], $c 1878-[1927?] $e (Gettysburg : $f J.E. Wible, Printer)

Related fields, etc. 008/7-10, 11-14, 15-17, 500, 550

indicator values, and subfield codes defined for that field or element; (3) repeatability codes for both the field and the subfields; (4) requirement codes for full and minimal level records for the field or element and all associated content designators.

The names of fields are those given in the *MARC Formats for Bibliographic Data (MFBD)*. All of the content designators defined for a field in the serials format are given. The asterisk and captions are used to indicate restrictions on use of various fields and elements. Consistent with its definition in the *MFBD*, the asterisk means that LC will not use the element, but will distribute if it is used by others. Captions are used to restrict use (e.g., LC use only; Not yet valid), to show those elements no longer used (Pre-*AACR2*; Obsolete), and to define CONSER practice (CONSER practice: not used). The latter identifies elements not used according to CONSER policy, as supported by a Library of Congress rule interpretation (e.g., $h in field 710) or those not used according to CONSER practice because they do not serve an identified need (e.g., indicator values in field 260).

Subfields that are currently valid or not yet valid for input are given in input order, followed by subfields that are no longer used, given in alphabetical order. This provides a useful reference for order of code input as well as separating those codes that are currently valid from those that are no longer used. (See Figure 2.)

The repeatability codes are *MFBD*-based and are given with the abbreviations "R" (repeatable) and "NR" (not repeatable).

A major change is in the requirement codes for the data elements. The minimum data element set (MDES) was discarded in favor of the requirement codes for both full level and minimal level records defined in the *National Level Bibliographic Record-Serials*. The MDES set had been developed before the definition of the NLBR codes and did not distinguish between full and minimal level records. A distinction that had been conveyed in the MDES code—whether an element is automatically generated or manually input—was no longer needed. Most elements are manually input. In cases where an element is automatically generated, this is stated in the description of the element.

FIGURE 2

	Rep.	Full	Min.
710 ADDED ENTRY--CORPORATE NAME	R	MA	OD
First indicator		M	M

  0 Surname (inverted) [Pre-AACR2]
  1 Place or place and name
  2 Name (direct order)

	Rep.	Full	Min.
Second indicator		M	M

  0 Alternative entry
  1 Secondary entry [CONSER practice: not used]
  2 Analytical entry [CONSER practice: not used]

Subfields

Name portion of heading

		Rep.	Full	Min.
a	Name	NR	M	M
b	Each subordinate unit in hierarchy	R	MA	MA
n	Number of part/section/conference	R	MA	MA
d	Date (of conference or meeting/of treaty signing	R	MA	MA
c	Place (including a name of an institution where conference held)	NR	MA	MA
e	Relator	NR	OD	OD
k	Form subheading	R	MA	MA

Title portion of heading

		Rep.	Full	Min.
t	Title (of a work)	NR	MA	MA
p	Name of part/section (of a work)	R	MA	MA
l	Language	NR	MA	MA
f	Date (of a work)	NR	MA	MA
m	Medium of performance (for music) *	NR	MA	MA
o	Arranged statement (for music) *	NR	MA	MA
r	Key (for music) *	NR	MA	MA
s	Version	R	MA	MA
g	Miscellaneous information	NR	MA	MA
x	International Standard Serial Number (ISSN)	NR	OD	OD
h	Medium [CONSER practice: not used]			

Control subfields

		Rep.	Full	Min.
w	OCLC AACR2 verification code [Pre-AACR2]	NR	MA	MA
4	Relator code	R	OD	OD
5	Institution to which copy-specific added entry applies	NR	MA	MA

Description/Instructions

Field 710 contains corporate names used as added entries. (For a definition of a corporate body see field 110.) Conferences are recorded in field 711 unless they are entered subordinately to a corporate body.

EXAMPLES

There are several cosmetic differences in the *MSEG* and *CEG* presentation of examples. First, subfield $a is explicitly given at the beginning of each example in the *CEG*. This eliminates any ambiguity when tracking from the text of the instructions for subfield $a to the examples showing how subfield $a is used. (A statement to the effect that subfield $a is not input on OCLC when it is the first subfield in the field appears in Section D.) The dollar sign is used as the delimiter sign, rather than the double dagger. (See Figure 1.)

The word processing package used in the preparation of the *CEG* has the capability to provide diacritics for German, Spanish, and French but cannot supply those used in other languages. Naturally, some of the best examples found were in Russian and Japanese! One of the early editorial decrees in preparing the *CEG* was not to hand-letter anything. Although it is of course preferable to give all diacritics in proper fashion, the illustration of proper tagging is not hindered by missing diacritics.

An overall aim was to provide more examples than in the *MSEG* and to make them serial-specific. Monographic examples are provided only for subfields defined for the heading fields that would rarely or never be used on a serial. Such monographic examples appear only in the general information section, and not in the text of individual fields.

Examples were taken from records added to the LC internal data base between 1981 and 1984. Examination of these records revealed tagging inconsistencies, pointing to misconceptions about the correct use of tagging, and thereby showing the areas most in need of further definition and instruction. Mistagging of the 245 field, in particular, showed that previous instruction had not sufficiently explained the correct tagging of complex titles. To remedy the situation, detailed instructions and examples are given for each subfield, as well as three additional pages of examples. The examples illustrate both simple and complex serial titles to instruct the beginning cataloger and to aid the experienced cataloger who is stumped by a particularly complicated title.

Changes to the Scope and Contents

In accordance with the objective to make the guide *AACR2*-based, fields and instructions pertinent to pre-*AACR2* cataloging were not retained from the *MSEG*. In particular, fields 247, 547, 400-411, and 840 were deleted, as were all instructions relating to retrospective conversion.

Also, only those fields that can currently be used in a CONSER record and that appear on a terminal display are defined. Three categories of fields were identified for omission: 1. those not yet valid for CONSER input (e.g., 773); 2. those never defined or implemented (e.g., 330); and 3. those not displayed on the terminal (e.g., record directory). Also omitted were most of the OCLC-defined local fields. One exception is field 069 – Other System Control Number – which is used by the National Library of Medicine and is the only new field added to the guide. A complete list of fields omitted and the reasons for the omission appears in Appendix A.

Instructions were omitted for any content designators captioned as "Pre-*AACR2*," or "Obsolete" (based on the *NLBR-S*). In some cases where an LC rule interpretation-based CONSER policy is stated in the text or an element is captioned "CONSER practice: not used" the RI is cited in the text. This, too, proved to be a controversial area. Some reviewers felt the inclusion of citations to RI's unnecessarily introduced cataloging to the guide, while others found it quite useful and wished for more cataloging instruction.

Once the necessary omissions were made, special attention was given to fields and elements peculiar to serials, to clarify and illustrate their use and to explain various problems associated with them. Detailed instructions are provided for use of the second indicator in field 246, for use of the formatted and unformatted 362 field, and for indicating relationships between the 580 and linking entry fields. The regularity codes have been more fully defined to illustrate proper use of codes "r," "x," and "u."

APPENDICES

Appendices were added, revised, or deleted relative to the appendices in the *MSEG*. Those that are new are Appendices A, B, C, E, G, I, J, and L. Perhaps of most general interest are appendices C, I, J, and L.

Appendix C provides instructions pertaining to punctuation, answering such nagging questions as whether or not it is necessary to add commas, periods, etc. It consists of the following: (1) OCLC system-supplied punctuation that is not input; (2) punctuation necessary for CONSER input; and (3) whether to add a period at the end of the field.

Appendices I and J pertain to subject headings. Appendix I gives LC's "division of the world" – namely the appropriate subject tagging for particular names of places, structures, groups, etc. The appendix gives the generic term, e.g., "cemeteries," and the tag that would be applied to the name of a cemetery when used in a subject heading. Appendix J is taken from LC's *Subject Cataloging Manual* and provides scope notes for subject subdivisions commonly used with serials.

Appendix L, "Special Types of Serial Records," lists elements that are unique to various types of serial records. Included are microforms, reprints, and newspapers. This section will be expanded by the addition of other types of serials, e.g., sound recordings and computer files, and by adding sample records to illustrate each type.

CHANGES TO CONSER PRACTICE

The discussion to this point has covered changes to the overall document. Several changes to CONSER practice at the field level, implemented with the issuance of the guide, are of significance to the interpretation of CONSER records.

The most important change—certainly a welcome one within CONSER—is the "regularizing" of second indicator values in the 1XX and 7XX heading fields. LC and CONSER will now use only value "0" in the second indicator position for these fields. As part of an overall attempt to integrate and simplify MARC formats, we in the Serial Record Division had earlier been asked to identify those elements no longer serving any useful purpose for serials. We first identified the indicator values in the 260 and 550 fields as ones that had outlived any useful purpose they might have had. Prompted by having discovered no CONSER need for these indicator values, CONSER practice was set to the effect that only value "0" would be used in these two fields (see Figure 1B). The decision about the 260 field, in particular, was greeted with relief by catalogers who had waded through pages of elaborate explanations, and for those of us who after ten years of preparing MARC records for serials could not remember the distinction between when to use 0 or 1 in the second indicator position of field 260!

At the same time, the second indicator values in the 1XX and 7XX fields were identified as likely candidates for the same type of "regularizing," but more research was needed to determine any current use. After querying different users it became obvious that the distinctions conveyed by the indicator values were no longer useful and that opinion was highly in favor of using the "0" (see Figure 2).

Also along the lines of tailoring requirements to usage, it was determined that the alphabet code (fixed field 008/33) and linking fields 760 and 762 (main and subseries linking entries) serve a useful purpose only for the National Serials Data Program (NSDP) and the International Serials Data System/Canada. These elements can continue to be used by others but it is not required that others use them. While not stating specifically "CONSER practice: not used" for the preceding elements, the requirement codes were changed to "optional." The alphabet code is defined as the alphabet of key title; under former practice, when there was no key title, the code was based on the title proper in field 245. Field 762 (subseries entry) was always "optional" and was never widely used; however, field 760 (main series entry) was "mandatory when applicable" and was routinely used with seemingly little purpose other than for the ISDS needs (the ISDS format does not have 4XX or 8XX fields).

The change from local (69X) to non-local (65X) subject headings was implemented before the publication of the *CEG*. The new instructions in the guide reflect general use of the 65X fields. The 69X fields have been removed and are no longer to be used for CONSER input.

A CONSER practice has been newly defined for the use of "frequency varies" in field 321. Pre-*AACR2* use of this phrase had caused problems when it was used in the 310 field. Rather than coding the frequency element (008/18) with the current frequency code, the character position was coded as "z" (other), a worthless code for those attempting to draw serials control information from the bibliographic record. When *AACR2* was adopted, use of the phrase was abandoned. This proved impractical. A compromise policy was established that requires use of the current frequency in field 310, along with the code for that frequency in fixed field 008/18. When more than three former frequencies have occurred, these may be combined into a "frequency varies" note, with the combined dates given in subfield $b.

Another CONSER practice has to do with the place of publication code in fixed field 008/15-17. It was decided that the fixed fields should reflect the most current information when known, as they are not tied to cataloging rules. The place of publication will thus be coded for the most recent place, when noted in the record, rather than the earliest place as given in subfield $a of field 260.

And last, but not least, use of field 247 has been forbidden for current cataloging. The *MSEG* had an instruction for use of the 247 field in successive records under one circumstance that is no longer applicable for *AACR2*. Current use of field 247 was considered for fluctuating titles, or other titles covered by LC's rule interpretation 21.2A that would not require a new successive entry record (such as those bearing "and" vs. "&"). To save possible confusion as to the status of the record as "latest" or "successive" entry, it was decided that field 246 will be used in all cases.

AVAILABILITY

The *CEG* base text, with binder, can be purchased from the Library of Congress Cataloging Distribution Service for $30.00. As cited on the verso of the title page, "This is a loose-leaf publication intended to be kept up-to-date by the periodic issuing of new and replacement pages." One update will be published this year. Future updates will be individually priced and can be ordered as they become available.

A companion product that might contain only Part II, published in personal computer documentation size (8 × 5-1/2 inches) has been contemplated. It could serve as a handy lookup when working at a terminal. If market analysis indicates that it would be a saleable product, the idea will be pursued further.

CONCLUSION

Adequate, if not excellent, documentation is fundamental to much of what we do in libraries. The consensus of those interviewed for the CONSER study was that CONSER documentation up to now has been adequate. It is hoped that the documentation contained in the *CEG* approaches excellence.

Nevertheless, because it deals with serials, the *CEG* of necessity will remain infinitely perfectable. Early comments are that the guide is a significant improvement over former documentation and a valuable tool for all involved with serials. Certainly the more the users of its products can understand what we within the CONSER Project are attempting to do, the greater will be the collective gain from the project for the library community.

NOTE

1. The CONSER Project: Recommendations for the Future. Report of a study conducted for the Library of Congress by Jeffrey Heynen and Julia C. Blixrud, p. 30. To be published as Network Planning Paper No. 14. Washington, D.C., Serial Record Division, Library of Congress, 1986. ISBN 0-8444-0535-3.

Life After Input:
Original Serials Cataloging Using OCLC

Beth R. Barrett, MLS
Olivia M. A. Madison, MA

SUMMARY. This article examines the original input of serials into OCLC by a medium-sized research library, evaluating both to what degree and in what way the records are used thereafter, as well as the role of CONSER in the upgrading of records. In addition, the impact of the OCLC Oxford Project on the original input of serials into the data base is explored, followed by recommendations for the future role of non-CONSER OCLC libraries in the maintenance of member-input serial records.

Anyone who has ever tried it knows that the original cataloging of a serial using a major bibliographic utility, such as the Online Computer Library Center, Inc. (OCLC), can be a complicated, time-consuming process. Certainly there must be many catalogers who, having spent a significant portion of time originally cataloging and inputting a title, wonder if any other cataloger will ever benefit from their labor. When a shared bibliographic data base is used, serials catalogers invariably spend much time looking at and using other catalogers' work. If that data base happens to be OCLC, they probably ask themselves, when they see a particularly lengthy string of characters representing libraries that have revised a record, just what has happened to that record since it was originally input. Who did what? How closely does the screen before them resemble the original record? How has the record been upgraded?

This article describes what happened to a test group of originally input serials records contributed to the OCLC data base by Iowa State University Library (ISUL) over an 18-month period. It also projects what original serials cataloging on OCLC will be like in the future, with the implementation of OCLC's Oxford Project. If OCLC's predictions and promises come true, serials cataloging should become an easier proposition, saving catalogers and inputters considerable time and effort over

---

Beth R. Barrett, formerly Instructor and Serials Cataloger at Parks Library, Iowa State University Library, is now living in Nashua, New Hampshire.
Olivia M. A. Madison is Associate Professor and Head of the Monographs Department, 204 Parks Library, Iowa State University Library, Ames, IA 50011. Ms. Madison is a member of both the OCLC Oxford Advisory Committee and the OCLC Cataloging Advisory Committee.

that required by the procedures used today. There is still room for improvement, however, and the end of the article includes recommendations for further ways serials cataloging on OCLC can be improved upon.

BACKGROUND

Iowa State University Library, while not a CONSER-participating library, fully catalogs and classifies its serials using the second edition of the *Anglo-American Cataloguing Rules* (AACR2) and the Library of Congress Classification System. Using OCLC as its bibliographic utility, ISUL catalogs approximately 1,630 serial titles a year, with about 180, or 11%, requiring original input. The cataloging records are later manually translated into a local, simplified, MARC-like format and input into a local serials data base, from which a computer-produced book catalog is created annually.

Currently the library is participating with the Iowa State Historical Department in the U.S. Newspaper Project, and through that project has partial CONSER status for newspaper bibliographic records. For the rest of its serial-cataloging interests, ISUL faces the same OCLC privileges and standards as any other member library. Briefly put, ISUL may do the following: input any non-duplicating serial title into the OCLC data base using OCLC's I (full) or K (minimal) input standards; replace the data contained in its own input records if no other library has used the record for cataloging and/or authentication purposes; edit the record at any time for additional card production or updating purposes; and submit to OCLC any changes that it would like made to the record if this has been used or authenticated by another library.

When ISUL began using OCLC for its cataloging of serials, it discovered, as many other libraries have, that the OCLC input standards are more extensive than its local needs dictate. As a consequence of differing data requirements between the ISU serials data base and the OCLC data base, differences often crop up between what is needed to satisfy the input standards of OCLC and what is needed for the local ISU cataloging record. In some cases information needs to be present locally that cannot be included in the OCLC record, and vice versa.

One example of the conflict between local needs and those of OCLC involves the construction of uniform titles. In this study there were four cases in which a duplicate title was found in the OCLC data base, necessitating the construction of a uniform title, even though no such conflict existed in the ISUL catalog. For instance, the serial title, *The Locator*, would have been entered in a 245 variable field (title main entry) for the ISUL catalog; however, the presence of a duplicate title in the OCLC database required, in addition to the title field, a uniform title (Locator

(Joliet, Ill.)) to be added to our new record in a 130 (Main Entry Heading Uniform Title) variable field. Other common, locally extraneous fields that needed to be input for OCLC were the 007 variable field (Physical Description Fixed Field) and the 776 variable field (Additional Physical Forms Available Entry) for microform publications. Altogether, in this study's records, 52 fields were input only to satisfy OCLC input standards.

After being input into the data base, OCLC serials records are subject to alteration and upgrading by participants in the CONversion of SERials Project (CONSER). Since its inception, CONSER has fundamentally changed the way serials are cataloged. It has created a national serials data base, which CONSER maintains and to which we all add records on a daily basis. With the creation of this vast serials data base, the need for substantial levels of original cataloging by individual libraries throughout the country has been alleviated. Secondarily, this means that any member-contributed record may be changed by any CONSER participant in the authentication process. Serial records are consequently not static, and may change substantially over time. The changes made are usually minor, but at other times they may be significant. Such major overhauls are useful in cases where the authenticating library holds a more complete run of the serial than the original library had when it input the bibliographic record. In these cases the project provides much needed information that the original library did not have. Similarly, if the original inputting library recatalogs one of its titles, it may find that the necessary changes have already been completed by the CONSER participant, thereby saving time and effort for the member library. CONSER may also correct errors in original records for incorrect form of entry for an access point, typographical errors, and tagging errors, among others. In other instances, changes may be made as a result of a revision in the form of entry for an access point by the Library of Congress. Other common changes come about because of a different cataloger's preference in the wording of notes, placement of bibliographic data in the record, choice of subject headings, or fullness of the bibliographic description.

DATA DESCRIPTION, METHODOLOGY, AND INTERPRETATION

While Iowa State University Library's total collection covers almost all disciplines, its serial collection is predominantly science- and agriculture-oriented. The library has an active international exchange program that results in a higher than average percentage of serials published outside the United States. The 235 original serial records that were examined for this article demonstrate both of these characteristics. The records were input over a 14-month period from June 1982 to August 1983, and had an average record length of 13.5 fields. The authors reviewed these 235 records in February 1985, eighteen months after the last record was input. The number of holding libraries that had been added to each record was counted and the upgrading of the records by the CONSER Project was checked. Copies of records that had been altered by other institutions were made, and these were compared with the cataloger's tag sheet from which the original input was taken. The changes by tag and type were then tabulated. It should be noted that, since this study concerns itself only with cataloging, interlibrary loan uses are not included.

Considering the scientific and agricultural orientation of the ISUL serial collection, it was not surprising to find that over half the original serials cataloging done at ISUL was classified in the Q, S, and T schedules of the Library of Congress's classification scheme. ISUL also did substantial cataloging in the H, L, and P schedules; these records were among the most heavily used by other libraries.

About 20% of original serials cataloging was of microform titles. Almost half of these had print records upon which to base the microform editions, and this cut down greatly on the time needed for cataloging. On the whole, the microform records tended to be little used by other libraries.

Of the serial records input by ISUL, 67% were used at least once by other OCLC member libraries as a basis for their own cataloging. Most of these records had been used only a few times: 71% had fewer than five holding libraries attached, another 16% showed between five and nine holding libraries in addition to ISU. Fewer than three percent had had heavy usage (that is, records displaying more than thirty holding libraries), but of these, some had extensive holdings. For example, the serial *PC*, a title concerned with personal computing, showed over 230 holding libraries. Table 1 shows the breakdown of records by number of holding libraries. Generally, titles garnering the most cataloging activity tended to be those most likely to be altered by a CONSER participant. Of

Table 1: Usage of ISUL Records by OCLC Member Libraries

No. of holding libraries	No. of records	%
0	78	33
1-4	112	47
5-9	25	11
10-14	9	4
15-19	5	2
20-29	2	1
30 or more	4	2
Total	235	100

the records displaying holdings, the altered titles had an average of about eleven holding libraries per record, while unaltered titles averaged 3.5 holdings. This is heartening, showing that those records generating the most cataloging activity are also more likely to be enhanced.

CONSER-altered records (64 titles) represented only 27% of the total test group. Of these altered records, about one third had been enhanced exclusively by one of three agencies: the Library of Congress, New Serials Titles (NST), or the National Serials Data Program (NSD). Another third had been altered by the Library of Congress, CONSER libraries and other agencies such as the Abstracting and Indexing Service (AIP), NSD, or NST. The final third showed recataloging activity by CONSER libraries and various agencies, but without a contribution from the Library of Congress. Table 2 shows the distribution.

The most common alterations involved the addition of the 010, 012, 042, and 850 variable fields. The last three fields, which can only be added by a handful of authenticating agencies, were included in half to two thirds of all the altered records. Indeed, over half the additions made to the records were of tags that could only be input by national libraries and authenticating institutions—not by other CONSER participants. Since it is impossible to trace what institution is responsible for what made by these few libraries. Table 3 lists the most commonly added tags and the number of times they were incorporated into the original ISU-input record.

AACR2 does not require the information included in a number of these fields, which can only be added by authenticating institutions. In practical terms, therefore, they increase the length of the record without increasing its usefulness, at least to the vast majority of OCLC's members. On the other hand, some of the additions are quite useful, making retrieval easier (the 010s, 022s, 222s, and 246s), or providing additional descriptive cataloging (e.g., frequency, physical description information, subject headings). Still, the number of changes that actually augmented information used for cataloging was smaller than might have been expected by those of us who look at those long strings of contributing libraries listed in the 040. Housekeeping takes up a good deal of space.

Unlike the many additional fields included when items were recataloged, the number of deletions was very low: only 14 fields were dropped out of the 64 sample records. The deletions tended to be for obvious reasons, as in three cases in which the ISUL-input 090 (Local LC Call Number) was dropped when LC added its own call number. Likewise, some local subject headings (690s) were dropped when LC input its subject headings (650s). Three of the deletions were at ISUL's request, to correct its own input errors. In the remaining cases, fields tended to be deleted when major recataloging had taken place, for instance, when frequency or issuing body changed.

Table 2: Recataloging Activity by CONSER Participant

Library or Agency	No. of Records Altered	%
Library of Congress (LC) only	1	2
New Serials Titles (NST) only	15	23
New Serials Data Program (NSD) only	7	11
LC with CONSER Libraries, NST, & NSD	20	31
CONSER, NST, & NSD (without LC)	21	33
Total	64	100

Table 3: Tags Most Often Added to Recataloged Records

Tag Number	No. Records Added To
010	44
* 012	31
022	14
* 042	45
* 050	6
* 210	12
* 212	5
222	18
246	17
265	12
310	11
362	5
500	4
650	4
690	4
730	4
* 850	43
* 936	16

* Can be input only by national libraries and authenticating institutions

The number of fields that had been changed was much smaller than the number of added fields, although greater than the number of deletions. Out of the 64 altered records, only 72 changes to existing cataloging were made. The majority of these were minor modifications that did not significantly alter the cataloging. These included changes such as adding or deleting marks of punctuation (brackets, question marks, parentheses), changes in the state abbreviation in ≠a of field 260 (Imprint) to or from the postal abbreviation, or changes in capitalization. Tags were occasionally altered, as in six local subject headings (690s) that were transformed by the Library of Congress to LC subject headings (650s). Indicators were modified, sometimes resulting in the addition or deletion of a tracing.

Roughly 40% of the changes were substantive and changed a field or series of fields significantly. A popular target was the =c of field 245 (Title Statement): in three instances the statement of responsibility was deleted, while in one case it was added. Corporate bodies traced in the 710s were qualified upon occasion. In one case, the corporate body main entry was changed to a uniform title main entry qualified by corporate body.

Some of these substantive changes unquestionably improved the cataloging, as in the case of the two titles that had changed their frequency since being originally input. Another title had changed publisher. There were also two titles that had ceased publication and been continued by other titles.

Not all the changes were necessarily for the better. Some clearly reflected a difference in cataloger interpretation, neither of which was wrong; others involved such minor points they hardly merited the time needed for them; still others were simply incorrect. Whether or not the subtitle should have been dropped in our cataloging for the serial *LAfile : The Landscape Architecture Catalog File* is questionable; a case can be made for either position. Likewise, the deletion of the statement of responsibility information, mentioned earlier, on two records is a matter of interpretation. Since neither case is absolute, however, it seems more logical to leave the record as it was input, especially since the deleted information was not subsequently added to the record elsewhere. It is also puzzling that the inclusion of a seemingly innocuous "the" in the =b of the 260 (Imprint) of one record was excised, as well as the added description "maps" in the physical description statement of the collation of another.

Similarly, the rationale behind switching the order of two 500 notes, which incidentally caused them to deviate from prescribed AACR2 note order, might be questioned. In another case, our cataloging, based on vol. 1, no. 2, of a title remained the same, except that the "Description based on" note was changed to vol. 2, no. 2. Perhaps most unfathomable, our place of publication for one title, "Sutton, Nebr.," was changed to "Sutton, NE (i.e., Nebraska)." I.e., Nebraska?

In all, the most striking observation about the altered records was how little they had changed. The records were longer, some by many fields, but the cataloging itself remained fundamentally the same. Our presumption that altered records in the OCLC data base were significantly enhanced simply was untrue. And while we were encouraged to find that two thirds of our records had been used by other libraries, we had expected that CONSER would have altered more than one quarter of what we had input. In sum, we found that while the use of the serials subsystem was active, the original character of most records remained largely intact over time.

OCLC OXFORD PROJECT

Leaving aside for the moment the benefits and shortcomings of CONSER's method of upgrading serial records, and turning from the specific to the general, some future OCLC system enhancements should make the process of original serials cataloging faster and more cost effective. The Oxford Project, an ambitious undertaking scheduled to be implemented by OCLC in 1987, will reconfigure the entire online system's hardware and software. The project will be installed in two phases, with the first phase largely consisting of four objectives: (1) major searching enhancements, (2) editing and inputting improvements, (3) capability to create holdings records and add authority records to a library's archive tape, and (4) duplicate record detection. When OCLC reloads its data base in its new configuration, it will also rerun its AACR2 conversion and execute certain error detection processes (e.g., correcting invalid data and deleting duplicate records). Original input of serial records will be most affected by the expanded searching capabilities, the facilitated input function, and the mechanism to add holdings records in the US MARC Holdings Format.

At ISUL, as at any other library using OCLC, considerable time is spent completing pre-catalog searching because current searching techniques are too limited to be efficient. Since serials often have short, nonspecific titles, it is many times necessary to wade through myriad summary screens and bibliographic records before discovering that an original cataloging record must be input. With the implementation of the Oxford Project, searching will be much more specific; in fact, there will even exist exact text searching, as well as searching by subject heading, classification number, and place of publication. A stopword list incorporated within the text of conference names will also be available. Combined with its Boolean and keyword search strategies, Oxford should provide search specificity that will greatly shorten the amount of time required to discover if original input is necessary.

The Oxford Project will also provide much more sophisticated input/edit functions, thereby significantly reducing the amount of time needed to input a new record. Instead of having to send each field added to a new record workform, inputters will be able to produce whole records with a single command, cutting the amount of communication necessary to create a record. In addition, OCLC will give much more specific error messages and plans to provide duplicate record detection before a record is added to the data base. The Oxford Project will also allow data to be transferred to a workform from another record (either a bibliographic record or an authority record). This will produce a substantial saving in the amount of time needed for keying in data as well as preventing simple typographical errors during the inputting process.

Finally, OCLC is planning to implement the US MARC Holdings Format during the first phase of the Oxford Project. Libraries that wish to take advantage of this option will be able to input their specific holdings into separate holdings records, which could contain location/copy information as well as piece-specific data. This capability will be available for all bibliographic records, serial or monograph; however, it will probably have more impact upon serial publications because of their more extensive piece-specific data. If a library, then, chooses to input this type of data and pay OCLC storage costs, it will have online access to its holdings data.

RECOMMENDATIONS

Because many of the problems associated with original input of serials on OCLC should be alleviated with the implementation of the Oxford Project, we found no need to make recommendations regarding the input mechanism. The following recommendations revolve primarily around the CONSER Project and the current privileges of member libraries regarding member-input serial records.

One of the major findings of this study was the low rate of authentication by CONSER participants of ISUL original serial records. The serial record file is second in size only to the books file in the OCLC data base, yet CONSER has only 22 active participants to maintain it. Considering the responsibilities and workload resulting from a file of this size, the CONSER participants seem overworked. We consequently strongly suggest that OCLC and CONSER implement mechanisms to lessen the CONSER workload, increase the opportunities for member libraries to upgrade their own records, ease restrictions for enhancing serial records by member libraries, and enlarge the number of records disseminated through the LC MARC subscription service. To these ends we make the following recommendations:

1. We recommend that an inputting library should be able to replace data on any of its own records that have been used only for cataloging purposes, but have not been CONSER-authenticated. According to the statistics gathered in this study, this would increase the percentage of records eligible for revision by the inputting library from 33% (percentage of records with no other holding libraries) to 73% (percentage of records with no CONSER upgrading). While not all ISUL original records represent ongoing titles, most continue or could potentially have earlier parts of the run added after original cataloging. In either case, due to the changeable nature of serials, each may be a good candidate for subsequent recataloging. For this

reason, it seems unfortunate that 40% of original input may not be upgraded except by the cumbersome, time-consuming process of submitting error reports to OCLC.
2. We recommend that CONSER review its current membership criteria and seriously consider expanding it. Besides helping correct some of the problems previously mentioned, such an expansion would significantly increase the total number of records distributed nationally through the LC MARC distribution process.

In conclusion, while recognizing the major benefits we all share through the CONSER Project, we also request that CONSER participants not change bibliographic data because of their individual cataloging preferences. Information should only be changed to correct invalid data according to AACR2 and national LC/CONSER practices or to add required or known data.

The Use of RLIN for Serials Cataloging

Mary Monson, MA

SUMMARY. This paper contains a description of the use of the RLIN data base for Serials cataloging. Specific information about searching the RLIN data base and cataloging in the RLIN environment is given, with reference made to uses of RLIN at the University of Iowa.

The University of Iowa joined the Research Libraries Group, Inc. (RLG) in 1979, and early in 1980 began cataloging materials using the Research Libraries Information Network (RLIN), the online data base of the utility.

Approximately 40,000 new items were cataloged last year at Iowa. Of this number, just over 1,700 were serials. In addition, Iowa participates in RLG retrospective conversion projects funded by the Hewlett and Mellon Foundations and the J. P. Getty Trust. In the first year of these projects (Sept. 1984-Aug. 1985), 96,000 literature monographs were converted into machine-readable form. During the current year another 60,000 literature records, 10,200 British history records and 13,500 art records will be converted. In 1983 the Retrospective Conversion Subcommittee of the Committee on Library Automation at the University Libraries recommended that, for serial titles, all records be converted to machine-readable form. Although Iowa does not yet have a formal serials retrospective conversion project, as recataloging of serials is needed, titles are converted to machine-readable form unless doing this is felt to be prohibitively time consuming. With two and a half FTE serials catalogers, the desire to put items online must be balanced with the reality of staff shortages. The combined efforts of Iowa's new-title cataloging and its retrospective conversion activity have resulted in the creation of approximately 450,000 machine-readable records for University of Iowa titles.

SEARCHING THE RLIN DATA BASE

The bibliographic portion of the RLIN data base is divided into eight separate files: Archival and Manuscripts Control, Books, Machine-Read-

---

Mary Monson is Assistant Head of Cataloging for Automated Activities at the University of Iowa Libraries, Iowa City, IA 52242.

able Data Files, Maps, Recordings, Scores, Serials, and Visual Materials. The file or sequence of files searched is determined by the default sequence set for each online account. This setting can be changed at any time during a searching session by using the SELect FILes command (each term in the command can be shortened to the letters indicated by capitals).

The basic format of search requests is FINd [index name] [search value]. The logical, or Boolean, operators "and," "or," and "not" may be used to enlarge or restrict searches. The pound sign (#) may be used as a truncation symbol to indicate to the system that a search request contains only part of a search value. Truncation can occur at the end of a value or within a value, but can be used only once with each search value.

RLIN records can be searched using a variety of types of indexes, such as number indexes, phrase indexes, name indexes and word indexes. The only exception is for records added or updated on the day of a search. These records are held during the day in a deferred queue for overnight processing and are available only through same-day status/activity indexes and ID indexes until the overnight processing has been completed.

Although RLIN searching offers the user both flexibility and precision, in formulating a search request it is important to choose carefully the index to be searched so the system can process the request as efficiently as possible. In general, for the type of searching done in technical services (i.e., known item searching) number indexes are the most efficient choice. For searching in the Serials file, the ISSN is usually an excellent choice. The ISSN index can be used in the Books, Maps and Scores files as well, where it retrieves items that have ISSN numbers in their series note fields.

If it is not possible to use a number index, phrase indexes are often good choices because they, too, use relatively distinctive information—phrases starting from the beginning of an entry. The title phrase index, for example, searches for the title, entered from the beginning, in correct word order. If the searcher knows how a title begins and cannot use a number index, a title phrase search is nearly always the most efficient choice, particularly for titles made up of common words.[1] In Example 1, the serial "International Journal on World Peace" does not have any truly distinctive words in its title, yet it is quickly and efficiently found using the title phrase index. (In all examples, the line that starts with the notation "SER/PROD" denotes the beginning of a new display screen on an RLIN terminal.)

For serials searching, the related title index may be used to retrieve information from the "linking entry" fields (fields 760-787). Using this phrase index, earlier or later titles can be found in records for serials that have changed title. As with the title phrase index, the related title being searched must be entered from the beginning, in correct word order. Ex-

```
SER/PROD  Serials                          Cat Maintenance   IAUG-MHM
FIN TP INTERNATIONAL JOURNAL ON WORLD PEACE# - 13 records in SER
MUL


SER/PROD  Serials       MUL                Cat Maintenance   IAUG-MHM
Result: 13 records
+
1) INTERNATIONAL JOURNAL ON WORLD PEACE. Vol. 1, no. 1 (autumn 1984)- (New York,
    N.Y. : Professors' World Peace Academy, [1984-)    c-9667   NYCT10310754-S

2) INTERNATIONAL JOURNAL ON WORLD PEACE. Vol. 1, no. 1 (autumn 1984)-
    ([New York, N.Y.] : Professors World Peace Academy, [1984-       .)
                                        c-9110   NJPG85-S1735    JX1901.I68

3) INTERNATIONAL JOURNAL ON WORLD PEACE. Vol. 1, no. 1 (autumn 1984)- (New York,
    N.Y. : Professors' World Peace Academy, [1984]-)
                                        b-9110   NYCG85-S4208    JX1901.I61

4) INTERNATIONAL JOURNAL ON WORLD PEACE. Vol. 1, no. 1 (autumn 1984)- ([New
    York, N.Y.] : Professors World Peace Academy, [1984-)   c-9650   NYBY85-S0

5) INTERNATIONAL JOURNAL ON WORLD PEACE. Vol. 1, no. 1 (autumn 1984)-
    ([New York, N.Y.] : Professors World Peace Academy, [1984-       .)
                          b-9110   COSG85-S1528    \JX\1901\.I54\PERIOD

6) INTERNATIONAL JOURNAL ON WORLD PEACE. Vol. 1, no. 1 (autumn 1984)- (New
    York : Professors' World Peace Academy, [1984]-)
                                        c-9110   CUBG85-S4109    JX1901.I59


SER/PROD  Serials       MUL                Cat Maintenance   IAUG-MHM
Result: 13 records
+
7) INTERNATIONAL JOURNAL ON WORLD PEACE. Vol. 1, no. 1 (autumn 1984)- ([New
    York, N.Y.] : Professors World Peace Academy, [1984-)
                                        c-9650   CSCW85-S276     JX1901.I53

8) INTERNATIONAL JOURNAL ON WORLD PEACE. Vol. 1, no. 1 (autumn 1984)- (New York,
    N.Y. : Professors' World Peace Academy, [1984]-)
                                        c-9110   NJRG85-S1450    JX1901.I68

9) INTERNATIONAL JOURNAL ON WORLD PEACE. Vol. 1, no. 1 (autumn 1984)- (New York,
    N.Y. : Professors' World Peace Academy, [1984]-)
                                        c-9110   CTYY85-S266     JX1901.I54 (LC)

10) INTERNATIONAL JOURNAL ON WORLD PEACE. Vol. 1, no. 1 (autumn 1984)- (New
    York, N.Y. : Professors' World Peace Academy, [1984]-)
                                                 b-9110    NYCX85-S643

11) INTERNATIONAL JOURNAL ON WORLD PEACE. Vol. 1, no. 1 (autumn 1984)- (New
    York : Professors' World Peace Academy, [1984]-)
                                        c-9110   CUBL84-S786     KJ851.A12I58


SER/PROD  Serials       MUL                Cat Maintenance   IAUG-MHM
Result: 13 records

12) INTERNATIONAL JOURNAL ON WORLD PEACE. Vol. 1, no. 1 (autumn 1984)- (New
    York, N.Y. : Professors' World Peace Academy,)
                                        b-9110   CSUP84-S4740    JX1901.I59

13) INTERNATIONAL JOURNAL ON WORLD PEACE. Vol. 1, no. 1 (autumn 1984)- ([New
    York, N.Y.] : Professors World Peace Academy, [1984-)
                                                 c-9110    DCLCSN847959-S
```

EXAMPLE 1: Title phrase search with result displayed on MULtiple screens.

ample 2 shows a related title search for "Nexus" and the first screen of results. Example 3 shows the FUL (tagged) display of the third record in the search result, illustrating how the related title is retrieved from the linking entry fields.

```
SER/PROD  Serials                                    Cat Maintenance   IAUG-MHM
FIN RT NEXUS - 13 records in SER
MUL


SER/PROD  Serials     MUL                            Cat Maintenance   IAUG-MHM
Result: 13 records
+
1) Nexus (CCPLS (System) ) NEXUS / Vol. 1, no. 1 (Nov. 1974)-vol. 2, no. 3 (June
   1975) (Denver, Colo. : Central Colorado Public Library System, 1974-1975.)
                                           c-9114    NYCG85-S5505    Z881.A12C65

2) THE JOURNAL OF ANTHROPOLOGY AT MCMASTER.  Vol. 1 (Jan. 1975)-v. 5, no. 2
   (spring 1980). (Hamilton, Ont. [s.n.])  c-9120    PAUG85-S2206    GN1.J687

3) BUSARA. v.1-  1968- (Nairobi, East African Literature Bureau.)
                                                     c-9110    DCLC72620460-S

4) TORONTO CLARION. Vol. 1, no. 1 (Oct. 15, 1976)- ([Toronto : Western Gap Co-
   operative, 1976]-)                                c-9111    OHCP8072184-S

5) BUSARA. v.1-  1968- (Nairobi, East African Literature Bureau.)
                                                     c-9665    NYCX1533268-S

6) TORONTO CLARION. Vol. 1, no. 1 (Oct. 15, 1976)- ([Toronto : Western Gap Co-
   operative, 1976]-)                                c-9110    DCLCCN8131025-S
```

EXAMPLE 2: Related title search with result displayed on MULtiple screen.


```
SER/PROD  Serials    FUL/BIB   DCLC72620460-S        Cat Maintenance   IAUG-MHM
Record 3 of 13
+
ID:DCLC72620460-S    RTYP:c    ST:p      FRN:      NLR:      MS:n EL:   AD:08-11-75
CC:9110   BLT:as     DCF:      CSC:d     MOD:      SNR:      ATC:       UD:01-01-01
CP:ke     L:eng  SL:0  GPC:    CPI:0     IDX:u     CMI:u     ALPH:    ISDS:z  TYP:p
PSC:u     D:1968/9999 FRQ:q    REG:r     PHY:      REP:      CNC:       IS:       TP:u
MMD:      OR:    POL:       DM:       RR:       COL:       EML:      GEN:      BSE:
010       72620460
022       0007-6376
035       (OCoLC)1533268
040       OKentU‡cOKentU‡dCU-CU‡dMUL‡dNIC‡dCtY‡dm.c.‡dMUL‡dOCoLC‡dAIP‡dNSDP
042       nsdp
050  0    PR9344.5‡b.B87
210  0    Busara
222  00   Busara
245  00   Busara.
260  01   Nairobi,‡bEast African Literature Bureau.
300       ‡c25 cm.
362  0    v.1-   1968-
510  2    MLA international bibliography of books and articles on the modern lan
          guages and literatures (Complete edition)‡x0024-8215


SER/PROD  Serials    FUL/BIB   DCLC72620460-S        Cat Maintenance   IAUG-MHM
Record 3 of 13
+B
550  1    Published for the Dept. of English, University College, Nairobi, 1968-
          69; for the English Dept., University of Nairobi, 1970; for the universi
          ty's Dept. of Literature, 19  -
650  0    English literature‡xAfrican authors.
650  0    African literature.
710  21   East African Literature Bureau.
710  11   Nairobi.‡bUniversity College.‡bDept. of English.
710  10   Nairobi.‡bUniversity.‡bDept. of Literature.
780  02   ‡tNexus
```

EXAMPLE 3: FUL1 screen with related title information in field 780.

Another phrase index useful in serials searching is the corporate phrase index, which may be searched for names of corporations or conferences. This index is particularly useful for searching conference names that include many common words inappropriate for word searches.[2] Example 4 illustrates this situation. The corporate heading International Conference on Social Welfare does not contain words that are distinctive enough to create an efficient word search. The corporate phrase search, however, works beautifully in this case.

Word indexes allow the searcher to find records when very little information is available. Words from a search value may be entered in any order. Since this search is less precise, however, to avoid inefficiency one must be careful to use words that are not too common. Ideally, three or fewer words should be used in a word search and each of these words should be distinctive. In Example 5 the searcher has used one distinctive word to achieve the desired result.

```
SER/PROD  Serials                                     Cat Maintenance   IAUG-MHM
FIN CW SOCIAL WELFARE - 1425 records in SER
MUL


SER/PROD  Serials      MUL                            Cat Maintenance   IAUG-MHM
FIN CP INTERNATIONAL CONFERENCE ON SOCIAL WELFARE# - 7 records in SER
+
1) International Conference on Social Welfare. WORLD REPORT / ([S.l.] : The
   Council,)                                         c-9114   CSCW86-S563    HV8.I553

2) International Conference on Social Welfare. PROCEEDINGS OF THE INTERNATIONAL
   CONFERENCE ON SOCIAL WELFARE. 14th-   1968- (New York, Published for the
   International Council on Social Welfare by Columbia University Press.)
                                                     c-9661   OHCP5294438-S

3) International Conference on Social Welfare. PROCEEDINGS. v.2-3;13-14.
   ([v.p.])                                          c-9665   ILNGAAN3252-S

4) International Conference on Social Welfare. PROCEEDINGS. 1st-   1928- (New
   York [etc.] Published for the International Council on Social Welfare by
   Columbia Univ. Press [etc.])                      c-9121   MIUG83-S11188

5) International Conference on Social Welfare. PROCEEDINGS. (New York [etc.])
                                                     c-1665   NYPG774829645-S

6) International Conference on Social Welfare. PROCEEDINGS.
                                                     c-9665   CUBG16566105-S    HV8.I55


SER/PROD  Serials      MUL                            Cat Maintenance   IAUG-MHM
Result: 7 records

7) International Conference on Social Welfare. PROCEEDINGS OF THE ...
   INTERNATIONAL CONFERENCE ON SOCIAL WELFARE. (New York, N.Y. : Published for
   the International Council on Social Welfare by Columbia University Press,)
                                                     c-9661   OHCP1607269-S
```
EXAMPLE 4: Corporate word search followed by corporate phrase search and its result, displayed on MULtiple screen.

```
SER/PROD  Serials      MUL                            Cat Maintenance   IAUG-MHM
FIN TW ENDOCYTOBIOSIS - 2 records in SER

1) ENDOCYTOBIOSIS AND CELL RESEARCH. Vol. 1, pp. 1-96 (Nov. 1984)- (T_ubingen
   [Germany] : T_ubingen University Press, [1984?-)  c-9661   OHCP3029120-S

2) ENDOCYTOBIOSIS AND CELL RESEARCH. Vol. 1, pp. 1-96 (Nov. 1984)- (T_ubingen
   [Germany] : T_ubingen University Press, [1984?-)  c-9110   DCLCSN8621086-S
```
EXAMPLE 5: Title word search showing use of one distinctive word to retrieve a record.

Subject searching is rarely used in the technical services environment, but if the need arises the serials file may be searched by subject phrase or subject subdivision. The subject phrase index provides the capability to search for subject headings, starting from the beginning of a subject entry, while the subject subdivision index allows searching for certain subheadings within subject headings, starting from the beginning of the subheading.

In some of the RLIN files, distinct records for the same edition of a work are grouped together when the results of a search are displayed. This grouping of results is known as "clustering." Although serials are not yet clustered, the Serials file is scheduled to become the next clustered file. Until this actually happens, serials search results will continue to display each individual record independently.

There are five different displays available to RLIN users: FULl, LONg, MULtiple, PARtial, and PRImary. The FULl display shows all of the bibliographic and holdings information with all MARC tags, indicators and subfield delimiters in place. The bibliographic or "BIB" segment (see Example 6) need not start at the beginning—the display can start from a specific range of the variable fields. For example, the command 5XX results in a display starting with the first field after 499. The holdings or "HOL" segment (see Example 7) of the FULl display contains detailed holdings information. The LONg (Example 8) display

```
SER/PROD   Serials      FUL/BIB    IAUG85-S1126         Cat Maintenance    IAUG-MHM
Record 1 of 1
+
   ID:IAUG85-S1126     RTYP:c      ST:p     FRN:      NLR:       MS:     EL:   AD:09-05-85
   CC:9110   BLT:as    DCF:a       CSC:d    MOD:      SNR:       ATC:          UD:09-05-85
   CP:nyu    L:eng     SL:0        GPC:     CPI:0     IDX:u      CMI:u   ALPH:       ISDS:1  TYP:p
   PSC:c     D:1981/9999           FRQ:a    REG:r     PHY:       REP:    CNC:        IS:     TP:u
   MMD:      OR:       POL:        DM:      RR:       COL:       EML:    GEN:        BSE:
   010       83646089‡zsn82021013
   022 0     0740-6657
   040       NBiSU‡cNBiSU‡dm.c.‡dHUL‡dNST‡dDLC‡dNSD‡dDLC‡dNST‡dIaU
   042       lc‡anst‡ansdp
   043       n-us---
   050 0     HB172.5‡b.M334
   082 0     339/.05‡219
   222 00    Introductory macroeconomics
   245 00    Introductory macroeconomics.
   260 00    Ithaca :‡bCornell University Press,‡c1980-
   300       v. :‡bill. ;‡c28 cm.
   310       Annual
   362 0     1980/81-
   500       "Readings on contemporary issues."
   570       Editor: 1980/81-   P. D. McClelland.
   650 0     Macroeconomics‡xAddresses, essays, lectures.

SER/PROD   Serials      FUL/BIB    IAUG85-S1126         Cat Maintenance    IAUG-MHM
Record 1 of 1
+
   610 10    United States‡xEconomic conditions‡y1981-‡xAddresses, essays, lectures

   700 11    McClelland, Peter D.
   780 00    ‡tMacroeconomics‡x0740-6665
```

EXAMPLE 6: The BIBliographic segment of a FULl display.

```
SER/PROD  Serials      FUL/HOL    IAUG85-S1126          Cat Maintenance    IAUG-MHM
Record 1 of 1
UPD
                                                  CIN CL    OID CM    FD 09/05/85
    CALL HB171‡b.M3
    VOL
    ANT
    INS              EXT
    HST 09/05/85  CT
    FNT                              PTH 7     FSP 16~700

      LOC MAIN      LCAL
      LVOL ‡vc.1: 1984/85
      LANT
      LINS          LEXT
      LHST 09/05/85 C
      LFNT                          LPTH      LFSP
        COP            MDES
       CCAL
       SHNT
```

EXAMPLE 7: The HOLdings segment of a FULl display.

```
SER/PROD  Serials      LON    IAUG85-S1126          Cat Maintenance    IAUG-MHM
Record 1 of 1
UPD
Introductory macroeconomics.
1980/81-
-- Ithaca : Cornell University Press, 1980-
v. : ill. ; 28 cm.

Annual
"Readings on contemporary issues."
Editor: 1980/81-   P. D. McClelland.
Continues: Macroeconomics 0740-6665
ISSN 0740-6657 = Introductory macroeconomics

  1. Macroeconomics--Addresses, essays, lectures. 2. United States--Economic
conditions--1981---Addresses, essays, lectures. I. McClelland, Peter D.
  LCCN: 83646089 sn82021013
  L.C. CALL NO: HB172.5.M334
  ID: IAUG85-S1126              CC: 9110       DCF: a
  CALL: HB171.M3
```

EXAMPLE 8: The LONg display.

shows the RLIN record in the catalog card format. MULtiple is a display of brief bibliographic citations (see Examples 1 and 2). Each citation is accompanied by four-character symbols of holding libraries and as many records or clusters as will fit on the screen at one time may be displayed. Appearing with holding library identifiers on the MUL display may be codes indicating that records contain microform information or CJK (Chinese-Japanese-Korean) characters. The PARtial display (Example 9) shows brief bibliographic information and holdings data for a single record. PRImary (Example 10) also displays brief bibliographic information but it does not show holdings data.

At the University of Iowa all pre-catalog searching is done by the Bibliographic Searching Section. This section is headed by a librarian who supervises five paraprofessionals. One of these paraprofessionals does all of the serials searching. Catalogers have access to an RLIN terminal for authorities searching and brief searching to solve specific cataloging

```
SER/PROD  Serials    PAR    IAUG85-S1126          Cat Maintenance  IAUG-MHM
Record 1 of 1
UPD
Introductory macroeconomics.
  1980/81-
  -- Ithaca : Cornell University Press, 1980-
  v. : ill. ; 28 cm.

  ISSN 0740-6657
  LCCN: 83646089 sn82021013
  L.C. CALL NO: HB172.5.M334
  ID: IAUG85-S1126              CC: 9110      DCF: a
- - - - - - - - - - - - - - - - - - - - - - - - - - - - - - - - - - -
HB171.M3

MAIN
  c.1: 1984/85
```

EXAMPLE 9: The PARtial display.

```
SER/PROD  Serials    PRI    IAUG85-S1126          Cat Maintenance  IAUG-MHM
Record 1 of 1
UPD
Introductory macroeconomics.
  1980/81-
  -- Ithaca : Cornell University Press, 1980-
  v. : ill. ; 28 cm.

  ISSN 0740-6657
  LCCN: 83646089 sn82021013
  L.C. CALL NO: HB172.5.M334
  ID: IAUG85-S1126              CC: 9110      DCF: a
- - - - - - - - - - - - - - - - - - - - - - - - - - - - - - - - - - -
IAUG (c-9110 IaU)
```

EXAMPLE 10: The PRImary display.

problems, but all other searching and re-searching is referred to the Bibliographic Searching Section. This arrangement allows us to make maximum use of our ten RLIN technical services terminals. Each searcher is scheduled daily for 1-1/2 to 2 hours online, and the remaining available times on these terminals is used for inputting of new titles and retrospective conversion activities. In addition to allowing us to take maximum advantage of a minimum number of terminals, we feel that this arrangement allows us to do the most efficient searching possible. All searchers are carefully and thoroughly trained in efficient searching techniques, making them specialists in this operation.

CATALOGING ON RLIN

In the RLIN system there are two basic cataloging functions: cataloging and catalog maintenance. Cataloging in RLIN means the entering of bibliographic data from whatever source (including a record already in RLIN) into the appropriate online file in conformity with: (1) field requirements as detailed in the RLIN field guides; (2) each individual library's cataloging conventions; and (3) certain standards required by

RLIN. Catalog maintenance in RLIN means making any changes to the catalog data in one's own records in order to improve their contents or keep them up to date—adding, deleting, or altering control, bibliographic, and/or holdings data. One's own records may be deleted as a maintenance activity also.[3]

RLG policy encourages creating and sharing records that meet as fully as possible the needs of RLIN's users for completeness, consistency, and adherence to national standards and conventions.[4] A special control field called cataloging category (CC) has been created in RLIN to indicate the source of a record and its content and cataloging level. This four-character numeric code appears in all commonly used displays. The first character indicates the level of authority control (currently there is no authority control in RLIN), the second indicates the level of cataloging, the third the level of content designation and the last the source of the machine-readable record. If an item does not meet standards for full level of cataloging and/or content designation this information will be reflected in the code in the CC field. When there are multiple records to choose from a searcher can quickly errors are found in RLIN records they can be reported to RLG's Bibliograeliminate less-than-full-standard records by checking the CC field.
phic Quality Assurance Specialist. Obvious errors in bibliographic data in records can be reported directly online. This is done by displaying the erroneous record and typing a brief (less than one line) error message on the command line of the terminal. Error reports requiring fuller explanations or documentation are submitted offline using the RLIN Record Error Report Form. All error reports are examined by the Bibliographic Quality Assurance Specialist. If there seems to be a pattern of errors at an institution, the Quality Assurance Specialist will notify the institution and pass on information indicating the nature and scope of the problem. If no pattern is apparent, error reports are simply forwarded to the appropriate institutions for corrections. Problems that seem to be of general concern to all RLIN users are discussed in the *Operations Update*, an irregular newsletter dealing with the operational aspects of using the RLIN system, while errors in LC records are reported to RLIN users in a document called *Cluster Error Reports*.

There are four types of RLIN cataloging activities: derivative cataloging, new entity cataloging, converting acquisitions to cataloging, and added copy cataloging. In derivative cataloging, bibliographic data are copied or "derived" from an existing RLIN record that represents the same title and edition one is entering.[5] During this process the bibliographic portion of the data can be modified and one's holdings attached to the record. The resulting record reflects one's own library's specific treatment of the record. This record, with all of one's modifications, can be recalled and displayed in its entirety at any time, as can all other records in the RLIN data base. New entity cataloging involves creating a bibliographic entity new to the RLIN data base. This may be done either by keying in a new record entirely from scratch or by basing a new record on another similar record already in the data base. Example 11 shows the BIB screen following the CREate command (to initiate creation of a new record from scratch) before any data have been keyed in. Converting acquisitions data into a cataloging record entails using a record already input by your acquisitions staff. (At Iowa as we do not use the acquisitions portion of RLIN, we never perform this particular activity.) Revision and updating of the bibliographic information may be necessary, and holdings are added. As its name implies, added copy cataloging involves updating of a library's existing records to show additional copies.

The catalog maintenance function is used for updating of a library's existing records. Since each library's unique record is stored in the RLIN data base in its most current form there is no need to repeat the original or subsequent modifications before the new updating is done.

As byproducts of cataloging and catalog maintenance activities, various types of output, such as catalog cards and tapes, can be ordered using the RLIN system. At the University of Iowa we don't have an online public access catalog, and so we order catalog cards for our union catalog at the Main Library as well as for the departmental libraries scattered across campus. These cards are produced nightly as a function of RLIN batch processing, which occurs after normal RLIN service hours, and are mailed from Stanford the following day. Each card shipment has cards sorted by destination catalog, with cards for each catalog prearranged according to our specifications. The union shelflist cards for our Main

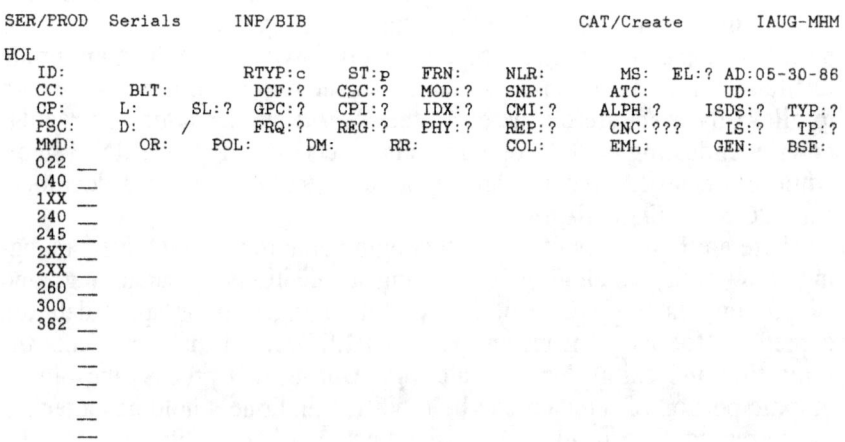

EXAMPLE 11: The BIBliographic segment of a new title input screen.

Library, for example, are prearranged in shelflist order, while the dictionary catalog cards for this location are prearranged in alphabetical order. The actual format of each type of catalog card as well as the arrangement of the cards in each shipment is specified in our catalog card profile, which was prepared at the time we joined RLG in 1979. When catalog maintenance is performed and only selected cards from a card set need to be replaced, it is possible to order cards individually for specific catalogs. These replacement cards arrive interfiled in the card shipment ready to file in the card catalog, with all notes and added entries supplied.

At the University of Iowa, we also receive a weekly tape of all of our non-CJK items cataloged or revised on the RLIN system that week as well as a monthly tape of all of our CJK items with activity that month. These weekly and monthly tapes are merged onto a master tape at our academic computer center. During this merging process, activity dates of RLIN transactions are checked and new occurrences of a record bump old versions of the same record, resulting in a master tape that contains the latest version of each RLIN record. NOTIS was recently chosen as the integrated library system for the University of Iowa, and our master tape will be used to create the local data base when implementation begins.

The great majority of cataloging at the University of Iowa is done on worksheets at the cataloger's desk and then input by typists. All professional catalogers catalog in this manner. Paraprofessional catalogers each have one hour of online time daily for inputting of their own records; the remainder of their work is done on worksheets, and input from these by typists. Straightforward LC and CIP copy is done by students, who shelflist and mark books and then search online for matching LC copy. If the LC record online has not been upgraded from CIP to full LC copy, the item is not cataloged on RLIN, although the book is sent on to the stacks. If full LC copy is found, the item is cataloged at once. Those items without matching full LC copy are re-searched approximately every two months, and are input as soon as complete LC copy is found. If researching continues for a year without the appearance of a full LC record, other appropriate copy is chosen as the basis for the cataloging, or the book is sent to a professional cataloger for original cataloging. Unlike monographs, however, serials are all cataloged by professional catalogers and input by typists. There are no paraprofessionals or CIP students working on serials.

Catalog maintenance is done online by two paraprofessionals who work from instructions created by catalogers. One paraprofessional is in charge of all but serials maintenance, while the other does only serials maintenance. This serials maintenance includes correction of errors in bibliographic and holdings portions of the records as well as additions and changes in locations and holdings data.

RLIN AUTHORITIES

The RLIN Authority file is separate from the eight bibliographic files in the RLIN database. This file is a reference file only, and consists entirely of Library of Congress Name Authority records. Since the September 1985 implementation of the Linked Systems Project, RLG has been using its computer-to-computer link with the Library of Congress for authority record distribution. Each day a computer program at RLG establishes a link with a waiting computer at the Library of Congress and retrieves the records LC has ready for RLG in its queue. The records are newly created or newly updated name authority records, representing work entered at LC during the day or during the previous day.[6] What this signifies for RLIN users is that the latest form of entry is now normally available within two days of the time it was established by LC.

THE FUTURE

At the University of Iowa we are looking forward to the clustering of the RLIN Serials file, an enhancement that should greatly increase our searching efficiency. With the contents of the Serials file nearing two million records, paging through search results consisting of individual records can be onerous. The implementation of clustering will bring about the grouping together in search results of records for the same title, with one record designated as the "primary cluster member." Bibliographic information from the primary cluster member will appear in the display, followed by library identifier codes for all libraries holding the title. Individual bibliographic and holdings records for any of the libraries represented in the cluster may be viewed by simply issuing the appropriate commands.

In addition, we are anticipating the day when we will be able to implement a formal serials retrospective conversion project. Maintaining simultaneous manual and automated serials operations is expensive and time-consuming, especially in the case of serials that are currently being received.

NOTES

1. Lavigne, Jonathan, Searching in RLIN II. 2nd ed. (Stanford, Calif.: Research Libraries Group, 1984-   ), p. 100.
2. Ibid., p. 124.
3. Khattak, Melodye M., Cataloging in RLIN II. 2nd ed. (Stanford, Calif.: Research Libraries Group, 1985-   ), p. 18.
4. Ibid., p. 18.
5. Ibid., p. 19.
6. "First Implementation of the Linked Systems Project (LSP)," Research Libraries Group. Library Operations Division. Operations update 34 (February 1986): 3.

EDUCATION OF
SERIALS CATALOGERS

The Education of Serials Catalogers

Mary Ellen Soper

SUMMARY. Past surveys of accredited library schools' efforts to prepare students to work with serials, and surveys of practitioners' attitudes toward their formal serials education are reviewed. The results of a 1986 survey of serials cataloging courses and units offered by library schools are then presented. Continuing education for serials work is covered, along with a consideration of whether or not special instruction for working with serials is necessary.

One of the things that draws those of us who work or have worked with serial publications together is the belief that few other librarians appreciate how different our "intended to be continued indefinitely" charges are from the rest of the materials in library collections. We read each other's writings about how unique we are, how misunderstood, and how we need special preparation for our work that our formal education failed to provide. There is an evident feeling among "serialists," based on various current writings and attendance at meetings, that we must stick together and fight for our place under the library sun. As a former serials librarian and now teacher for some years of a separate course on serials management I understand and even share in some of these feelings. All aspects of serials, including administration, collection development, acquisitions, organization, preservation and public service, are often considered by serialists to have characteristics that require activities different from those used with monographic materials. It is perhaps too easy to forget the

---

Mary Ellen Soper is Assistant Professor of the Graduate School of Library and Information Science, University of Washington, Seattle, WA 98195.

© 1987 by The Haworth Press, Inc. All rights reserved.

commonalities all library materials share, and instead focus increasingly upon those features unique to each pattern of publication, to each format.

There are differences of opinion among library educators and professionals concerning the need for special preparation and training to handle specific types of library materials and for performing certain library activities; it appears to depend upon a person's own experiences as to what side he or she supports. The purpose of this article is to review some of the surveys made in the past twelve years of the need for special preparation for serials librarians, and to report on a survey made by the author in 1986 of the accredited library schools and how they educate their students for the specific task of cataloging serials.

PREVIOUS SURVEYS AND DESCRIPTIONS OF SERIALS COURSES

Benita Weber conducted a national survey of serials librarians in the spring of 1974 to determine the state of the art in training for serials librarians, and to evaluate Drexel University's Graduate School of Library Science serials course against the actual needs of the profession.[1] Six hundred five academic and special libraries were randomly selected; 361 responses were received for a 60% return. Most of the people working with serials were in the areas of acquisitions, binding and selection. Only 20% of the college group and 10% of the special libraries group actively sought a serials position; Weber interpreted this to indicate that few people felt prepared to assume a serials position because of lack of specific education for the work. A minority of both groups received some specialized on-the-job training directly related to serials handling and control.

An inquiry as to the areas of serials work not adequately covered by library school courses elicited the following list, in descending order: automation, manual handling, acquisitions, cataloging, selection, indexing/abstracting, reference and copyright. Continuing education was particularly requested in the areas of automation, cataloging, indexing/abstracting, manual records, and selection and acquisitions, in that order. Many felt that special serials courses should be taught by experienced serials administrators, as only such persons could be familiar with both the theory and the practice involved. Hands-on experience in classes was also mentioned as mandatory.

Weber concluded that many working serials librarians felt there were severe deficiencies in their formal education. A survey she did of the ALA accredited library schools found only 8 schools offering a course on serials in spring, 1974. She recommended that the ALA Serials Section Policy and Research Committee issue a position statement expressing concern over the lack of special courses for serials librarians, and encouraging the schools who did not offer such courses to do so.

During the 1976 ALA annual conference a panel discussion on serials training was sponsored by the Joint RTSD/LED Committee on Education for Resources and Technical Services. The results of a survey by an Ad Hoc Committee on Serials Education, under the direction of Hal W. Hall, were reported. Only 13 of the 65 library schools responding reported having a serials course of any kind.[2] The panel members agreed that as long as the primary orientation in libraries was to monographic publications, serials work would remain localized and improvised. Serials work was described as depending on oral tradition, handed down from person to person as a kind of folklore. Patricia Oyler, from the School of Library Science, Simmons College, pointed out three problem areas that impeded widespread introduction of dedicated serials courses in library schools: library school programs were too short to include many specialty courses; few faculty members had the necessary knowledge and experience to teach such courses; and library school administrators often raised questions as to budgets, size of class enrollment, fragmentation and overextended curricula. The panel agreed that the problem must be made more visible to the profession and to library schools before solutions could be found.

In 1978 Marion Szigethy described a concentrated three-week serials course offered at Columbia University during the summer of 1977.[3] A more permanent serials course at Loughborough Technical College in Leicestershire, England, was described in 1983 by D. P. Woodworth.[4] The Loughborough course had been offered for some years and was believed to be the only separate year-long option offered in England. All aspects of serials work were covered, with emphasis on selection, acquisitions and public service.

Though not specific to serials work, a 1978 survey of cataloging practitioners conducted by Cynthia C. Ryans to determine their feelings about the importance of cataloging courses in library school and the most useful approach to teaching such courses in order to prepare students to be qualified catalogers, is interesting for what it reveals about practitioners' attitudes toward library school curricula.[5] Sixty questionnaires were sent out to the heads of catalog departments in the libraries of each university that had an ALA accredited library program; 42 were returned, for a 70% response.

The majority of the respondents believed that students coming out of library schools were not as well prepared for cataloging positions as the administrators would like. In spite of this, the respondents preferred to hire new graduates and train them, rather than hire experienced catalogers. A strong background in theory was wanted, but it had to be combined with practical training. However, only a few of the cataloging departments cooperated with the schools by providing on-the-job experience for students. One interpretation of the results of this survey appears obvious: as library schools are failing to instruct their students in the techniques needed by specific catalog departments, the libraries have to do their own training. To blame the schools for such lacks, however, is very shortsighted, and in reality is actually praise for the schools' curricula. Library schools cannot train students for specific libraries and specific positions; if they did, they would soon lose all credibility in the profession, as well as their accreditation, students, and university support.

In 1980 a very thorough dual survey of library school administrators and of instructors of serials courses to determine the current status of education for serials librarianship was made under the auspices of the ALA Resources and Technical Services Division Serials Section Committee on Library School Education.[6] Forty-five of the 68 accredited schools responded, for a response rate of 66%. The administrators reported that 5 schools offered separate courses that attempted to cover all aspects of serials work, with little attention given to serials in other courses; 7 schools offered separate courses plus units in other courses to cover specific topics omitted from the separate course; and 22 schools offered only serials units within various other courses. Responses from the instructors of the serials units in the schools revealed that 18 (40%) out of the 45 schools had separate serials courses. The difference between the two groups' responses is intriguing; it was apparently caused by some administrators failing to answer the specific question.

The presence of resources to teach special courses or units on serials was given as the most important factor for curricula development in this area. Resources meant faculty who could teach the subject and facilities such as a serials unit in the parent institution's library. The lack of such resources was the most influential factor working against serials emphasis in library schools. Some administrators said serials should not be singled out for special emphasis, but instead students should learn about serials in an integrated general curriculum; others appeared to believe such treatment would result in only limited exposure to the subject.

Collection development was selected as the most important aspect to be covered; cataloging was a strong second, followed by acquisitions, public services, resource sharing, microforms, recording of holdings, and preservation. Courses were predominantly technical services oriented. Contact with professionals, implemented through tours of serials operations or with guest speakers, was the most popular teaching method. Assignments designed to develop skills were heavily used. Reading assignments, with emphasis on textbooks, along with seminar papers and reports on journal articles, were also utilized.

If the school only offered units in other courses, the most frequently offered topic was serials cataloging, as the courses containing the units were most often basic and/or advanced cataloging. Since advanced cataloging courses are usually elective and the majority of serials units were offered in them, many students graduated from library schools with little or no exposure to serials. Many administrators reported that as there was a lack of student interest in serials, special courses or units could not be offered. But if there are no courses offered, how are students to find out enough about serials to be interested in them?

In the fall of 1984 another survey of the ALA accredited library schools was conducted by Diane Stine.[7] She wanted to find out whether progress was being made in adding serials courses and units to the curricula. Sixty-two questionnaires were mailed; 50 (80%) were returned, but only 44 contained useful information. Eighteen of the 44 respondents indicated that they had a course specifically devoted to serials; one of these schools could not complete the rest of the questionnaire because the instructor was on sabbatical. Twelve of the courses covered all topics relating to serials; 5 excluded cataloging and automation, which were covered by other courses in the schools. Cataloging, automation and collection development were the primary topics of the separate serials courses. Many of the schools also had other courses that devoted some time to these aspects of serials. Fewer than 10% of the students of 10 of the schools offering separate courses took them. Twelve of the courses were offered either annually or every other year; the 5 schools that offered their courses only occasionally possibly used adjunct faculty for them.

Twenty-six of the schools indicated they did not have a specific course, but many offered units in more general courses. Cataloging, collection development, and union lists/resource sharing were the most popular topics. Administration and public services received the least emphasis. Many of the serials topics were offered in elective courses, and so the percentage of students being exposed to serials work of any kind was low. Stine suggested that serial topics be covered in required courses in order to insure that library schools produce graduates prepared to be serials librarians. This appears to be an appropriate suggestion, based on the survey results, but any library school can point to many other areas of specialization whose practitioners urge the same solution. As long as most schools maintain a one-year program the number of special courses and the variety of topics covered in the curriculum must be limited.

1986 SURVEY OF EDUCATION FOR SERIALS CATALOGING

On March 10, 1986, a questionnaire was sent to 62 accredited library schools specifically inquiring into how serials cataloging was taught in these schools. Responses were requested from the people responsible for teaching the subject. Data from the Graduate School of Library and Information Science, University of Washington, were added by the author. On May 2, a follow-up was sent to the non-respondents. Of the total 63 questionnaires, 53 were returned with some usable data, for a response rate of 84%. (See appendix for questionnaire.) Sixteen (30%) of the respondents offer separate serials courses. Nine of these courses had prerequisite cataloging courses, ranging from core courses required for all students, to one or two other courses. Five schools had no prerequisites for the course, while the other 2 had non-cataloging prerequisites. The percent age of time in the separate courses devoted to cataloging ranged from 0% to 25%. See Table 1 for the figures.

As two of the questionnaires contained responses only to questions 1 through 3, the total of respondents dropped to 51 with question 4. The aspects of serials cataloging covered in the separate courses ranged from none, to a general overview, to coverage of AACR2, MARC(S), and practice inputting records into a utility. This great variety in attention paid to serials cataloging in separate courses was similar to the amount of time spent on the subject in units offered in other courses; 33 schools, including 3 of the schools with separate courses, offered such units. Sixteen covered the subject only in advanced cataloging courses; 8 offered a unit only in their introductory courses; while 9 offered coverage in both an introductory and advanced course. See Table 2 for the breakdown of time

TABLE 1
Time devoted to serials cataloging in separate serials courses

	0%	less than 5%	10–15%	20–25%	Total
Number	3	2	3	5	13*

*2 schools left this question blank; one reported that the time spent varied, depending on who taught the course.

TABLE 2
Time devoted to serials cataloging in other courses

	Less than 10%	10–15%	20–33%	Total
In Introductory course	4	3	1	8
In Advanced course	3	6	7	16
In two courses				9
Introductory	6	2	1	
Advanced	3	4	2	
				33*

*3 schools appear in both Table 1 and 2.

spent on cataloging. Of the 7 schools that had neither a separate course nor a unit on serials cataloging in another course, 4 said their curriculum made no provision for covering the subject, while the other 3 could provide some exposure in workshops, practica, or special projects.

Question 8 asked if the instructor felt that serials cataloging was different enough from monographic cataloging to require special training. "Training" was an unfortunate choice of word; it was pointed out many times that graduate programs should educate, not train. In spite of this many responses were received to this question. Twenty-six of the respondents felt that serials were different enough in details to require special preparation for students. Four felt that special instruction was needed, but that there was not enough time in the curriculum to provide it. Eleven responded that the general principles of cataloging were sufficient, and no further preparation for specific formats or patterns of publication was needed. Seven answers seemed undecided; they said general principles were sufficient, but special instruction was also required for some materials. Three had no opinion or left the question blank.

Twenty people felt automation made no difference in the requirements for special instruction in the cataloging of specific materials; one felt it decreased the need. Twenty-five felt automation increased the need for more preparation; four of these pointed out that the bibliographic utilities tended not to include a great number of records for non-monographic and non-book formats. As a result, more original cataloging was required in libraries. And for this reason more instruction in these more unusual formats was needed. Two respondents felt that it was public service personnel who needed the special instruction so they could interpret the contents of online data bases, and not catalogers. Three people had no opinion.

Only 9 of the 51 schools indicated they offered any continuing education opportunities in the area of serials cataloging. Three of these schools offered workshops when AACR2 was introduced. One school offered a course, but no one signed up for it. Serials were also included as part of several cataloging update workshops. Evidently there is little need expressed by the profession to the accredited schools for such offerings, in spite of the enthusiastic response generated whenever a unit of ALA or some other library organization offers instruction in serials. Perhaps the profession does not often think of the schools as a source of such opportunities.

CONTINUING EDUCATION FOR SERIALS CATALOGERS

Continuing education is vital in serials work, but opportunities designed specifically for serials catalogers have been rather limited in the past. However, there have been many workshops, institutes, conferences, etc., that have covered a variety of aspects of serials work; many of these would be of interest to serials catalogers since the more that is known about serials the easier it is to organize them for use. A good survey of continuing education programs offered in recent years has been done by Elaine K. Rast.[8] She covered offerings in Illinois, the rest of the United States, and concluded with programs given in Canada and the United Kingdom. She listed many of the institutes covering serials cataloging that resulted from AACR2 and the growing use of automation in libraries.

A very useful source of information about the work of the RTSD Serials Section committees, including the Committee to Study Serials Cataloging, is the "Serials News" column by Gary Pitkin, that appears regularly in *Serials Librarian*. These committees also report their activities in *RTSD Newsletter* after each Midwinter and Annual ALA Conference.

The bibliographic utilities, such as WLN and OCLC, provide training for their members, and include regular reviews and advanced workshops covering serials cataloging in the network environment. Many workshops were given by state organizations on AACR2 after it was published; some of these focused on the specific application of the new code to serially published materials. One example of such state efforts was a workshop on serials cataloging, sponsored by the Washington State Serials Roundtable, given in 1980, first in Bellingham, and repeated in Cheney.

In addition to the committee work and regular conference programs of the Serials Section, RTSD recently sponsored a preconference: "Who's Afraid of Serials," held June 21-22, 1984, in Dallas. Ellen Siegel Kovacic delivered a paper on serials cataloging. RTSD was also a cosponsor of the "LC Road Shows," held around the country to introduce AACR2. Most recently RTSD and its Council of Regional Groups is cosponsoring another regional institute with the Library of Congress, that deals specifically with serials cataloging. The Serials Cataloging Regional Institute was first held in Minneapolis on May 7-9, 1986; it will be repeated in Pittsburgh in the fall, and in 1987 in Oxford, England, Atlanta, San Francisco, San Antonio, and Boston. Any beginning or experienced serials cataloger should find this institute valuable, as it is to cover all current aspects of the organization and automation of serials.

A description of the various publications that serialists, including catalogers, should try to keep up with has been compiled by Susan Matson.[9] Lastly, there is a new organization for serialists to be aware of and possibly join. In 1985 at the ALA Chicago Conference the organizational meeting of the North American Serials Interest Group was held. It is patterned after the successful United Kingdom Serials Group, and is designed to provide a forum for librarians, publishers, vendors, library science educators, binders, etc., to exchange information and opinions and discuss issues of current interest. Its inaugural conference is being held June 22-25, 1986, at Bryn Mawr College.

ARE SERIALS REALLY DIFFERENT?

Any consideration of whether the handling of serially published materials in libraries really does or does not require special education and abilities must begin with a definition of what is being discussed. "Serials" is a term applied to material in any physical format, published in consecutive parts, and intended to be continued indefinitely. Thus any serially published item can be expected to continue to come for an undetermined period of time; each new issue of the item can contain bibliographically significant changes from its predecessors.

As a result of the continuing nature of serials, all aspects of library work are affected. Collection development personnel should be aware that the addition of a serial title results in a continuing demand upon the budget, and should make their selections carefully. Acquisitions has to select sources that can be depended upon to continue to supply the title and clear up any problems that come along, and it must also develop some way of recording what has been received and what should continue to be received. Cataloging must create records that can accommodate possible extensive changes as time passes. Shelf maintenance has to develop ways to preserve serial titles by binding, microfilming or some other method so that all issues retain their usability. Since serial publications traditionally have been valued over monographs for their currency, public service personnel have to insure that issues are made easily available for use, see that the necessary indexes to and abstracts of the contents are at hand, and be able to interpret bibliographic descriptions of serials. And circulation staffs have to develop routines for the circulating of unbound and bound issues.

It seems apparent that serials really are different in many ways from monographs, but since serials make up a major part of many libraries' collections, to treat them as something unusual and out of the ordinary run of library activities is completely wrong. Ideally all library school graduates should be equally familiar with both serial and monographic patterns of publication and value each for its contributions to meeting the users' needs. But since most library schools are limited to one year programs, many of the special features of serials may perforce be excluded from the curriculum.

In the specific area of cataloging of serials, students should be introduced to the intricacies of Chapter 12 in AACR2, the meaning of rule 21.1B2, and the extensive additions that have been made in Chapter 25 concerning uniform titles for serials. These special features of serials cataloging can be covered fairly easily if students have a good grounding in cataloging theory and practice. Students often say there is not enough time to cover everything they feel they need to know, and not nearly enough practice work to make them comfortable with the multitude of cataloging rules and the requirements of automated systems. But if they are taught how to interpret the rules, given the basics of automation, and cautioned concerning the inevitable changes, they should be able to cope satisfactorily in any position in which they find themselves, and be able to grow in knowledge and abilities as required. The need for continual learning after the MLS must be stressed. Students should expect that most of their future education will be informal, rather than formal.

CONCLUSION

The majority of accredited library schools do not have separate serials courses, but they do offer instruction in many aspects of serials, including that of cataloging. There is no agreement as to whether serials cataloging requires special training in addition to instruction in general principles of cataloging; about half of the schools feel that it does. As most of the extended instruction in serials cataloging takes place in advanced courses that are likely to be elective, many graduates are probably not exposed to the specific problems involved in the organization of serials. Moreover, the schools offer relatively few continuing education opportunities for graduates and other librarians to receive additional instruction in the subject. A slight majority say that automation is increasing the need for attention to be paid to the cataloging of special formats.

Serials continue to be part of library schools' curricula, but probably will never be stressed as much as many serialists would like. Evidently the schools do not agree with the vocal part of the profession on this subject; whether they should will no doubt continue to be debated as it has in the past.

NOTES

1. Weber, Benita M., "Education of Serials Librarians: A Survey," *Drexel Library Quarterly*, 11 (July 1975):72-81.
2. "The Education of Librarians for Serials Management Positions," *American Library Association, Library Education Division Newsletter*, no. 88 (March 1977):6-8.
3. Szigethy, Marion C., "A Course in Serials Librarianship at Columbia University," *Serials Librarian*, 2 (Summer 1978):387-390.
4. Woodworth, D.P., "Serials Education," *Serials Librarian*, 7 (Spring 1983):63-65.
5. Ryans, Cynthia C., "Cataloging Administrators' Views on Cataloging Education," *Library Resources & Technical Services*, 24 (Fall 1980):343-351.
6. Hanson, Elizabeth and Germaine Linkins, "Serials Education in Library Schools," *Journal of Education for Librarianship*, 23 (Fall 1982):83-95.
7. Stine, Diane, "The Adequacy of Library School Education for Serials Librarianship: A Survey," *Illinois Libraries*, 67 (May 1985):448-452.
8. Rast, Elaine K., "Formal Continuing Education for Serials," *Illinois Libraries*, 67 (May 1985):453-458.
9. Matson, Susan, "Informal Continuing Education for Serials: Keeping Up with the Journal Literature," *Illinois Libraries*, 67 (May 1985):458-462.

APPENDIX
QUESTIONNAIRE

1. Does your school have a separate course devoted to serials librarianship? Yes_____ No_____
   If you answered no, please go to question no. 5.
2. Are there prerequisite cataloging courses for the separate serials course? Yes_____ No_____
   If yes, please list the title(s) of the course(s), and briefly describe their content.
3. What percentage of course time of the separate serials course is devoted to cataloging?
4. What aspects of serials cataloging are emphasized in the separate serials course?
5. If you don't have a separate serials course, is serials cataloging taught as a discrete unit of another course? Yes_____ No_____
6. If you answered yes to question 5, please indicate of what course it is a part, and the percentage of time devoted to serials cataloging.
7. If you answered no to question 5, does your curriculum make any other provision for teaching whatever might be unique about the cataloging of serials?
8. In your opinion, is serials cataloging different enough from monographic cataloging to require special training, or are the principles of cataloging broad enough to cover all types of material without any unique preparation based on formats? Please give your reasoning.
9. Do you feel the increased application of automation in libraries decreases the need for special training in cataloging of specific formats, or has it increased the need?
10. Has your school offered any continuing education opportunities for your graduates and other librarians in the special area of serials cataloging?

Index

A

AACR2
  bibliographic utilities, impact on 88
  chief source 38,48
  comparison to AACR1 21-22,86-88
  drafting 27-30
  lack of explicitness 31-32
  level of description 35-36,44-45
  public services, impact on 22-24
  serials cataloging 21,30-40,44-52,68-69,
    74,86-91,96-97,143-144
American National Standard Z39.44,
  serials holding statements 112
American National Standards Committee
  on Library and Information Sciences and
    Related Publishing Practices, Z39 2
  Subcommittee E 7-8
American National Standards Institute
  (ANSI) 1-2
Automation 13-14,21-23,44,76,88,90,97-99,
  102,110,113-114,121,128,147-168

B

Bilingual cataloging 53-62

C

CONSER 43-47,56-57,67,134-135,147-156
CONSER Editing Guide 131-145
CONSER Manual 133
Card catalogs 14,19-20,23-24,65-66,73-74,
  84-90,94-95
Cataloging codes, comparison 11-12,21-22,
  75,84-88
Cataloging Service Bulletin 31-32
  no. 5 32
  no. 10 33,36-37
  no. 11 32,35
  no. 12 32,35
  no. 13 33,36
  no. 14 32,35-36,38
  no. 15 35-38
  no. 16 38
  no. 18 34,37-38
  no. 20 32-33,39
  no. 22 34
  no. 23 32,35,37-38
  no. 25 32,34
  no. 26 34,37
  no. 29 39
Clarke, Andrew 73,80-81
Cole, Jim 67,69-70
Committee to Study Serials Cataloging 29-30
Cooperative cataloging 11-13,16,43-44,
  46-47,97,134-135

E

Earliest entry cataloging 83,88-91,93-95,
  98-99

F

Filing rules 73-74,110,113

H

Headings 53-54,56-58
  subject 16,58,142-143
Holdings statements
  newspapers 112
  serials 7-9,155

I

ISBD (International Standard Bibliographic
  Description) 4-5,40

This Index is compiled by Nancy S. Hanks, Assistant Professor and Head of the Documents Processing Section at the Washington State University Libraries, Washington State University, Pullman, WA 99164-5610.

© 1987 by The Haworth Press, Inc. All rights reserved.

ISBD(S) 3-9,34,40,51,64-65
ISDS Manual 5-7,46,51,67,75,80-81
ISSN 3-5,15-16,65,104
International Federation of Library
    Associations and Institutions (IFLA) 2
International Organization for Standardization
    (ISO) 2
  Technical Committee (TC) 46
    (Documentation) 2
International Serials Data System (ISDS) 3-9,
    13-16,43-44,65,67,104
Iowa Newspaper Project
  budget 120-121
  onsite visits 118-121,125-126
  planning 118-122
  publicity 128-129
  staffing 120-124
  union lists 124-125

K

Key title 3-5,12,16,46,51,63-68,104-105

L

LIBRIS (database)*11-14
Language
  multilingual editions 54-56,58-62
  of description 54-55,58-62
  of headings 53-54,56-58
  of subject headings 58
  separate language editions 55-56
Latest entry cataloging 83-86,93-99,
    110-111,144
Library of Congress
  serials cataloging 43-52,131
Linking entries 6,16,38,45,49-50,126,143

M

Main entries 11-13,16,21-22,28,32-33,35,45,
    50,63-82,104,106-109
Microforms, serials 8,32,111-113,142,150
Monographic series 13,37
Monographic vs. serial treatment 38-39

N

National Endowment for the Humanities
    (NEH) 117-118
National Information Standards Organization
    (NISO) 2
National Library of Canada (NLC)

bilingual cataloging, serials 53-62
National Serials Data Program (NSDP) 43-44
New Serial Titles 44,74-76,81
Newspapers
  CONSER Editing Guide 142
  cataloging projects 117-129
  holdings statements 112
  OCLC (database) 119,121,124-125
  union lists 124-125
Numbering, serials 7-8,37

O

OCLC (database)
  newspaper cataloging projects 119,121,
    124-125
  Oxford Project 125,154-155
  serials 147-156
  union lists 102-104,110-115,124-125
Organization of American Historians
    (OAH) 117

R

RECON 13-14,133,157
RLIN (database)
  authority file 168
  searching 157-164
  serials cataloging 164-167
Rast, Elaine K. 176
Reprints 39,48-49,111-113,142
Rule interpretations, formulation 47
Rules and RIs, AACR1
  6 46,107
  6A 104
  6D1 86
  160B 86
  167G 86
  167Q 86
Rules and RIs, AACR2
  0.12 56-57
  1.0D 44-46
  1.11A 39
  1.11B 39
  1.11F 39
  12.0B1 38,48-49,86
  12.1B1 37,49
  12.1B2 49
  12.1B3 34
  12.1B4 34
  12.1B5 34
  12.1E1 49

Index

12.1F3 35
12.3 37
12.3B1 48
12.3G 37
12.7B 49-50
12.7B5 34
12.7B6 89
12.7B7 38,86
12.7B7g 48
12.7B7k 50
12.7B9 38
12.7B17 50
21.1A2 35,50
21.1B 107
21.1B2 35,177
21.2 51,86
21.2A 34,51
21.28B 50
24.3 57
25.2A 106
25.5B 32,45-46,66-67
Rules and RIs, ALA, 5C(1) 84
Ryans, Cynthia C. 171-172

S

Serials
  AACR2 treatment 21,30-40,44-52,68-69,
    74,86-91,96-97,143-144
  acquisitions 98
  alphabet code 143
  automation 13-14,21-23,44,88,90,97-99,
    102,110,113-114,121,128,147-168
  CIP records 15
  CONSER 43-47,56-57,67,134-135,
    147-156
  cataloging policy 43-62,131
  checkin 98
  chief source 38,48
  consistency of publication data 14-15
  data elements 136-142
  dates 8,37-38
  definitions 93-94,102
  earliest entry 83,88-91,93-95,98-99
  edition statement 6
  frequency varies note 143-144
  holding statements 7-9,112,155
  imprint 7
  indexes 50
  indicator values 143
  key titles 3-5,12,16,46,51,63-68,104-105
  latest entry 83-86,93-99,110-111,144

  level of description 35-36,44-45
  linking entries 6,38,45,49-50,126,143
  main entries 11-13,21-22,28,32-33,35,45,
    50,63-82,104,106-109
  microforms 8,32,111-113,142,150
  numbering 37
  OCLC (database) 132,147-156
  parallel titles 34
  personal authors 35,50
  place of publication code 144
  punctuation 6-7,142
  RECON 13-14,133,157
  RLIN (database) 157-168
  record consolidation 135
  record modification 44,135,147-156,
    165-166
  reprints 39,48-49,111-113,142
  series linking entries 143
  standards 1-9,131-145
  successive entry 86-88,91,94-99,111
  supplements 50
  Sweden 11-16
  title
    changes 6,21,34,48,51,75-76,86-89
    generic 46,65-67,74-81
    initialism/full form 36-37,49
    page 38,46,48
    proper 32-33,45-46,64-67,
      76-82,89
  uniform titles 32-33,45-46,63-82,105-109,
    148-149,177
Serials catalogers, education 169-179
Standards, serials
  ANSI 1-9
  CONSER 131-145
  ISO 1-7
State Historical Society of Iowa 117-118
Stine, Diane 173
Subject headings 16,58,142-143
Successive entry cataloging 86-88,91,
    94-99,111
Supplements, serials 50
Sweden, serials cataloging 11-16

T

Title
  changes 6,21,34,48,51,75-76,86-89
  generic 46,65-67,74-81
  initialism/full form 36-37,49
  page 38,46,48
  proper 4-5,33-34,49,64-67,76-82,89

U

Uniform titles 32-33,45-46,63-82,105-109, 148-149,177
Union lists 11,101-115
  access 104-110
  definition 102
  guidelines 103
  microforms 111-113
  newspapers 124-125

OCLC (database) 102-104,110-115
  online 113
United States Newspaper Project 117-118
Universal bibliographic control (UBC) 15
University of Iowa
  serials cataloging 157,163-164,166-168

W

Weber, Benita 170-171

For Product Safety Concerns and Information please contact our EU representative GPSR@taylorandfrancis.com
Taylor & Francis Verlag GmbH, Kaufingerstraße 24, 80331 München, Germany

www.ingramcontent.com/pod-product-compliance
Lightning Source LLC
Chambersburg PA
CBHW052121300426
44116CB00010B/1758